D1805760

The Scots Way to Santiago de Compostela

Marvels and Wonders
Encounters with Strange Humans,
Beasts, Birds and Insects

Patrick Farnon

WANDERER PRESS

Copyright © 2015 Patrick Farnon

All rights reserved. No part of this text or any of its contents may be reproduced, copied, modified or adapted, without the prior written consent of the author

ISBN 978-90-76660-40-0

For more information see patrickfarnon.com

Cover illustration adapted from *The Last Judgement* (c 1505-1506) by Hieronymus Bosch

Wanderer Press is an imprint of WordBridge Publishing, Aalten, the Netherlands
www.wordbridge.net

Contents

To Rick from
Patrick with
affection!

To Santiago de Compostela and back: Camino Frances, Camino
Fisterra, Camino del Norte

1
The Scots Way to Santiago de Compostela

Looking at the maps of the traditional pilgrim routes to Santiago de Compostela in the Middle Ages, it is noticeable that there are no roads from Scotland. I thought it might be a good idea to invent one. After all, of the various well-trodden roads to Santiago we have the French way (El Camino Frances), the English Way (El Camino Ingles), the Silver Way (La Via de La Plata from Seville), the Northern Way (El Camino del Norte, along the Cantabrian and Basque coasts) and the Primitive Way (Camino Primitivo, from Oviedo). There's also a Portuguese Way.

Whether they are the same routes as in the Middle Ages is open to question since asphalt has swallowed up many of the paths, especially along the northern coast, although efforts are being made to regain them. So why not the Scots Way to Santiago? Scotland already had well-established pilgrim's routes that were popular in the Middle Ages and are again receiving attention. No one these days is expected to walk all the way from Iona to Santiago de Compostela, if they ever did, although it's not a bad idea. Pilgrims traditionally stepped out their front door and went walking clad in a robe, carrying a stick and a bag with all their essentials in it. The journey might take months. The same is true today. The routes on the map are indicative. Basically you can start where you like and take as long as you like.

King Duncan of Scotland went on a six months trip to Rome to meet the Pope in 1050. James IV of Scotland went regularly on pilgrimage in Scotland. For his sins: his involvement in his father's death. And The Bruce too wanted to make the trip. The Confraternity of St James in a little booklet on Pre-Reformation Pilgrims from Scotland lists about 55 pilgrims who made the journey. The greatest number of pilgrims from the British Isles tended to go by sea.

Years ago the *Sunday Post*, published by D.C. Thomson in Dundee, had a column on traveling in Britain. It was written by someone called the HON man. Apart from the delights of looking forward each week to the adventures of Oor Wullie and the Broons, there was the HON man to look forward to at the week-end in the Sunday Post. I loved the HON man and for many years lived under the delusion the name was short for HONOURABLE. He was an honourable traveller going round Britain and exciting places abroad giving you tips on nice places to stay. Or so I imagined. To my dismay, while travelling down the Camino, I discovered there was nothing honourable about the HON man. It meant Holidays for Nothing, or so I was informed by an old journalist friend who had worked for the Dundee Courier.

Which made me feel guilty about the whole enterprise. Where was the spiritual quest? The desire for nobler things? To rise above petty every day preoccupations. Fortunately along the way I ran into such a motley bunch of lost souls, cheapo tourists, bemused pilgrims, sundry backpackers, wanderers, bullshitters, French Santa Clauses, a bum pinching Cajun, freeloading Koreans, slurping Japanese gentlemen, a Norwegian, a Finn and a Dane, two Icelanders, a Rastafarian Spaniard, a volunteer French fireman, a Harvard college student, Americans, barbecuing Argentineans, Brazilians, five Czechs pulling a wheelchair, half a dozen Bulgarians, an Italian choir, and a bald German stuck in a grove who couldn't find the signposts to Berlin. And that is just a selection.

Among that motley bunch I soon started to feel normal. Particularly when I ran into Muldoon. Seamus Muldoon, that is. There's nothing like the company of another Scotsman to assure you you're not the only screwball in the universe. The dogs, cats, mules, donkeys, crows, ants, flies and other creatures of the earth that I met along the way also kept me on the right track. As always, unlike humans, they were behaving well.

And returning along the Camino del Norte, I made a few more discoveries. That cavemen had a higher IQ than us. That the Basques were descended from Neanderthals and that the Basque language came from the Neolithic language spoken in the caves of Altamira. That was one of life's problems solved for me. Where the Basque language had come from had kept me awake for years. I also discovered a delicacy called the Balls of the Antichrist and that the most interesting facts about the sumptuous castle of the richest man in 19th century Spain are that visitors are capable of peeing behind the door of the main salon and stealing the tacks from the leather chairs when the guide is not looking.

Adding spice to the journey, the *Codex Calixtinus*, the illustrated medieval manuscript of St James was stolen the year before. The police were hard on the trail of the thief and there were regular updates in the press. I had never heard of the *Codex Calixtinus* of course, let alone the fact that there was a Pope of that name, Pope Calixtus II. Being self-educated in my formative years on a diet of Captain Marvel, Bugs Bunny and G.I. Joe, the *Codex Calixtinus* had as much appeal as counting cabbages in the moonlight. What I needed was a new soul, not a just change of scenery.

But needs must. Even moles occasionally dig up a gold coin. I ended up reading the manuscript online. Whether that was a good idea or not, I don't know. My training in *The Horrors of the Vaults* and *The Walking Dead* left me unprepared for what its 12th century writer had to say about the Scots, the most horrible race on earth by all accounts. At that time, I must add. When they were disguised as Spaniards. From Navarra. And wore kilts. They came to Scotland from Scythia originally and had been brought over from Scotland by the Romans, it seems.

The *Codex Calixtinus* or The Book of St James was the first travel book. For pilgrims. It was written or compiled around the year 1150, by a French hack, known in medieval times as a scholar, called Aymeric Picaud. The population of Scotland then was between 200,000 and 400,000 people. They were already causing trouble. Part of the problem was the language. In the 12th century, Norse Gaelic and Scots were being spoken, together with the French the Anglo-Normans brought with them. By the 16th century when Scotland's borders were mostly defined, Scots was spoken in the Lowlands, Gaelic in the Highlands and Norn (from Norse) in the Orkneys and Shetlands. Over the centuries the language shift can be read in the names of the kings. From Kenneth MacAlpin who founded the kingdom in 884 AD to Alexander II's death in 1286, for over four centuries their names came from the Gaelic. Queen Margaret brought an end to that when she came to Scotland from Norway in 1290. After that the Normans arrived with John Balliol first and then Robert de Brus who was crowned king in 1306.

By the time we get to the Stewarts, or the Stuarts, who can also be traced back to Normandy, the names have changed mostly to Robert and James. The name James comes from Gemmes in Norman French. It is the name James we are interested in terms of the Way of St James to Santiago de Compostela.

On the continent, going on pilgrimage to the tomb of St James had been building up since the 9th century and by the 15th century it is estimated that as much as two million pilgrims or 5,000 a day were visiting the cathedral at Santiago de Compostela, the third most important place of pilgrimage for Christians in Europe after Rome and Palestine.

Relief was probably the most common expression on their faces. At having arrived sound and well. The Dutch painter Hieronymus Bosch has a telling portrait of a pilgrim on his way to Santiago. Painted around 1500, it depicts a pilgrim with long dark curly hair and a beard. Over his shoulder he has a long, sharp metal-tipped pole from which a blanket is hanging, reaching nearly to the ground. He is wearing a long grey-coloured robe. Behind his head is a floppy hat with the brim turned up showing the scallop of St James. At his side is a scabbard with a long knife. He is slightly stooped as though the weight of the book in the bag hanging over his crotch is pulling him down. The book looks bulky, heavy and cumbersome. Probably it is a breviary written in Latin. Breviaries were very popular at the time and contained prayers to be said during the day at fixed times. The expression on his face speaks volumes. Not only is he looking very worried, he is asking himself what in God's name he is doing there? Closer inspection reveals he has good reason to be asking. He has just come down a hill and is standing by a little stream. Perhaps he is thinking of jumping in. In the distance behind him to the right, there's another pilgrim spread-eagled on the ground about to croak his last. A robber is standing over him wielding a wicked looking knife. Further up the hill to the left, two pathetic looking pilgrims are descending the steep slope. The one at the front is on crutches and the one behind is in no better shape. The lame leading the blind.

Behind them further up, sitting under a tree, is another pilgrim with a hood pulled over his head who is reading a book and is ignorant of the tragedies being enacted round him. The message is clear. Why go to all that trouble in this evil world?

A few paces below the two *desperados* is a hump of earth. It is a grave. Newly dug by the look of it. Someone has recently been buried. A crude wooden cross made of two sticks; the broken staff of a pilgrim perhaps, has been stuck lopsided in the earth beside it. Further down almost at the mesmerized pilgrim's elbow is a barren stump of bush on which a magpie sits. The magpie is looking across in the direction of the robber. Perhaps the glint of the metal from the knife has caught its attention. Perhaps it is waiting for the robber to finish his dirty business so it can hop over and pick out the eyes of the victim.

2
On the Road, the Sun Also Rises

To get on the road, all you have to do is step out the door and start walking. The road can take you anywhere. Things stick in your head. Decades ago a childhood friend of mine said to me a propos of something: "Old Jimmy when he was 83 got his bag on his back and went walking. Just got his rucksack on his back and walked out the door."

I'm not that age yet but it stuck in my mind ever since and those words come back constantly as if foretelling the future. Maybe they plant a seed in your brain that becomes a tree when you get older. Because one of the recurring images "Old Jimmy" inspired was a man under a tree in the sun. On a grassy verge by the side of the road, the bees buzzing and the butterflies hovering over the flowers. In a warm country where the sun shines. In a place like Spain or India. Because there is no way you can imagine a man sleeping peacefully under a tree in Scotland. Memories of the rain lashing down, the thunder cracking and the lightning flashing, or midges biting you to death in a freak hot summer, put such dreams to rest.

Jimmy would have had much the same problem. He lived in the north of England, near York, close to where my friend lived. Maybe the weather there is not as bad. It's further south than central Scotland so it's probably a bit warmer. But it doesn't conjure up fond pastoral memories at my stage in life, though I do have idyllic memories of the yellow corn and the haystacks, coming out of the freshly mown cornfields on the back of a tractor in the shadow of the pine forest in the West of Scotland as a child.

Where Old Jimmy was headed, I've no idea. I didn't ask. It didn't seem necessary. At that age where else would he be going with a bag on his back? And walking. There was no answer to that and none necessary. When you reach the third stage in your life, or so they say in India, it's time to pick up your bag and take to the road. The first third of your life is for getting yourself together and the second is for raising a family. When you've done that, you've done what the gross of mankind does with their lives. For better or worse.

So whatever stage you're in, take to the road when you can. There's not a minute to lose. And all the better if you find yourself on the road to Santiago de Compostela, the Way of St James (Camino de Santiago), travelling through France or Spain with a map of the route, a guide book in your hand, or none of these but only but your official hostel card (and your wallet). All you need to do is to keep putting one foot in front of the other and keep going. You'll meet some wonderful people on the way. You'll cross some marvellous landscapes and seascapes, pass through hundreds of fly blown villages and big towns. You can walk alone or you can walk accompanied. It doesn't matter; you'll realize after a while that you're in a stream; that you're being carried along in the flow of people heading for Santiago de Compostela, the shrine of St James

I recently read that there are over two million people in the air at any moment of the day. Over seven billion on the ground and two million people in the air. Just think of that! All over the globe at this moment nearly two million people are passing overhead from one place to another in a jet plane. And once you're on a jet plane you can't get off till it lands.

The road is a bit like that. Once you're on it, you're part of a flow. You're never really alone because you're connected to other people doing the same as you. With the same purpose and maybe even the same reason as you. But when you're on the road you're different. Because you're free. You're free from what you left behind. Physically anyway. And free for the time that you're on the road. The length of which you determine for yourself. As well as the time you wish to spend. And when it comes to spending just remember that if, as the saying goes: Time is Money, Money is also Time.

I'm not saying it's easy but from ancient times people have crossed the hidden paths of Spain to see the sun die at the end of the world in Finisterra – Finis Terrae as the Romans called it: Land's End – and resurrect in the morning.

Today over a hundred and fifty thousand people travel the routes to Santiago de Compostela every year, some walking for months at a time, others rushing to get there in a week or two, on foot or by bike. On donkeys and horses too reportedly, though I saw none of those in two months. Then there are others, that get stuck on the road just about forever like Forrest Gump, and when they finish one route, start another.

There are plenty of books on the route, personal journeys mostly, spiritual guides, and there are quite a few films on the subject too. Luis Buñuel, friend of that other Spanish luminary, Salvador Dalí, filmed *La Vie Lactée* (The Milky Way) in 1967, with travellers disputing obscure points of doctrine as they follow the direction of the Milky Way, a by-name for the Camino since it served as an overhead compass for travellers from the earliest times. Martin Sheen, the American actor, whose father was from Santiago, updated it more recently with *The Way,* directed by his son Emilio Estevez. Well received in the U.S., it opened the floodgates to American visitors. Or as one young American kid said to me in Burgos, "You know what Americans are like, they want to see who can get there first."

And we agreed that, before you know it, they could be thunderballing down the Camino on motorbikes. The end could well be in sight. These days it's more popular than ever as the world's backpackers: from kids to octogenarians, take to the road. The Koreans discovered it in recent years after Paul Coelho's book *The Pilgrimage* was translated into Korean.

Apart from North and South Americans, you'll come across people from just about every country in Europe. In the course of a two month trip I met people from England, Ireland, Scotland, Iceland, Germany Finland, Holland, Hungary, Czechoslovakia, Australia and New Zealand, Bulgaria, France, Austria, Switzerland, Italy. You'll meet a few Asians too, Japanese mostly. No mean walkers themselves on their own trails. And American walkers who will tell you about the 2,200 mile Appalachian Trail running down the east coast of America.

The Camino pales in comparison. Maybe because it's more amenable for wimps as they go strutting down the road, rising often before daylight for weeks on end. There are two kinds of hiker. Some have time and some have no time. Take as long as you like or as long as you can afford. You can start from anywhere. There are enough maps of the routes to follow or not, through continental Europe, the British Isles and Ireland. But the pilgrim's ways were sufficiently known from medieval times onwards, whether they led to Rome or Palestine or to the Field of the Star, Santiago de Compostela.

And as regards the rising and setting of the sun, or the resurrection and the life, I came across Ernest Hemingway once more as I passed through the Basque country in Northern Spain. And re-read *The Sun Also Rises* in San Sebastian, where he stayed. *The Sun Also Rises* is about the lost generation, as it was called, after World War I, and how they managed their lives in the aftermath that would eventually scoop up much of humanity and send it crashing like swill against the sea wall of Wall Street in 1929, the ripples of which we still feel to this day. I wondered where the title came from and looked it up. It came from the Bible. It says:

> What profit hath a man of all his labour which he taketh under the sun? One generation passeth away, and another generation cometh: but the earth abideth for ever. The sun also ariseth, and the sun goeth down, and hasteth to his place where he arose.

El Camino Frances

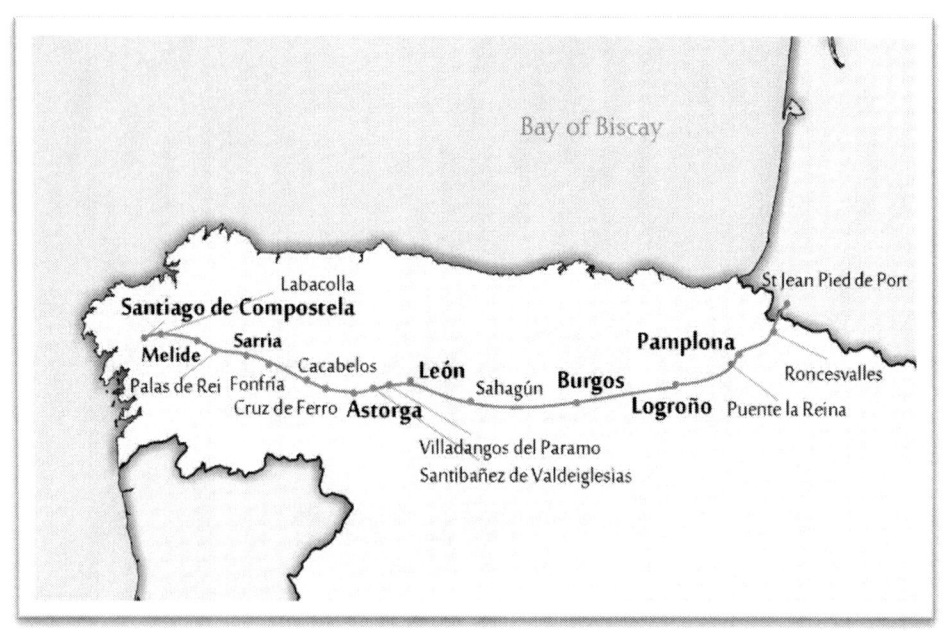

Camino Frances From St Jean Pied De Port to Santiago de Compostela

3
Step and Gaily Off We Go

Roads are like furrows: as furrows produce wheat, so do roads produce people, inns, languages, nations. With a road, you can travel along it, or sit beside it or take your harvest in. This road I'm talking about now is rather like an old beggar, even though each traveller who treads it, re-news it, and manages to revive some portion of early youth on its bro-ken, dusty surface. From Miranda, I can see a stretch of the French Road, the Pilgrims' Way, the way of St James...

Alvaro Cunqueiro, "The Road is Like an Old Beggar," *Merlin and Company*

I am about to step onto the path, dip my toe into the water of the flowing stream, so to speak, but something is holding me back. Another message has come, the third of fourth now, from one Muldoon who says he will see me soon.

"See you soon," the message says. The messages are all the same. They provide no further clues apart from where the Muldoon person is. I get one from St Jean Pied de Port on the other side of the Pyrenees, a day or two ago. Then another saying, "See you in Pamplona." After which nothing. I don't know Muldoon from Larry but before I leave home I get a message from a friend who calls off at the last minute but has met someone who wants to do the trip and has given him my mobile number. That, I suppose, pending further clarification, must be Muldoon.

That is also why I am in a book shop in Pamplona, leafing through the books, wasting another day, flicking the pages of *Fiesta*, or *The Sun Also Rises*, by Ernest Hemingway who hung about these parts in the twenties and wrote about the bullfight.

Pamplona, a beautiful city, is best known for the running of the bulls. Which takes place every year and starts on the feast on Saint Fermin, the patron saint of Pamplona on the sixth of July and lasts for a week till 14th July during which time six bulls chase after six steers and whacked out revellers through the cobbled, narrow streets to the bullring. More than a million people come to see the festival every year these days.

In Hemingway's day it was different. Leafing through a book on the San Fermin *corrida* in the 1930s, which was when Hemingway was here, what strikes you is the amount of space between the runners and the bulls. Apart from the fact that the photos are in black in white there is plenty of space between the bulls and the runners as they flee or look back over their shoulders. Today there is practically no space. The streets are jam-packed and there is little distance between the tips of the horns of the bulls and the white shirts of the runners.

Another one or two people will get gored or killed this year again. The spectacle is shown daily on television with the runners scrambling up barricades or hiding in doorways as the stiletto horns of the bulls whizz past their paunches. Mesmerized viewers follow the spectacle daily hoping to see the bull make off with a string of blue entrails and a piece of white T-shirt on its horns.

It is said by those who have a close acquaintance with bulls and know their ways that they are stubborn, morose creatures most of the year but brighten up no end when the feast day of St Anthony, patron saint of animals, arrives on 17 January. They then start flicking their tails compulsively in joyful anticipation of St Fermin's day six months later. The bulls fortunately hold no prejudices and bear no grudges. True, they may have justification for the treatment received through the ages at the hands of Spaniards, but they are blessed with short or no memory. They gore all and sundry without distinction, young and old, male and female. Since male idiocy is global, they are supplied with a steady stream of willing victims every year. Female idiocy, although in lesser supply, adds extra spice to the spectacle and a piquant touch to the afternoon and evening menus in bars and restaurants up and down Spain during the goring season. Between one spoonful of paella and the next the tourist can unite with the locals and gape open mouthed at the screen above the bar as yet another white shirt gets the downside of the liquor fuelled fiesta.

There's a poster on a wall advertising a bullfighter called El Cid. It's nice to see El Cid (from Sidi, Arabic for Lord) is still around. He's been gone but not forgotten for nearly a thousand years when he was known as Rodriguez Diaz, apart from a short interval in the 1960s when he was called Charlton Heston riding along the beaches of Valencia on his horse in a Hollywood film of that name. Upright in the saddle but very dead after the stubborn Moors gave siege to Valencia which he captured in 1094. The painter Goya did an etching of him in 1816 called El Cid Campeador Spearing Another Bull. In it he is on his horse, spearing a bull with a long lance. He's wearing a funny little hat with voluminous feathers, is dolled up like a dandy with a cape and has a dark beard and moustache. If it weren't for the macho lance bit, he'd be more Boy George and the steed more Charlton Heston. But that's a side issue, why did Goya call it another bull? If he'd just said El Cid kills a bull, everything would have been alright. But another bull? Was El Cid up to nothing else but killing bulls all day long?

There were plenty of bulls around in El Cid's day. They were descended from the aurochs that Neolithic man painted on the caves of Altamira not far from Pamplona and that roamed the plains all over Europe 70,000 years ago after the Ice Age. The skull of one was dug up in Northumberland, England in 2009 and the last survivor died in 1627 in Poland. They stood six foot high to the shoulder and weighed between 700 and 1,000 kilos, compared to between 500 and 700 kilos for a fighting bull these days.

That's what I'm pondering as I head out of Pamplona, down through the campus of the university, pack on back, looking for the signs with the scallop of St James and the yellow arrows that point the way out into the countryside and the hills. I've also bought a handy Michelin guide of the Camino de Santiago running from St Jean Pied de Port just over the Pyrenees, a popular starting place. From there to Santiago is 777 kilometres. The guide is structured into distances you can walk easily in a day (20 to 25 kilometres) and shows the elevation of the terrain, the villages in between, where the hostels are and what kind of facilities are in the place, whether a bus stops there, that sort of thing. It's just as well. I get a message saying "In Cizur Menor," the first place on the route on the way to Puente La Reina which is 24 kilometres further. The path winds through the rolling Navarran landscape of wheat grass, high and waving in early summer, with a sprinkling of trees along the path where you can stop and rest in the shade.

When I get to Cizur Menor there's no sign of Muldoon so I dip my feet in the fountain in the square, have a sandwich and lay down on a bench on top of my pack. But the early June sun is too hot around midday so I move on through the little villages of Guendulain and Zaiquiegui and onto the highest point on this stretch, the Alto de Perdón, so called because it's a halting place. Alto is halt. And Perdón is pardon or forgiveness. There's a line of cut metal figures representing pilgrims, rusted and carrying long poles, on the crest of the hill. One is mounted on a little donkey with a dog running alongside. Bringing up the rear is a pilgrim with a mule and behind those, three of four other figures walking in line. About a dozen or so travellers have stopped for a break before heading down the other side of the rise, down the slope towards Puente La Reina.

When I see the kilt, the hairy grey woollen socks stuck into the hiking boots in the sweltering heat, the feet rested on the backpack and the can of beer in the hand, I take a chance and call out "Muldoon?" I say I take a chance because you never know these days, you can't necessarily deduce someone is a Scotsman because he is wearing a kilt, but with the rest of the paraphernalia, there's a good chance he is. And first thing he says, when he stands up and I see the sporran – if that's what you want to call it, because it looks more like a home-made pouch tied round his waist with elastic binders – is "Here's tae us," raising a can of beer in his hand.

"Aye, you're right there," I say. Then without further ado, we get going, down the steep slope between the vineyards and the almond trees, Muldoon in front leaning on his stick in case he slips on the loose stones and falls and skins his bare arse. Two things I notice. He's got a bag exactly like mine: black. And there's a lump burnt out the arse of his kilt. Another thing, and I'm no expert at tartans, but I can make a decent guess at one or two: a Stewart or Douglas or a Cameron. But a Muldoon tartan? I don't recall having heard of a Muldoon tartan. But that's of secondary interest. At the moment it's step and gaily down the Hill of Forgiveness into uncharted territory on our quest for salvation.

O young Lochinvar is come out of the west,

Through all the wide Border his steed was the best;
And save his good broadsword he weapons had none,
He rode all unarm' d, and he rode all alone.
So faithful in love, and so dauntless in war,
There never was knight like the young Lochinvar.

Sir Walter Scott, *Lochinvar*

4

Robbed and Gutted in Puente La Reina

A disorderly, screeching, noisy, dirty, cheerful, rowdy bunch of rogues. Gypsies, fortune tellers, magicians, pseudo alchemists, wanderers; Coquillards, marauding hawkers, acrobats, tricksters; wanderers disguised as pilgrims, crooks with fake sores, professional beggars, phony cripples, couples living in sin, charlatans, mimes, buffoons, jugglers, clowns, comedians, dancers, contortionists, prostitutes, hustlers, street preachers, the humble poor, wandering friars and clerics, gentlemen down on their luck, outcasts, hermits.

Pablo Arribas Briones, *Picaros y Picaresca en el Camino de Santiago*

Muldoon and I arrive at the hostel in Puente La Reina just after one, having walked for about five hours. It's drizzling as we come over the bridge and into town. The hostel has just opened for the day so it's nearly empty. We select a couple of bunks in the corner. Muldoon up, me down, away from the patio and kitchen the entrance to which is blocked by two clothes horses. A Japanese girl – or maybe she is Korean – is drying her clothes. Muldoon's kilt is soaked so he hangs it out in the patio, under a plastic awning, where, he hopes, it will be out of reach of the rain. Two Bulgarians come in, wheel their bicycles through the dormitory and park them against a bunk. Slowly the place fills up with odds and sods. By evening there's a group of noisy, young Catalan cyclists quacking like ducks and next to us a couple of friendly Australians. The girl of the pair is pregnant. We have a walk around town, have a meal in a restaurant and watch the Germany versus Spain match on TV for a bit. Then it is back to the hostel and lights out about ten and all's well with the world.

Till the next day that is and I start getting things together. And, my dear brothers and sisters, what's this? I can't believe it. Robbed! Jesus Christ! Everything gone from my little bag. The little bag I carry round my waist with my passport, my credit cards and money. And my mobile too, the scumbags, naves, the wicked poltroons in this province of Navarra in this rain soaked town of Puente La Reina.

I look everywhere: under the mattress, under the bed, in the rucksack, in all the pockets of the rucksack, under the bed, on the unslept bunk on top, over and over, and in defiance of all logic, under the T-shirt where I usually keep my money belt, squeezing my stomach as if my panicked mind believes the bag is inside me, under the flesh and just needs a few more prods to make it jump out and miraculously reveal itself round my waist where it usually is when I am not asleep. Muldoon looks everywhere. Under the mattresses. In the bags. Gone, gone. Gone!

Now I'm at the desk explaining to the warden, a lady of about fifty. "Gone!" I tell her and my empty hands flap up in the air. I give her the details. How I had it last night when I went to bed and woke up in the morning and it was gone. "Gone."

We've been getting some strange people lately, she says. Thieves and robbers that mix with the pilgrims. You could be sitting next to them at the table and they're smiling at you, their next victim, sizing you up, thinking about your money bag, you poor innocent traveller. She gives me a mobile phone left behind by a pilgrim and box of all sorts of sorts of appliances and cables to rummage in for a charger for the phone. Then I get on the internet to see where the nearest embassy or consulate is. I may have to get a train down to Barcelona or Madrid to get a passport. Otherwise how can I get across the French border? The train maybe. But the police sometimes check on the train. Or the bus? Do they check the bus? Not as far as I can remember. But going through France that last time? Years back when the police came on and took the North African kid away? Well, I don't look like I'm from North Africa but I still have to show a passport. So that's hazardous as well.

I go to the police station, make a *denuncia*. On the way back to the cafe where I left the Young Lochinvar, through the window of an otherwise empty restaurant, I see the two Australians having breakfast.

"It must have been the Australians," Muldoon says when I get back,

"How otherwise would a pregnant woman be taking the top bunk?" That sounds logical. "Another thing was they were very nice and friendly."

"There you go," Muldoon says. "Wiz 'Dead giveaway. Thieves are always nice tae ye. That's why they're good at bein' thieves."

That sounds plausible so I go back down the street to where the two thieves are having breakfast. And confront them.

"Look into my eyes." the young guy says, "I'm telling you we didn't steal it." He invites me to look through their bags. I have an uneasy feeling about this. I'm on shaky ground.

"Look intae ma eyes?" Muldoon says back at the café when I tell him.

"Wiz 'ie tryin' tae hypnotize you?"

Muldoon will bankroll me for a few days. The passport is the biggest problem but we'll get that sorted out too. A bit inconvenient is all. I pick up a copy of the *Diario de Navarra*. There's more to this Way of St James than meets the eye. The *Codex Calixtinus*, the illustrated early medieval manuscript, named after Pope Calixtinus, describing the route for pilgrims, and worth a fortune, disappeared from the Cathedral of Santiago de Compostela on 7th July 2011, and they're on the track of the robbers, it says on the front page. There's also a longer article inside about the manuscript itself and some quotations from it. And since we're in Navarra (Navarre) they've selected a reference to the Navarrans.

"Listen to this," I say, translating bits of the article to Muldoon who has his nose in a dog-eared book of crossword puzzles. "Navarrans dress in black clothes that are short and to the knee like the Scots ...They are a barbarous people, different from all others in their customs ... lewd, drunken, aggressive, fierce and savage ... cruel, quarrelsome, devoid of any virtue, and taught to every vice and iniquity."

"Sounds familiar." says Muldoon. "Mibae they came doon in their kilts an didnae go back up, 'cause ae the weather."

5

Meet the Scallop Gang

After the truce of 1444, the king sent part of the *"skinners"* – some 30,000 mercenaries – back to Switzerland and Alsace. But there still remained a considerable number scattered throughout the kingdom, unable to revert to peace. They turned into gangs of bandits. The most famous are the Coquillards, put on trial in Dijon in 1455 and sentenced. The gang had about five hundred members who adopted the rallying symbol of the scallop (coquille) carried by the pilgrims on the Way of St James… The Coquillards were led by the *"King of the Scallop"* and dominated by a complex hierarchy of *"masters,"* of *"subtle things"* and of *"long masters."* The apprentices were killers, pickpockets, flimflam artists and card sharps… Their social mix was as varied as their geographical origin: Spanish, Parisians, Scots, Bretons, Savoyards, Normans, Picards, Provence soldiers recruited from the unemployed and the wretched but also from among the clergy, the choir of the Holy Chapelle in Dijon, students…

Encyclopedie Universalis

Imagine this: It is the year 1455 and the Hundred Years' War has recently ended, James II is on the throne of Scotland and you are a pilgrim and you have been walking for months: down through Scotland, on into England through York and Canterbury till you get to one of the Channel Ports and on to France. Then another month or two passing through France, over the Pyrenees and now you are in Spain. You are in Navarra, in the Basque country. You've got a smattering of French and that has got you by so far but no Spanish, which does not help anyway because the language the heathens speak here on this side of the Pyrenees is nothing like Spanish and is understood only by the locals themselves, the Basques and the Navarrans, they and their mules. Fortunately you attend mass regularly so you have some Latin, which helps a bit. Down the muddy paths when it rains and the dust in summer, the stinking dangerous inns where you don't know what to expect, the monasteries where you are at least safe and have a bed for the night and are fed by the monks and the brothers.

And now it's early morning in Puente La Reina. You have heard some pretty horrific tales of robbery and murder in the inns, but so far you have been lucky apart from that Gasconard you spent two days walking with. That you'd caught with his hand in your bag and who disappeared with a whore at the last place you stopped. But you have just woken up in the hospice, had a crust to eat for breakfast and a drink of water from the wooden bucket and now you're approaching the main square of Puente la Reina, heading on for Estella where you hope to reach the monastery in time for a meal.

So it's just as well to think of getting another travelling companion. Because the road is dangerous and the pitfalls many. Before you reach the square you hear a voice call out in Latin, the *lingua franca* of the day "Deus, adieuva, Sancte Jacobe. Deus adieuva, Sancte Jacobe," or God Help, Saint James, God, help, St James." The cry is familiar and you have heard it dozens of times on the way down. It is the cry of pilgrims looking for someone to accompany them on the road for the day. It is dangerous to walk alone. The young man is dressed in a long cloak, has the scallop of St James hanging round his neck and is carrying a long staff. He greets you pleasantly. He seems a decent enough fellow and you head out of town together, talking about this and that as far as the language barrier allows. About half an hour later you halt on a grassy knoll under the trees, and you wake with a mouthful of grass, unable to move, your face in the earth. You are being raped by a band of Gasconards, Basques in fact, ex-mercenaries, some of whom fought in the Hundred Years' War. That is when you hear mention for the first time of the King of the Scallops (Coquillards) that they're talking about, and how pleased he will be with the contents of your bag.

And if you could speak they would tell you you have the honour of falling into the hands of the Coquillards, a band of over five hundred thugs of all ages, organized like a medieval trade guild, each with his own specialty. At the bottom of the league is the apprentice learning the tricks of the trade. Then there is the *vendimiador* who specializes in slitting the bags of pilgrims and stealing their contents, the *beffleur* or baffler, skilled in games of chance. And there's the *blancoulon* (white shirt) as he's called, who attacks traders and commercial travellers in the inns and if he's skilled enough becomes a dispatcher a *remitente*, a skilled assassin, whose favourite weapon is the knife or the dagger.

And there's also the woman. The woman who tells you she's a widow and strangles you in your sleep or takes you to the inn which is really a brothel and the brothel owner strangles you there. And before you die, you listen to snatches of their conversation and wonder at the strangeness of the world and at these men and women whose sole concern is to get on, as they say, in life, get better off from what they are good at doing. To aspire to rise through the ranks, to become masters of their trade, become masters or *maestros* and then go on to become *largos*, or seniors.

And for some strange reason, you recognize the same structure in the church all the way to the top. To the Pope, where they don't rob you but sell you indulgences. But they are good men and these men are evil. And as the light is waning in your head, a great joy fills your heart. You are leaving this place. You are leaving this hell. You have been in hell all your life and now you are going to heaven. But you will not come back. If you could, as a bird, as a crow, even as an ass, you would know the world. But you never will, because you have come from the world of men where you were robbed and cheated and killed a thousand times a thousand every day on the roads that your life passed along. From the time Cinaed mac Ailpin was on the throne of Scotland and Gregory was on throne of God in Rome or the day the Basques murdered Roland at the pass of Roncesvalles and stole Charlemagne's gold and poets wrote the Song of Roland and blamed it on the Saracens. And you see yourself again this morning coming over the stone bridge into the town, thankful to the saints, San Juan Ortega or San Jesus, or even the kings of Castille, Navarra and Aragon, who had the bridges built so you could avoid the predatory boat men who could charge you up to ten maravedis for the crossing as well as for any valuables you were carrying, on the pretext they were protecting you.

And in your ears as you are breathe your last, you hear the clink of the coins in the hands of your assassins who are counting them and remember the coins in your bag from the time you left home: the bawbees, the groats, the silver shillings, the English quarter nobles, the half leopards, some of them minted in Berwick or Edinburgh, and see the money changers turning them over, examining them, when you pass from one territory into another, from one region of France into another, from one region of Spain into another, see the money changer place your coins alongside others you have never seen before, never imagined existed, German thalers, Italian ducats, and you hear about white money and black money like you hear about good and evil and see one last time Jesus cast the money changers out of the Temple and understand just before you close your eyes why the birds sing and the donkeys bray when they could have learned the language of men a thousand years ago but refused to do so but waited for St Francis to appear so they could come down out of the trees and rest on his arms and shoulders and speak to him in the language of birds. Or maybe a miracle is happening as the white light flashes in your head and you go flying through the universe.

6
But Not to Worry

But not to worry. Or as it says in the horoscope in the newspaper: "Be of good cheer, this is your lucky day, help is on its way from a well-wisher."

It happens like this. "Oh ma back?" Muldoon groans, sitting down on the bench in the square. We've just come over the hill and stop in the square of this one horse town. The place is deserted in the early morning and the tourist office at the other side of the square is not yet open. The provincial highway runs through the place like the blade of a dull knife made of some cheap, low grade material. One of those places where the buildings on either side of the road are grey and bald with their surface flaking off like dandruff, and when you look back the way you came, the highway disappears over the crest of the hill behind you. And when you look forward you see it run for four of five kilometres in front of you across the landscape between the fields before it dwindles to a thin line and disappears over the horizon. There are no cars on the road. Maybe one will pass after a while, maybe not. When it rains the surface of the road is slippery and if you're driving you've got to be careful. That's about as much as you can say about the place. There's also a bus stop further down from the square with a timetable pasted to the wall of the shelter. It is under a little tree that no doubt provides relief from the hot sun for the one or two passengers waiting for the bus. But there's no one waiting in the shelter at this hour of the morning. The next bus isn't till late afternoon.

On the other side of the square the shutters of the tourist information office have just gone up. A cyclist comes over the hill with his head down peddling furiously as if trying to get out of the place fast as he can. The bike tires hiss on the road as he streaks down the blade. The sun is trying to get through the morning haze but you can look up at it without hurting your eyes and follow the cyclist. Soon it'll get pretty hot and the haze will clear. Muldoon stands up, groans, says "Ah'm off for a coffee," picks up his bag by the strap and heads for the café on the corner. I watch him go through the door and look across the square, pick up mine and head for the information office. The office is open and there's a desk but there is no one behind it. I check out the brochures and pick up a map of the region. Then I wander round the town, find a bench and open up the map. That's when the phone goes. It's not a call but a message. And it comes as a shock. The message says: "Sandra asking when ur back."

It's not my phone. Who in God's name is Sandra? It must be a friend of the owner of the phone. The girl who left it behind in the hostel. Probably recently, because it doesn't need charging. Young probably and not too savvy because she hasn't coded the phone so it's no problem for another person to use it. Mary, we'll call her, has a few messages from her parents, asking how she is and why she hasn't been in touch these last days. It is weird. I feel like a Peeping Tom.

Then I get another message. From Muldoon. "Found bag," it says so I hurry back to the café where Muldoon is sitting at the bar looking proud as punch with the missing bag on top of the bar.

"Wiz in the back," he says.

I open the bag and everything is there. Nothing's been touched. "Where was it?" And he shows me. At the back of the rucksack there's a compartment. An open compartment you can slide things into but not anything too bulky. It's reinforced with hard rubber and its purpose still eludes me unless it is for sliding maps or papers into, stuff that you can easily access when you stop and take the bag off your shoulders. And since Muldoon has the same type of bag as mine, I must have put my valuables in the wrong bag the night before.

A miracle is an event that appears inexplicable by the laws of nature and so is held to be supernatural in origin, or an act of God, the dictionary says. But what are the laws of nature?

"Eh?" Muldoon is silent on that one.

The laws of nature are empirical truths, dictated by reason, I explain. So in this case they don't apply if you don't know there is a secret cabinet in the rucksack. And if you don't know there is a secret cabinet in the rucksack you cannot be held to blame. Strictly speaking it does not qualify as stupidity either, as stupidity implies a lack of perception.

"If ye look at sheep a think thur goats, yir no right in the heid." is Muldoon's contribution to the polemic.

I think of divine intervention, but I'm not too hot on that topic and strictly speaking, it doesn't qualify for that either. Not miraculous enough. "Maybe it was the pain," I say. "Because if you hadn't felt the pain in your back, you wouldn't have known. Sooner or later you'd have to take a look." Muldoon agrees that's a pretty reasonable explanation so to celebrate we order a nice big baguette with *jamon serrano* and watch the barman cut slices from the leg of smoked *pata negra* hanging on a hook on the tiled wall and layer it with a liberal sprinkling of sea salt and olive oil. Muldoon orders another beer; I have another *café con leche*.

We check the map. I pay the bill. Then we shoulder up, hit the road, pass the bus shelter and take to the road. We can be visualized as getting smaller and smaller and smaller, dwindling into the distance as we glide down the long dull grey blade evaporating into the morning sun, the sort of thing you see in second rate road movies when "The End" comes up on the screen and you get this desolate landscape under a grey sky being sucked into the far horizon. About all it tells you if you even care to think about it, is it's the best the director can come up with. You've seen it all before. And so has the director.

7

An Ancient Miracle

The Poitevin whom the Apostle sent an Angel to Help in the Guise of an Ass

In the year one thousand one hundred of Our Lord's incarnation, in the principality of Count William of Poitou, under Louis, king of the Franks, a deadly plague lamentably invaded a town of Poitou to such an extent that fathers of entire families together with all their dear ones were taken away to be buried. Then one day, a certain gentleman, mortified by so many deaths and wishing to avoid this scourge, determined to go to Santiago, passing through Spanish lands. And with his wife and two children, mounted on his mare, they arrived in the town of Pamplona. But there his wife died and his wicked unjust host iniquitously kept the wherewithal the gentleman and his wife had brought with them.

Desolated by her death and stripped of all his money together with the mare he carried the children with, he took them by the hand and continued the journey with great difficulty. And along the way, sunk in the greatest distress and concern, on the road he encountered an honourable looking man being carried along on a very sturdy looking donkey.

This man, when he heard the many and great adversities that had befallen him in his misfortune, said in commiseration:

"In view of your extreme distress, I will lend you an ass of mine who will be very good for taking your children to the town of Compostela where I live, provided you give it back when you get there."

Accepting the ass then, and mounting his children on its back, the pilgrim came to the sepulchre of Santiago. Finally, when he was devotedly at vigil during the night in a secluded corner of the venerable basilica, the most glorious Apostle appeared in radiant attire and said,

"Do you not know me, brother?"

"Not at all," he replied.

"I am," he said, "the Apostle of Christ that lent you his ass in the midst of your grief in Pamplona's lands. Now you can borrow it again until you return to your home, and your wicked host, for having unjustly taken from you what is yours, will fall from his chair and be beset by ill luck; I tell you this, and also that all unjust innkeepers, established on my road, who iniquitously steal the goods of their guests, living or dead, which are to be given to the churches and the needy for the repose of the departed, will be damned forever. "

And just as the pilgrim bent forward to embrace the feet of he who spoke to him, the most reverend Apostle vanished from the eyes of man.

And so it was that the pilgrim, rejoicing at the vision of the Apostle and receiving so much consolation, departed from the town of Compostela at dawn with the ass and his children, and on arriving in Pamplona found the innkeeper had died of a broken neck when he fell from his chair at home just as the Apostle had predicted.

And arriving happy and content in his own country and lifting the children down from the ass at the door of his house, the animal vanished from sight. Many who heard him tell of this were amazed more than can possibly be said and commented that, either it was a real ass, or an angel in the form of such as the Lord often sends to help those who fear him.

This was done by Our Lord, and is admirable in our sight. And so therefore, as is clearly shown by this miracle, all malicious innkeepers are condemned to eternal death for unjustly taking the goods of others. Give alms to the churches and the poor of Christ in suffrage for the dead. May it serve also to remove all blame and condemnation from all believers through the merits of Santiago, Jesus Christ our Lord, who with the Father and the Holy Spirit, God reigns through the endless ages of ages. So be it.

The Book of Miracles, Codex Calixtinus, Book II, Chapter VI

8
Sleazeball Spaniards were Scots

Oh my dear brothers and sisters, especially you my dear brothers, that this may serve as a warning when venturing abroad in foreign climes, but it has come to my ears that we are not descended, as has oft been told, from that great Celtic hero Fingal, whom the great bard Finn McTool calls the king of shields and the king of shells, or from the mighty Wallace, six foot seven in his shoon, and hands like a palm tree if we are to believe Blind Harry, but brought in bondage to Spain by the same Romans who invaded our lands all the way to Aberdeen whence they transported our brothers to Spain to inseminate the poxy Iberian tribes and convert them into sleazeball Navarrans.

And I tell you this, among other things, my dear brothers and sisters, so that you may take note and assist in these barren lands, at opportune moment, my dear friend and companion Seamus Muldoon who is much affected by the dreadful revelations of our true origins and is sunk in deep misery, not knowing which way to turn.

There has come into my possession a document of no small import written before Alexander was our King as you will remember from that well-known poem which begins:

Qwhen Alexander our kynge was dede…Our golde was changit in to lede.

And changed into lead indeed we are, my dear brothers and sisters, Muldoon and I, wading through the sludge of the world's iniquity larding these slippery byways for over a millennium, and whenever we pause for a break on our pilgrim's way I take out a page or two and study it.

I am unable to give you – at this point – a translation in its entirety of the extract in question from the *Codex Calixtinus* and so have omitted all references to evil ferrymen, thieving innkeepers and horse-skinning thugs lying in wait by poisonous streams for innocent pilgrims, all of which will be familiar stuff, in different guise, to those of my dear brother and sisters who are faithful readers of the daily press.

In this mountain, before Christianity spread throughout Spanish lands, the wicked Navarrans and the Basques would not only assail the pilgrims going to Santiago but mount them like asses and kill them...Next to this mountain, to the north, is the valley known as Valcarlos (Valley of Charles), in which Charlemagne himself was encamped with his armies, when his warriors died at Roncesvalles.

Many pilgrims on the way to Santiago pass through it when they do not want to scale the mountain. Continuing on down you get to the hospice and the church where you find the rock that the mighty hero Roland split with his sword down the middle, from top to bottom, in three strokes. Then comes Roncesvalles, where the great battle took place that killed King Marsilio, Roland and Oliveros with another forty thousand Christian and Saracen combatants.

After this valley comes the land of Navarra, rich in bread, wine, milk and cattle. The Navarrans and Basques are very similar as regards food, dress and language, but the Basques are more pale skinned than the Navarrans. The Navarrans dress in short, black garments down to the knees in the manner of the Scots and use a type of shoe they call brogues, made of hairy, untanned leather, tied at the bottom with straps that only cover the soles of the feet, leaving the rest bare. They wear black woollen cloaks with a fringe that come down to their elbows.

As is plain to see, they dress badly, just as they eat and drink badly, because at home the Navarran usually eats together with his entire family, the servant together with the master, the maid with the mistress, mixing all the dishes together in a single pot, with no spoons because they eat with their hands and they all drink from the same jug. If you saw them eating you would think they were dogs or pigs. And listening to them talk makes you think of the barking of dogs, so barbarous is their language. They are a barbarous people, different from all others in their customs and nature, full of evil, dark in colour, vile-looking, malevolent, perverse, treacherous, disloyal, lustful, drunken, aggressive, fierce and savage, ruthless and reprobate, pitiless and crude, cruel and quarrelsome, devoid of any virtue, and versed in every vice and iniquity, partners in evil with the Getae (Thracians or Dacians, neighbours of the Scythians) and the Saracens and sworn enemies of our Gallic nation.

For a miserable coin, a Basque or a Navarran will put paid to a Frenchman when he gets the chance. In some of their counties, in Vizcaya and Alava for example, when they are warming themselves by the fire, Navarrans will flash their private parts: the man to the woman and the woman to the man.

Furthermore in some impure and unclean communities where they abuse their animals, the Navarrans fornicate incestuously with their livestock. And it is also said that the Navarran puts a chain on the backside of his mule or his mare so that no one but he may have at it. He also imparts lustful kisses to the vulva of his woman and his mule. Because of all this, people of breeding and education cannot but condemn the Navarrans. However, they are considered brave on the field of battle, if bad in besieging fortresses. They are praised for their payment of tithes, and in persevering in their offerings to the altar. Every time a Navarran goes to church, he offers God bread, wine, wheat, or any other substance.

Wherever a Navarran or a Basque goes, he hangs a horn round his neck like a hunter and usually carries two or three javelins... And when he enters or goes back home he warbles like a thrush. And when lying in wait to ambush his prey, he will call silently to his companions, hooting like an owl or howling like a wolf.

It is said they descend from the lineage of the Scots, because they are similar in their habits and appearance. The story goes that Julius Caesar sent three peoples to Spain: the Nubians, the Scots and the men with the tails from Cornwall, to subjugate the people who refused to pay tribute, with the order to put all the males to the sword and spare the life only of the women folk.

They came by sea to that territory and with their ships destroyed it and devastated it with fire and sword from Barcelona to Zaragoza and from Bayonne to Montes de Oca. But they were unable to pass beyond these boundaries, because the Spaniards united, fought and repulsed them from their borders. In retreating, they fled to the mountains of the coast, situated between Nájera and Pamplona, that is to say, towards the sea, in Vizcaya and Alava land, where they settled, raising numerous fortifications and killing all the males, took their wives with whom they had children to whom posterity gave the name of Navarrans.[1]

As I say, I only give Muldoon the gist which means I've got to pull out the pages I downloaded every time he asks a question. And carefully check the Spanish. He doesn't say anything at first. He's in denial, mulling it over. He'll seize on any inconsistency. Take the kilts. We're sitting outside a little café in a one-fly-blown village having a drink and the word kilts come up.

"Ach, away ye go. They wernae kilts," he says, "Jist wee short skirts. There's nae mention ae tartan so they couldnae a been kilts."

But it would be a foolish man would write off Muldoon. He has his insights. Later, I tell him – we've stopped for a break on a long boring stretch between the wheat fields and are sitting on a little bridge over a watercourse – it was the Basques or the Navarrans attacked and killed Roland after Charlemagne's army razed Pamplona and went back over the mountains into France with Roland trailing behind in the rear, and he says,

"That means it wiz the Scots killed 'im."

"How'd you arrive at that?"

"Ye said the Navarrans wir Scots. So it wiz the Scots killed 'im."

I've got him sussed. A blood-thirsty loon like the rest of his race. He seems to like the idea the Scots were a murderous bunch and killed Roland. This is a new turn of events. Almost a positive slant on things, you might say. But I keep my peace, bide my time. And when we're hoofing it again through the wheat lands, I say to Muldoon, I say, "Funny thing about the kilts."

"Whit d'ye mean?"

"The Navarrans. Them being black and that. The kilts." Because Muldoon said the Navarrans couldn't be Scots because they didn't have the tartan.

"Aye ah ken," he says. "That's jist it. Mibae that wiz the tartan."

"What d' you mean?"

"Black."

"Black? Black! You're kidding?"

---

[1] *Book of the Pilgrim, Codex Calixtinus*, Book V, "Names of the Regions and Characteristics of the People of the Camino de Santiago."

"Naw. Black. Jist aw black. A black tartan."

"But you can't have tartan without stripes."

"Not at a'. Not at a'. That jist it. That wiz before they come up wi the stripes."

9

Sunday the Wolf

"Sunday the Wolf," I tell Muldoon as we step and gaily again on the road towards Estela, "was the one who ratted when they caught the Coquillards, the Scallop gang. Him and the barber spilled the beans."

"Solly Bean?"

"No. Not Sawney Bean, the Galloway cannibal.[2] The barber. The barber was seen going into an inn in Dijon, frequented by ne'er-do-wells. Run by a guy called Jacquot de la Mer. A fence. Later got hung. Barber went by the name of Perrenet le Fournier.

"So the magistrates raid the place. They're fed up to the teeth with all the pillaging, break-ins, ripoffs and God knows what else this murderous bunch of lipey-loos has been up to in the manor for the last couple of years. Find half a dozen of the villains with their faces pressed flat against the wall in the cupboards of the inn, the idiots. Reckon them in and try to charge them but nobody is talking. Sealed lips is the order of the day.

"So then the magistrate gets to talking to Dimanche le Loup, Sunday the Wolf and offers him a wee deal if he'll sing. So Sunday, who's the youngest of the bunch, tells them a thing or two in exchange for getting off the hook. Explains how the Coquillards operate. They've got their own language, use fake names so nobody knows who they are most of the time. There's about five hundred of them although the barber says there's over a thousand. Nobody knows for sure.

"They have a king. King of the Coquillards. The one they've got at the moment is called Regnault Dambour and is a stone cutter in the service of the Duke of Burgundy. So the magistrate's listening to this, taking in everything Sunday's saying and before you know it, he's written down about two hundred words of their jargon and the terms they use in their business. There's talls or

---

[2]Sawney Bean was head of an incestuous clan of cannibals who, according to legend, lived in cave in Ballantrae, Galloway, in 15th century Scotland.

"longs" – "longs" is what they call them in French – who come under the king and they're sort of like masters of their trade, specialized. Under them come the rank-and-file, the everyday, common and garden tea-leafs. They're into everything. They've got spies, buying and selling information, purse cutters, lock-pickers, confidence men, counterfeiters and their assistants, flimflam artists sharper than a brace of Mississippi gamblers, counterfeiters making fake gold or silver ingots, with assistants that ply the inns looking for patsies, softening up the soft touches with tear jerking tales about the tribulations of their sad masters who may or may not be disguised at that very moment as rich fat merchants blowing their trumpets in the inn about how much money they've got on them to attract the attention of the gullible fools lapping it all up, all the baloney, their tongues hanging out in wonder. So they can "dupe" them. That's where the word dupe comes from. Did you know that? From the Coquillards.

"And they're having a grand old time of it at the inn. That's where they hole out. Honking, rooting and gambling the night away. Dice and cards. On the batter. Shafting the whores and when they've blown the ever readies, including the gelt of the tarts, they scarper, hit the trail and the inn's silent as the tomb for month, maybe two while they're out on the road doing the dirty, disguised as pilgrims going to Santiago, stripping their victims bare as new born bairns when night falls, cutting their throats.

"Come from all over the ship. Go under all sorts of nicknames. All sorts of names to disguise themselves. One day they're called this, the next day they're called that. Keep changing them. Colin the Breton (Colin le Breton) William the Norman (Guillemin le Normand) Andrew the Provençal (André le Provençal). Even a Scot among them. John of Scotland (Jean d'Ecosse). Mercenaries probably who'd fought in the Hundred Years' War.

"Regnier the Spaniard (Régnier dit l'Espagnol) or Little John the Sword Master (Petit Jean dit Maître de l'Epée). Roaming troops who had broken up with the army, former mule skinners or criminals run afoul of the law. Like Perrenot Cropped Ear (Perrenot l'Essorillé). They cut off your ear if you got caught nicking stuff. Or loped a lump off it."

"Chris," Muldoon says, "Sounds like Reg the Whistle used tae gie his greyhound a sniff a coke afore it bolted oot the trap at Carntyne."

"Long and short of it is they can't make the charges stick. Got their cake holes buttoned. Most of them anyway. But they hang three of them just the same. Dambour the king gets his, Jacquot de la Mer, a sergeant-at-arms working for the magistrates is another and Sunday the Wolf too, despite the promises made if he sang.

"Sunday the Wolf?"

"Another two get done for counterfeit. You know what they do to you for that? Boil you."

"Boil ye? Yir kiddin?"

"No! Boil you! In a big vat. Fill it up with water, stick you in and boil you like a chicken. Over the fire. Can you believe it? Christoph le Turgis and Denisot le Clerc, two 'planters' who tried to palm off fake silver and gold ingots, stuck in a big cauldron and boiled over a fire. Hours on end."

"Wee Sunday... how auld wiz he?"

"Doesn't say. Only the youngest."

"Hung?"

"Aye, afraid so."

"And do you know what they did beforehand? Stuck you in a cart used to carry all the shit and paraded you through the town on market day. If you were a noble you got your head chopped off first. Then you got hung with all your gear on. But don't ask me how they did that without a head, because I don't know. Your furs and spurs. And the commoners, the rank-and-file they got striped down to their shirts and strung up."

"Wee Sunday? Maybe jist a boy."

"Aye, bastard isn't it? Mind you, you don't know do you? I mean: Sunday the Wolf? Come on. A wolf on a Sunday and a sheep during the week?"

"Still an a', the youngest."

"Maybe a bad wee bastard."

"Aye, there's that as well."

And so it goes as we plod further west along the road towards the ends of the earth. Trouble is you never know with Muldoon. Whether he's leading you on and just taking the piss.

10
Rollerballing Dudes in Burgos

To Hare is Human.

Merrie Melodies[3]

Lucas is from Kansas and he's with his girlfriend Louisa and they're doing the grand tour to Santiago through the villages, towns and watering holes to the Holy of Holies. In two weeks. That's all the time they've got and to do that they need a need a bike. They've just arrived in Burgos and want to rent a couple of bikes but I can't help them on that. We're in the Albergue Municipal in Burgos up behind the vast white stone Cathedral. The hostel is spread over six floors and has two lifts. The common room with the cooking facilities is gigantic. Totally modern, it's like a small-sized aircraft hangar you could get three or four Piper Cubs in. Reputedly it is the best hostel between Roncesvalles on the border to Santiago. It even has Wi-Fi, what more can you say?

Lucas and Louisa are happy bunnies and raring to go. Life is looking great for them. You can see that from their faces. They're in love. I know that because they agree with each other no matter what either of them says. And whatever is said is just great. They're of one mind, as they say. That's how it goes. They've probably finished college, but we don't go into that. We don't want to spoil the conversation by talking about work. Lucas is a sort of blonde kid, round faced and Louisa is dark haired. He could be originally from where blonde faces like that come from. Sweden? Denmark? Holland? Some place like that. She might have a touch of Irish or Mexican or maybe even Italian, but that's just a guess. You're not going to do grandmothers and grandfathers when you've just met.

---

[3]"The Road Runner cartoon represents the existential nature of man. The coyote is always making his plans, always thinking that he will finally win. Then the Road Runner comes up behind him and 'Beep', 'Beep': the sound of the universe laughing."

Anonymous quote on the internet

What we're talking about, which is what interests me most, running into these two dudes, is the influx of Americans on the road. Is that a recent thing? Has something happened out there in transatlantic space I should know about? Has there been a mind change thing? These last few days I see more and more Americans. Alone, in pairs, in groups with bicycles. Getting mounted up outside hostels and heading out into the hinterland, the countryside, the outback or the badlands, whatever you want to call the space out there, outside the towns and cities. With firm purpose and noble intent. Young kids mostly. Teenagers. In groups at times, accompanied by their mentors.

What's it all about? Have they been flicking the feel-good pages of Paul Coelho, looking for their swords? Or has some other gombeen man guru wisdommed them a DIY manual of the Seven Secrets to Happiness and Success? Or was it that film by Martin Sheen. *The Way?* I haven't seen it yet, but someone mentioned it. It's been a big hit in America. Maybe they've been up late watching that. Maybe that's why they've come?

But no, Lucas is keen to distance himself from that popular stuff. Yes, he has seen the film but that was much later. That didn't affect their decision. No, no, he insists, he has had it in mind for some time. Got the lowdown from friends.

"It's getting busier and busier," I say, but I don't really know what busy means in these terms since I have never been here before. But I've got some figures handy. Over 272,000 visitors in Holy Year 2010, and 183,000 in 2011. Of which. Yes, of which over 7,000 Americans against less than four thousand Brits and about the same for the French.

Lucas says, just you wait till they really get started. The Americans, he means. Because Americans need to do things faster. They can't help it. They have to be competing. Racing down the Camino to the finishing line. To see who gets there first.

Lucas is pretty laid back so he's not going to be into that.

"Motorbikes," I say "Thunderballing like in Thunder Ball Express?"

"You mean *Cannonball Express*, that film with Burt Reynolds?"

"Is that what it was called?"

"Yes, Burt, the guy with the white teeth and the toupee? Sounds about right. Thunderballing, Rollerballing, Cannonballing? It's all the same. No?"

"Rollerballing? You mean rollerblading?"

"Rollerblading too. Right. Good one. If they get the bumps smoothed out."

So, I'm sorry to say, my dear brothers and sisters, we could be looking the beginning of the end straight in the eye. Give it a year or two at the outset and its curtains. With every man Jack, his dog, cat and granny in search of peace of mind and escape from the machine. If the Americans get a taste for the action, it could get pretty crowded down this way. Trailer parks. Souvenir shops. Hot air balloon trips, pilgrim skydiving. And who knows, Karaoke in McDonald's, Good Old Boys singing "Ah wish ah wahz in Dixie," The Sister Rosetta Tharpe Singers belting out "Up Above Ma Head." And the Brits, don't underestimate the Brits when it comes to bad taste, whiteys all micked up as coons hovering carpets to the sound of Freddie Mercury with wings, singing "I Want to Break Free" from the clouds on high. Or reciting the Book of Job dressed as Moses holding the tablet of the Ten Commandments. And just think what they could do with a Book of Revelation Theme Park. The earth cracking and spewing fire. Demons winging in on par gliders. Angels giving them the one two up the hooter with a sword thrust.

The Spanish municipalities are all well aware of pilgrim potential on the road, but they still have some sinking to do to reach transatlantic (or cross-channel) levels of venality. "It will be sausage to me," as the Dutch say (*het zal me worst wezen*) which is what the revellers last night were also thinking as they tanked up late into the wee hours on wine, Coca Cola, beer and everything in between, making more noise than when Spain won the World Cup. They call it the noisiest hostel in Spain. There was a non-stop racket deep into the night, till – I don't know when – maybe four or five when the dawn started to come up in the sky. But I was in a pit of deep exhaustion by then. I got up from bed three or four times and looked out the window to see where the din was coming from. Maybe a disco next door or downstairs, though they had locked the big main door before twelve and you couldn't get in after that.

It was only when I left in the morning to go down the stairs again, past the Cathedral, to look for a coffee, I saw the scene of depredation. A small square littered with beers cans, jumbo-sized plastic Coca Cola bottles, wine bottles and here and there an empty bottle of vodka, sherry, *Larios* gin, and I'm pleased to say, since I used to drink it in Edinburgh, *Ballantine's* whisky.

If you were an archaeologist you could probably make a good stab at who had been drinking what. And their nationality. But not a lot of the heavy alcohol stuff, which is not what the under eighteen's can afford: the young braves, the students, the out-of-work, anybody, in other words under the age of twenty five with no other reason on God's earth to be abed on a Friday night and nothing better to do than get gutted, smoke dope and shoot the breeze.

Yes the *botellón* struck during the night. Botella is bottle and Spanish. And if you put the letters on at the end of some words you get *botellón*, literally a big bottle. A big booze up. I had never seen the aftermath of one this size before. Like one of those tornados we get to see on TV, regularly sweeping across the Great Plains, that swirl like crazy across the landscape and you only know the meaning of when they have passed and you wake up dead among the debris of your prefabricated cabin or your trailer.

There have been reports enough in the papers about the *botellón*. The trouble it is causing up and down the country with kids drinking en masse in the public squares into the wee hours babbling like loons under octogenarian windows. This was the biggest one I'd seen, although I am only talking as an amateur archaeologist, surveying the aftermath of The Marriage Feast of Cannae, trying to determine from the crusts of bread and the wine stains how many guests were there. A hundred? Two hundred.

Three hundred?

Do you have any conception of the sound a bunch of kids can make in the middle of the night in a little park sloping downhill, dwarfed by three or four storey medieval buildings with six foot thick walls? Put it this way. Just imagine you are a mole in a hole deep in the earth and the ants are on overtime through the night lugging and stacking eggs in a cave half an inch from your little pink ear. And there's no other sound on the earth. So with Spaniards botelloning all over the ship and Americans rollerballing down the camino, things could get pretty hairy up ahead. And with the progeny of the nouveau riche from China, Japan, Europe, Russia, and not to forget Korea, headed this way too with bad habits, that should put an end to this little pilgrim lark. Look what happened to Sloppy Joe's in Key West when the punters found out Hemingway dropped in one day to use the toilet.

But mankind needs new challenges to rise to. And with Everest so strewn with tourist trash the Sherpas are moving into the recycling business, we have to be on our toes. Yes, the future is already here. Spiderman competitions. Scaling the Cathedral with sticky fly feet. An electronic sign on the highest spire flashing the fastest time to Santiago on LED display. Mountain bikes revving up in the square in the early morning. Flags of the world waving. Banners fluttering in the breeze saying *Santiago Annual Thunderball Rally 2030*. Or maybe even sooner, the speed things are going. With the winner getting to pull the rope and swing the incense-burner from the roof in the Cathedral. And then there's the St James Scallop. No *Ferengi* has patented that. You remember the *Ferengis*? Those ugly little dwarves with the big eyebrows and the square heads in Star Trek? Greedy little vermin obsessed with making big bucks at somebody else's expense. And since there are more *Ferengis* in the good old US of A than anywhere else on earth, some of them are going to get into a screaming rage if they can't satisfy their greed.

But no sweat, there's still time to replace the scallop. Replace the logo. With Wile E Coyote or Road Runner. Or maybe Speedy Gonzalez, he at least spoke Spanish.

Sorry, got to go now. Just got a message saying God is coming to Glasgow and I'm one of the lucky ones been chosen for the welcoming committee to meet him at the airport. Got to make a few phone calls, see if I can raise the 100,000 dollars and wire them immediately to Nanggala in Nigeria to get him to reveal the day and the hour of the Second Coming, send me the ticket and get his cousin Mumbaluma to bless the holy gloves I need to shake God's hand at no extra cost.

11
Once Upon a Time in Sahagún

A sad and decayed town, Sahagún belongs to a vanishing Spain, with decrepit houses mainly of the early years of this century (20th) and streets and a central square lined, as with so many towns and villages of this region, with blackened, splintering, wooden porticos.

Michael Jacobs, *The Road to Santiago de Compostela*

Remember *Once Upon a Time in the West?* The film? Where they're waiting for the train to arrive? In this godforsaken hole out in the desert with nothing nowhere, not in a thousand mile radius or anything near it? Utter desolation? Well Sahagún is a bit like that. The only difference being it has a little railway station. And next to the railway station there's a bar. With big rough-hewn wooden tables you can sit outside at and have a beer. But if it's drizzling, you'll want to sit inside. Which is what we're doing now. The place is otherwise deserted on an early Sunday afternoon.

We're sitting inside looking at our boots and studying the woodwork. And the bar. And the panelling. And the big casks, head high behind us. I don't know about Muldoon, who's got his crossword puzzle book out again, but I'm wondering what they have in them. Pure boredom is going to force me eventually to get up and investigate the casks more closely and read the labels. At the moment, I'm fighting the urge.

And talking about trains, the place also makes you feel like you're a character in another Western: *3:10 to Yuma,* where everything hangs on that three-ten train coming to take the bad guy to Yuma Territorial Prison. That's what I'm thinking about, eyeing the wooden panelling and the woman who has just appeared behind the bar to pull us two cold beers. Out here you are really and truly nowhere. You are waiting for something to happen and know that if it does, if things start moving, taking direction, unlikely as it may seem, you could be out of your depth. So you get your head down and check your Michelin map again for the name of Sahagún in case you got it wrong. From the promotional bumph you have read it is supposed to be a gem of a place, not this dump. So where is it? So you look at the name again but it still means nothing. You're disconnected from the grid. You've been short-circuited. And like the place you are not connected to anything in this world.

Before we come up to the station to check on the times of the trains, we are at the hostel, sitting at a table having a cup of tea. Herman the German is wearing nothing on his upper body but a sleeveless sheepskin tunic. He looks like he has just come out of the Black Forest where he has been killing wolves. He has a big staff leaning against the wall. When he picks it up later you see it goes over his head and is about a half a foot taller than he is. And he's tall. Tall and muscular and fit from knocking down trees and killing wolves. If you had to put a name on him, you'd say the Jolly Green Giant you see on the back of a can of green peas, but minus the Jolly bit.

The other three guests are the Catalan trio, the would-be gypsy Catalans. The Catalan harpies are arguing about the plates or something or maybe they're moaning that there aren't enough knives and forks to go round. Muldoon is lying on his back on a bunk. He's been pretty silent of late now I've run out of inspirational stories.

Herman tells his story. In German, since he speaks no English. It roughly goes as follows. He leaves home one day and goes walking. He'll be in his mid-forties, walks for a month till he hears that his wife has died. Then he goes back quickly and stays for a few more months to sort out things with the kids. Then he takes off again. He gets the big curly stick he cut from a bush in the Black Forest and sets off again. That was about three months ago.

He has a big crucifix round his neck. He's a serious guy, religious, and he is suffering. That's the way I see it.

It's an old church, the hostel. And they haven't made a very nice job of renovating the place which makes you feel like a piece of flotsam and jetsam among the rest of the flotsam and jetsam.

Later Francisco comes in all smashed up. I met him some days ago back at the bar in the square in Fromista just before we left (where I also ran into Rien the Dutchman with the trolley. You remember Rien?) Now he's all cracked up and broken. He's been walking over 100 kilometres with a broken leg. He cracked it up and has kept going since, refusing to listen to his friend's advice to give up. There's tears in his eye telling me all this, the poor bastard. He's headed back tomorrow on the train to Barcelona. He's been walking two or three days. After he fell on the hill way back coming down, slipping on the little pebbles. On El Perdón? Where I met Muldoon.

And we've come some distance since then.

Sahagún is an important place, the tourist guide says. But nothing holds it together. The old has been mingled with the new. There are fine old monasteries and churches but the buildings have been done up in so many conflicting styles you get to thinking maybe a posse of cowboy builders from the scrublands came in and raped the place regularly in times gone by, architecturally speaking, leaving the town with a load of miscreants. The barmaid is now showing off the barrels and telling how "they" took the place over and did it up. It's stopped raining so we go and sit outside at one of the rustic tables and take in the empty car park. The sun comes out. Muldoon gets out his book of crosswords. There's no newspapers in the bar and the only book I've got with me is *The Pilgrimage* by Paul Coelho, about his walk to Santiago de Compostela in 1987. I picked it up in a little store this morning but I can't quite get into it so I go back to studying my boots at the end of my legs on the chair and try not to tap with my fingers on the table.

All the same, it's kind of nice up here at the station. It's got that nice nothingness feel about it. As I say, like that opening scene in *Once Upon a Time in the West*.

Yes. Sahagún is a real joy of a town. It'll be dark in an hour or two. I can't wait for the night to cover it up and to stay that way till the 3:10 to Yuma or in this case, Leon, roars in tomorrow to take us away. This stretch of the Camino has got so boring we've decided to hop on the train to Leon. But that is not the only reason. Something has come up. Muldoon left someone looking after his dog and something has come up. Some problem.

What exactly he doesn't say. He plays his cards close to his chest does Muldoon. Only that that he has to call it a day. Get back sooner than expected. And get to Leon to make a connection.

"What's on the menu?" he says later.

"Leeks."

"Leeks?"

"Grilled leeks. Says it's a specialty."

"Leeks?"

"Aye, leeks. Puerros de Sahagún a la parrilla. Sahagún grilled leeks."

"Must be a lot a leeks aboot here. Hivnae seen any."

"Me neither."

12
Shooting the Crow in Leon

For most of the province of Leon, the pilgrims' route continues to make
its way across the same desolate plateau which it entered after Burgos.
Michael Jacobs, *The Road to Santiago de Compostela*

We're sitting on the kerbstones outside a new supermarket in Leon, eating sardines and *chorizo* in the blazing sun, not a full grown tree in sight. I'm giving
the can of sardines the business and Muldoon is demolishing a baguette with
chorizo – you know the red sausage with the big lumps of white fat in it. That's
what Muldoon likes best: *chorizo*, though looking at him you'd never guess he
was a *chorizo* man. Thing is they're a bit a stringy and the fatty bits stick between your teeth so you have to dig them out with one of those wooden tooth-
picks you get free in the bars. Either that or you have to carry a supply of your
own. If you must eat *chorizo*.

Only two memorable things to say about Leon apart from *chorizo*, and
that is the absence of El Cid and the disappearance of Muldoon. El Cid, the
great Celtic warrior who drove the Moors out of Spain, is not on his horse in
full charge, as promised in the guide book, holding his sword at arm's length.
The reason is he is on his horse in Burgos in full charge holding his sword at
arm's length, his cloak flapping in the slipstream of the traffic whipping by on
both sides. That is where I took a photo of him.

I tell Muldoon all this, show him the photo I took of the plaque on the
floor of Burgos Cathedral where El Cid is buried. When we visited it a few days
back. "Remember?"

But all he says is: "Mmmmm."

Since his head is mostly inside his mobile phone or in his book of crossword puzzles, it doesn't absorb much external information. Plus, Muldoon
doesn't do maps or guide books.

"Whair ir we?" he'll say just about every five minutes. And when we arrive it's "Whair's the bog?" or "Whair's the kitchen." A dozen times a day. If he

knows he's in Spain, it's news to me.

We've just done the cathedral visit. Leon cathedral that is, not Burgos. A beautiful cathedral with glass windows reminiscent of the Notre Dame in Paris. We enter together but Muldoon wanders off and hasn't come out yet. I'm sitting outside a café in the square, keeping an eye out for our global traveller, having a *café con leche* and a *mini con queso*, reading the local paper. There's a bunch of young American kids, college kids, with their tutor, singing their lungs out on the benches in the square to the left – some sort of folksy song. Noreen, the Irish woman I was walking with a few days back before Sahagún, appears out of nowhere. She's just booked into a nice hotel across the street, she says, but has to go because she's made appointments for a massage for her back and for a physiotherapist for her leg, and off she goes again.

Finally Muldoon appears. He has just come out of the cathedral about a hundred yards away across the square. Even at that distance I see him halt for a moment, turn his head from side to side to get his bearings, before advancing in my direction. He has only gone a few paces when the cathedral guide comes running after him. She stops him. He turns round. He's got something in his hand. He gives it back to the guide. She goes back inside and he crosses the square.

"What was that all about?" I ask when he takes a seat.

"Audio guide. Furgoat ah hud it."

He orders a coffee and when it comes he stirs it and says. "El Cid's no in the Cathedral, ah looked."

"What do you mean?"

"El Cid. He's no in the cathedral."

"I know he's not in the cathedral" I say, "El Cid's not here. He's in Burgos."

And he says, "How did ye no tell me?"

"No tell you?" I say. "I pointed it out to you. You were standing over the plaque where he was buried. You probably weren't listening." So I get out the guide book, look up El Cid and read a few snatches to placate him.

"El Cid, that's Spanish-Arabic for the Lord. Rodriguez Diaz. Had a sword. Tizona it was called. One hundred and three centimetres long. Weighed

1.1 kilos. That's 2.4 pounds. Supposed to have been forged in Cordoba of Damascus steel, the strongest steel you can get."

That gets his attention. "And on his sword on one side it said in Spanish. 'I am Tizona made in the year 1040' and on the other side 'Ave, Maria, Gratia Plenum'…Hail Mary, Full of Grace."

"Tizona, whit's that mean?"

"Doesn't say. Had a horse called Babieca …*babo* is a fool in Spanish. Means the stupid one. That's what he called it. Because of his godfather. His godfather was a Carthusian monk. *Pedro El Grande.* Big Pedro. So one day he wants to make him a present of a horse. Invites him to choose one from the corral, can have his pick of any one he likes. Big Andalusian horses, one of the oldest breeds. Famous among the Romans and the Greeks. Homer mentioned them in the Iliad and William the Conqueror is supposed to have rode one when he invaded England... There he is on the horse."

And I show him some more of the photos I took of El Cid. Up on his horse.

From both sides and from the front.

"Mair than a kilo?"

"What?"

"The swoard."

I let him ramble on for a bit about how nobody can hold out a sword at arm's length for any length of time, no matter how strong they are. Never mind on horseback. And at full charge with your arm shaking up and down.

"Artistic licence," he says finally and we leave it at that. Next day we head down to the railway station in the afternoon. Muldoon has to get back home because of the dog. It's gobbled a lump of plastic or some piece of junk on the beach and is at death's door. Or so I surmise from our conversation about his "dug," which runs as follows:

"Your dog?"

"Aye."

"Didn't know you had a dog."

"Aye. A whippet."

"What's happened?"

"He's swallied somethin'."

"What?"

"A bit a plastic."

"Oh aye?"

"Aye."

"How'd he do that?"

"Oan the beach?"

"What beach is that?"

"The beach near where ah live."

"Oh aye?"

"Aye."

"Where's that?"

"Whit?"

"The beach."

"The beach?"

"Aye, the beach?

"Troon."

"Troon?"

"Aye."

"Troon? That where you live?"

"Aye."

"What's he called?"

"Who?"

"The dog. The dug."

"The dug?"

"Aye, the dug."

"Rocky."

"Rocky Raccoon?"

"Naw, jist Rocky."

See what I mean? It's like trying to lever a tyre off the wheel rim of a Jeep with a spoon. After that exhausting exchange and the detailed revelations of his private life, he gets his nose into the crossword puzzle book and I read *El Diario de León*, the local rag. Next day we go down to the railway station and

Muldoon shoots the crow. Goes off on the train to Alicante to get the EasyJet flight back to Glasgow to succour Rocky Raccoon. But he never gets there. Alicante, that is.

"Book a place before you go," I tell him. "You never know." But does he listen? All he says is:

"Nah, be OK."

"I'll do it for you."

"Nah."

Doesn't do internet, doesn't do telephone calls, Muldoon. Turns out he arrives in the middle of a big festival in Alicante and there's nowhere to stay except sleep on a park bench or the beach. Everything is booked full to the gunnels. So what does he do? Hightails it down on the train to Benidorm which has more hotel beds than Las Vegas and New York combined. Texts me next day, says,

"In Bellydorm."

And so for his sins Muldoon has to hang out in the last place on earth anybody in their right mind would want to be spring, summer, autumn or winter unless they're a meat-eating seagull or a barfly alcoholic. For four more days before going back to Alicante to get the flight for Glasgow.

13
Crazy Cajun, Snoring Catalan

I'm sitting at an ancient IBM Think Centre computer from the year zero and a little router. On the internet. Which is free, for goodness sake, since it's so ancient. In this hostel in Villadangos del Paramo. A *paramo* is a high plain, an unpleasant place, the dictionary says. I don't dare pursue the word *dangos* too long in case I come up with something worse than dead dogs. So in a dead-dogs, high-plains, one-horse, no-horse town, not even town, not even village, a line of streets and a bar and a little shop, I'm sitting looking out onto the highway from the hostel patio high above the road at the occasional car whishing by in the searing hot merciless sun, not a tree or a shadow in sight.

After washing the bits and pieces that compose my wardrobe, I hang them out on the clothes line behind the hostel. The wind keeps blowing them off as there are no clothes pegs to hold them. I tie the shirts together by the arms and stick the towels through loops of loose cord hanging from the poles, all sorts of crazy combinations that only a desperate man will invent. Still the wind keeps blowing them off, I discover each time I go check. Luckily the sun is very hot and they dry quickly. Even lying on the ground.

At the computer again, Daniel the French Canadian, is trying to put a USB stick into one of the portals of the router, which is equivalent to sticking two fingers into the electric power supply to see if the power is on. He has as much knowledge of technology as a raccoon up there on the North East Coast of Canada.

In the afternoon I go up to the shop and buy some sausages and some *tortellini* and an onion and prepare them in the kitchen. I get an electric shock from the oven. To avoid getting more electric shocks I go put on my rubber-soled boots. Then I go for another walk up to the little shop in the village to get some yoghurt to put my vitamin powder into. But the guy says you have to buy four and I say I can't eat that much so I take a two pack of custard and a cookie and come back and fill a cup with water and put it in the micro and then get a tea bag out of my *mochila* and make a cup of tea and to give myself a pep, add some of the Guaraná powder Lisa, my housemate, brought back from Brazil.

When I'm in the garden behind the hostel picking up the washing, most of which is on the ground or has blown onto the wire-mesh fence, the Cajun appears with his wife. He's whistling some crazy tuneless tune, so tuneless I can't possibly guess what it's supposed to be even though I give it my undivided attention. But flog me with a horsewhip, I haven't a clue and that's the truth.

He's still whistling blithely against the low wall with his back to the house with a can of beer in his hand and his eyes on his wife's bum as she hangs up the washing. Bum is obviously what's got his full unadulterated attention. Presently he gets up from the wall, takes a few paces across the green and squeezes his wife's bum.

My washing is dry by then and the Cajuns have just started to hang theirs up. Judging by the crazy look in his eyes, God help us, what else is he planning? His English is pretty incomprehensible because he speaks it with a French-Canadian accent. His French, or rather his French-Arcadian is even more incomprehensible. It's ten times worse than that of his two side-kicks, the two portly Santa Clauses he has walked with all through France and into Spain. Starting from Le Puy in central France, two months back. They might just be French but it is difficult to tell. When the two white beards utter a few words I usually understand, but they are few and far between. I can only conclude Le Puy, which is where I assume they come from, is one of those isolated places where true mountain men live who have all but lost the power of speech and spend the day grinning wisely, grunting and tentatively trying out the ten remaining words of the French language they can muster.

When I get back from the shop I remember I have to phone Jacotrans to pick up the backpack and bring it to the next hostel. I change a five euro note for coins with a girl lying on the couch beside the coffee machine for the seven euros I need to put in the envelope and attach it to the bag tonight so Jacotrans – a couple of guys with two vans who run a backpack delivery service up and down the Camino – can come collect the bag in the morning and bring it to the next place. It's a solution if the bag is too heavy or your legs have gone or you're simply decrepit, lazy, hate inconvenience or don't have any other option.

But there's a little problem later because when I phone up Jacotrans to tell them I want the *mochila* sent to Villares de Órbigo, Jacotrans tells me the hostel doesn't accept bag packs of any kind. So I have it to change my destination, to the next village which is Santibañez de Valdeiglesias, sixteen kilometres distant.

I hope I've got it right on the mobile. It looks like another 6:30 rise or maybe even before. Because some of these mindless so-called pilgrims get up about five in the morning and start rummaging about in the dark when the sun in still sitting under the South Pole. So you're obliged to get up as well when the noise invades the inner recesses going right through the ear plugs you pressed deep into your ears the night before to cut out any noise other than angels singing, and the bastards start snoring.

When I arrived at the hostel in the morning about eleven, the girl opened up for me. There was no one else in the else in the place so I took a bed next to the window by the door, at the top of the dormitory the best spot in the whole room among the single beds with their dark blue covers and pillows and the two-tier bunk beds at the far end.

When the French Canadians and the French Santa Clauses arrived, the four of them, that's where they parked their stuff. On the beds at the far end. So I had a nice bed next to the window at the top. But what happens after I come back from eating? There's a guy in the bed next to me and the cunt is stuck in his sleeping bag, knocked out, snoring. And what's worse, he's with those two other Catalan harpies, those two phonies I ran into the last time in Sahagún and before that in Fromista with their noses in my tin of vitamin powder where I had to suffer the embarrassment of watching them later in the evening clacking their castanets and their heels in a fiery flamenco dance in the reception hall, while sister Margarita played the guitar, half a dozen sisters wailed *cante hondo* and those two Barcelona city-gypsies let rip, whirling and whipping up their skirts like the best of them to show their spindly old barnacle-encrusted ankles, *Olé*, to try to convince us that Catalans, contrary to popular conception, are really Spaniards at heart from the deep south of Spain, and don't deserve their reputation for arrogance and meanness.

They keep turning up regularly like demons to haunt me. But those crazy

Cajuns, as I like to call those French Canadians, can do no wrong in my book. Jack Kerouac, that old beat Ti Jean (ti from petit) as he liked to call himself was born of French-Canadian parents, and spoke incomprehensible French too, which is another recommendation.

I gather up all my stuff again and put it on another single bed near the door. And that's it for today. Unless something else comes up and I have to move bed again. Pity the Cajuns are up at the far end of the dormitory. They probably know a few songs. Maybe that song of Cleoma Breaux and Joe Falcon. The song that's in my head now that they sang in the 1930s. Cleoma on pedal steel guitar and Joe on diatonic accordion. *Ils Ont Vole Mon Traineau* (They Stole My Sledge). Cajun French is pretty incomprehensible. Took me ages to work out the words since they swallow most of them. If they were within ear-shot I'd sing it to them, I surely would. You'll recognise the tune when you hear it. Goes like this:

> Y'ont volé mon traîneau cher,
> Y'ont volé mon traîneau cher
> Quand ça a vu j'étais chaud cher
> Ils m'ont ram'né mon traîneau.

Says: They stole my sledge, love. They stole my sledge, love. When I saw it I was livid. They stole my sledge.

14
Busted Dutchman, Busted Taxi Driver

Leave the hostel in Villadangos del Paramo heading for Astorga, before seven in the morning when it's still dark and head off into the not-yet day. It's a bit chilly so I have to wear my flannel-fleeced jacket. Water is gurgling and racing past fast in the irrigation channel that runs along the path. Then I'm going downhill into Hospital de Órbigo. The town has a lovely, long medieval bridge going over the river Órbigo. It seems to have about a hundred arches, it's so long, rising and falling in curves all across the river bed which is dried up now except for one channel where the water is trickling.

There's a nice cafe at the other end where I have a *tortilla* with bread and a *café con leche*. That's where I meet Kees from Woerden near Utrecht, a big tall fellow with long white hair, in his late fifties. He has a busted knee which he got from skating in March in Holland and it's supported by a tight bandage. The other knee is also bound to keep a balance between the two. He's quite glad to be talking Dutch again, he says. He checked with the doctor in Holland before leaving so it's okay about his knee. He's been on the road for nearly three months walking from Utrecht, through France, over the Pyrenees and into Spain. As it's quite early I read the local papers in the bar and chat with the barman. Then I head out through the village and encounter no one. Not a light in a window. No one getting up for work. Or for a coffee. Or just to turn on the radio. No one. Till I see a little newsagent's shop. I go in and buy a copy of today's *El País*, stick it as best I can between the straps of my pack to stop and read when I find a pleasant spot to sit down.

The countryside is quite flat now with fields of maize and what looks like sugar beet being watered by sprinklers that spread so much water there are puddles on the otherwise dry earth of the track. A frog croaks as I cross a ditch, leaving Hospital de Órbigo behind as lifeless as the occasional scarecrow in the surrounding maize fields. The sky is overcast. It's about eight thirty in the morning. The hills rise in the distance but for the rest the landscape is very flat and will become boring in a few days when I realize I am on the flat plain of the *Meseta Central* that runs across a huge tract of central Spain.

Cars and trucks race past on the highway alongside the Camino till I get to the sign saying Santibañez de Valdeiglesia and head towards that. But I'm waylaid by a tempting sign saying Nature Reserve pointing into the trees and away from the highway. An alternative path. There's a board with an illustration of a crow of some kind saying there's a colony of them here. It's quite a rare crow the text on the board says. No, it's a rook (graja) my dictionary says. Since I seem to have entered some sort of spiritual dimension, out of respect I spend a few minutes reading about Mr. Rare Rook.

But I don't see anything unusual about him. He's just another black crow. Still, it's a nice touch. I wonder if Mr. Rare Crow can read and if he knows that Mr. Nature Reserve says he is a colonist living in a rook colony.

The road loops through Rook Land and before you know it the Trickster has trumped me. Bamboozled. Like in one of those Paul Coelho tales where you think you're going one way but it turns out a secret organization whose members are disguised as dogs, has other plans and sends you in another direction. It's only a little clump of trees. That's the extent of the nature reserve, Mr Rook's country estate, and I'm back on the trail again running along the highway just when I thought I'd given the highway the slip for today.

Far up ahead I see the two Cajuns and the two French Santa Clauses. I call out and greet them as I approach. As always the Santa Clauses peer at me from under bushy white eyebrows and say nothing. The Cajun has an orthopaedic foot, I notice just before I pass them. He's been walking all through France and Spain with a gammy foot.

It's just after eleven when I arrive after about 16 kilometres in Santibañez de Valdeiglesias. And it doesn't look good. It's dead as a dodo. The hostel is easy to find because there's not much else in the place. A few houses, some sheds and farm buildings and the unmistakable smell of cow and pig.

The hostel is on the road uphill leading out of the village. A sign on the door says it doesn't open till one thirty. A few doors down is a bar. The Centro Social it is called. And when a bar tells you it is called the social centre you need look no further for anything better. This is as good as you are going to get.

Inside it's empty. The surly lout smoking a cigarette at the entrance is the barman. Spain has a smoking ban in bars and restaurants except if they're divided by a partition. The Centro Social is too small for that.

Now that he's got a customer, the surly lout at the door metamorphoses into Mr. Social about ten minutes later when his lungs are nicely charged up and takes his place behind the bar.

"There's coffee but the kitchen isn't open yet for a sandwich," he says.

And that's about it. He looks at me and I look at him. Impasse. So I adopt my ant pose. That is, I place my hands on the bar, open my eyes wide as I can, let my jaw drop and fix on a point somewhere on his thick skull, roughly between the bushy eyebrows of the beast, and ply him with stupid questions. Being an ant or any other form of beast or insect is a good excuse.

Is there a bus? He doesn't know. Has he seen the Jacotrans van come with my bag? He doesn't know if he has seen anything. How far is it to the next place? He doesn't know. I'm about to ask him if he knows the date of birth of Sancho Panza, Don Quixote's sidekick but we ants have our protocols so I order a *café Americano* and a *Madalena* instead and sit working the cookie out of its plastic wrapping while he's getting the coffee machine to make the usual hissing sounds. Is there a taxi out of here?

There's an undetectable pause at this point, one that only the highly sensitive antenna of the ant can pick up. A hint of suspicion – you might say of distrust – passes across his countenance. Maybe some other ant has tried the *non-sequitur* technique on him before. That's the one where when the dumb asses don't answer; you tell them some piece of nonsense to see how they react, see if they're listening. First thing comes into your head. You have a granny fell out of tree at ninety six and goes shopping to the supermarket in a chauffeur driven Rolls Royce for bagels which she is very fond of, ten of which she eats a day. These facts give you enormous scope for embroidery. Like the colour of the Rolls Royce and why she likes that colour. Or the difference between cream bagels and cheese bagels.

As I say you can go on forever with this technique, and if they try to get out of earshot, that's no problem either because once you're in fully charged, friendly-friendly mood you can always shout the details after them as they flee for the door.

Yes, there's a taxi out of here, he says, but it isn't in the village, it has to come four kilometres from Villares de Órbigo. And he gives me a card from the shelf behind the bar. That's when I know he wants rid of me. So I take the card and go and sit outside with the coffee at the little table. Then I get up and do a quick tour of the place. At the bottom of the street, round the corner there's a bus stop and a house with a beautiful bush of red roses hanging over the garden wall. They're so beautiful I almost want to clip one off, stick it somewhere on my jacket. But I don't have a suitable button hole. I study the timetable on the pole and as far as I can understand these things, there's not going to be a bus for quite some time. Perhaps two a day.

I walk out of the village as far as I can go, and in each direction. It is a farming community. With a few barns and houses but no shops and little sign of any inhabitants, unless they're indoors gasping their last.

I run into two French ladies wandering about like lost sheep. When I tell them there's not even a shop in this hole of a place and they would be best advised to clear off *post haste* they become enraptured with this piece of bad news and continue on their merry way blithely admiring the broken doors of the cattle sheds and the crumbling stonework of the houses as though I'd just told them we were in the gardens of Versailles and the Sun King had passed this way two minutes ago with his Mistress Madame de Maintenon on his arm.

I go back and sit at the table outside the bar where my coffee cup is still undisturbed and my newspaper is where I left it. Later a small bus appears at the stop round the corner. I jump up and go round. An old man with a stick is getting off. I ask the driver if he's going to Astorga, the next watering hole down the line, but he isn't. There's no other bus till five thirty he says. You have to get it a kilometre or so on the outskirts of the village.

So I ask him if he can take me there and show me the stop since he's headed that way anyway. He's a friendly guy. I get on the bus and stand talking to him on the step and he drives me out of the village and points to the yellow-sided farm house about four hundred metres away, on the crest of the slope, on this side of the trees that hides the highway along which you can hear the cars buzzing faintly.

I walk back to the Social Centre again. There's a bit more activity. Three or four other pilgrims, a couple of girls and a beardy have arrived and are consuming cheese sandwiches at the small tables waiting a voice from on high to tell them when the heavens will open up to receive them.

Later a little electric car appears with an Italian number plate and stops further up the street outside the hostel. I walk up. The two French ladies are sitting on a bench outside with their bags wondering whether to continue or stay for the evening meal advertised on the door. Señor Italia is loading goodies from the car into the hostel, drinks by the look of it. And food. I follow in after him. He protests saying they're still closed. I tell him I just want my bag which I had sent on with Jacotrans from Villadangos del Paramo. So I get the bag – it's still about an hour till one thirty. If I wait long enough and stay I can get the evening meal. But unless I can go into a coma till night falls or run round the village a couple of hundred times, I'm going to have to find another solution. When I get back to the bar, the surly nave has a rose stuck in his lapel. He must have plucked it from the garden at the bus stop.

There is something indecent about the rose in the shirt pocket of Mr. Rosebud and something indecent too about our Mr. Rosebud, our former Señor Social and come to think of it, something indecent too about our Señor Italia.

Maybe it is indecency by association because they're now standing at the entrance to the Centro Social smoking and mulling over the percentages they'll be making on the sandwiches the wayward strangers are consuming inside and who will, with luck, also be present this evening at the eight thirty dinner. From the way the two wolves study the burning ends of their cigarettes and search for something to focus their eyes on, it is plain they are not giving each other much rope either. So as the man said before putting a gun to his head, I'm out of here pronto. Also I need to get to a cash machine.

I phone the number of the taxi on the card and sit down at the end of the road till the taxi comes about ten minutes later from the village further up and we head for Astorga. Once we're out of the village and hit the highway, I slump down, settle into low gear and chat to the taxi driver from the back seat. The usual ant babble. How are things in your colony? How are things in mine? Yes, glad you asked. Then he whips out a sheet of prescription medicines he says he's taking and passes it back to me. There's about a hundred items on the list by the look of things. The medicines might just as well be for horses or pigs. The names mean nothing. One of the medicines he's taking costs over 500 euros a month, he says, and he's paying about 80 euros a time for the subscriptions since the government announced a few days back you have to pay a euro for every item on the prescription.

He's a walking apothecary. He doesn't look too healthy either, come to think of it. He's a decent man, maybe in his late fifties, and he looks pretty stressed out. We've been buzzing down the highway for some time. There is not much traffic on the highway, even though Astorga is a fairly big town. During the gaps in the conversation you can hear the hiss of the tires. The rest of the conversation you don't want to know about. It's about keeping up with your mortgage and paying for the medicines you need because of the stress of making a living to pay for your mortgage. The usual crap you hear all over the place, except maybe you're lucky and living in a mud hut on the Nile Delta or running about bollock naked in the Congo and have got better things to do with your time like chasing monkeys up trees for the evening meal.

15
The Wolf that Hanged Himself

"This is a new story about something that happened last winter in the Kingdom of León, in an oakwood called Dueñas, some nine leagues from Astorga. People are singing songs about it already in León and Palencia, but it's not known hereabouts as yet. What happened was that a wolf hanged himself.

"The story goes that there was an old wolf of the kind they call 'brigands', because they're always prowling round villages and farm-steads and have no fear of men. He caused havoc among the dogs, attacked people and killed a soldier and a little girl who was taking a donkey out to pasture. He paid special attention to the girls, particularly if it was a certain time of the month with them, and he came to howl at them right under their windows

"The village priest and a famous hunter called Don Belianís – he's a half-brother of the Archpriest of Los Vados: he buys books about gun-powder from me, and last year I sold him Biringuccio's Pyrotechnics – these two, with the men from the Santa Hermandad patrol and the Marquis of Astorga's servants, armed with shotguns, assembled to hunt him down.

"Once one of the king's hounds named 'Segovia' had picked up the scent they got on the wolf's tracks in the scrubland, and followed him night and day through the hills, and at dawn they had him surrounded in the Dueñas oakwood. This was a triumph for Segovia, but also for the men who had so laboriously followed on.

"Don Belianís went into the wood with his gun at the ready and there watched – he still hasn't got over the shock – while a naked man hanged himself from an oak-tree, tying a rope round his neck and then to a branch and letting himself drop, and as he fell, turning into a wolf, the same old wolf as had been causing all the trouble.

"So it was that people realized the fearsome beast had been a werewolf after all. The priest, a worthy and compassionate man, organized a funeral for him, and as he was saying an 'Our Father' over the body – he might have been in time, you never know – while he was still praying, the wolf turned back into a man and everyone recognized him as Romualdo Nistal, who had kept a shop over in Manzanal: a well-thought-of chap, who never gave short weight.

"Those then" said Mr. Elimas "are the first three tales and I generally tell them the first night in the inn. Naturally I dress them up a bit, giving details about people: saying that some character was lame, or had made a second marriage with a deaf woman who had money, or had a law suit going on about the water supply, things like that. And I add bits about the towns, their size, how many squares and streets they have, what the fairs are like, what the local fashions are. Stories, you know, like women, like dishes, need some decoration. About this Romualdo Nistal, to take him as an example, I might tell about his life when he went off as a soldier, and how he fell for a drum-sergeant's wife, and how he found two ounces of gold in the street, which is what he used to start up his shop in Manzanal"

My master loved Elimas's stories, He bought seven books from him, gave him some money on top of that and a cheese for his journey, and let me take Norés the dog with him as far as Belvís, where he was going to sell the girls of the Countess's family a new story he had with him, then all the rage in Paris, entitled *Paul et Virginie*.

Alvaro Cunqueiro, *Merlin and Company*

16

Brierley is the Bee's Knees for the Irish

The Irish are in a flap. Noreen is in a flap and Lorna is in a flap and Lorna's wee pal, Claire is in a flap too. We're coming to the most difficult part of the route, just after Foncebadón, the highest and most dangerous. It says so in the book and since it says so in the book, everyone is in a flap.

Noreen is taking it quite stoically though her little nose twitches occasionally like a rabbit catching the whiff of a fox on the breeze coming down the hill. Lorna's sucking so hard on her fags, they're burning faster than those fuses Wile E. Coyote lights in the cartoons and wee Claire is saying nothing as usual, only twisting the silver rings on her fingers and looking like she'll break down and cry any minute.

Noreen has been in a state of semi-shock these last two days since she consulted the book. Lorna, the fat one, the nurse, that smokes non-stop also has the book. And wee Claire too has the book. They've all got the book and the book says we are coming to a difficult spot. A 'danger, bad bit ahead' light is flashing. The exact wording I cannot give you, as I do not have the book. But it says in the book that this part of the route is the most difficult, if not dangerous, that's what it says in the book.

Trouble is, all the Irish, or just about all, have the same book: John Brierley's *A Pilgrim's Guide: From St Jean Pied de Port to Santiago de Compostela*. Spiritual exercises are included and there are little places along the route associated with spiritual moments. It's the bee's knees for the Irish. Now so that there is no misunderstanding between us, Brierley's book is a good book (I find one later left behind in a hostel). On the downside it obviously doesn't mention the possibility of spiritual lows if you don't get the spiritual highs. But you don't need to be a hedge fund manager to know that. Thing is the printed counsel can give rise to collective hysteria as is happening now with the Irish contingent.

So now as we slog uphill, Noreen and I are – what else? – talking about the tribulations of the Catholic Church in Ireland, where, or in which, or so it would appear, half if not all of the sadists, child molesters, pederasts and other untermenschen in the country, driven by less than spiritual motives, have found shelter for decades if not centuries. The Catholic Church, it seems, is a covert organization for perverts. But you can say that about a lot of organizations public and private.

Noreen is retired. She was a civil servant working for the health department in Cork. She walks a lot and has a wide circle of friends. In short, she is an intelligent, informed woman. I no longer recall exactly what her diagnosis was of the Irish disease or how the Irish Catholic Church managed to control the minds of the Irish population for centuries through fear. In the early 1970s, she tells me, over 90% of the Irish were still going to mass. That's now down to fewer than 25%. Whether the mentally warped in Ireland constitute a higher proportion of the population than in Spain is an open question. One Spanish paper I read said 30% of Spanish *machos* were psychopaths. That's maybe a bit harsh, my dear brothers and sisters, but do not lose heart. As always proceed with caution, let not the toxic sludge cling to the flesh or poison the mind. Just remember as a species the human being is more dangerous than the beasts of the forest.

We've now arrived at the Iron Cross (*Cruz de Ferro*). Brierley's book has much to say about the Iron Cross, but since I have not been informed in advance of the associations, the significance of the Iron Cross or of its spiritual emanations, ignorance is bliss. I perceive only a tall, five metre-high, wooden pole with a little iron cross at the top, on a mound of stones at the top of a hill. It is of no particular beauty, apart from the fact it stands out well against the sky at the highest spot on the hill, 1504 metres. Half a dozen young Spanish billy goats are careering among the stones amid a scattered debris of cans, ribbons, bits of T-shirt by the looks of things, and maybe even – God forbid – ladies' underwear, so I don't dare go any nearer to investigate the junk has been offered up to the God of Christendom by the feeble minded who pass this way. A few years back one of the herd cut down the pole and nicked the Iron Cross. So much for spirituality.

As it turns out, going uphill is a piece of cake and going downhill is not as bad as forecast. The slope is hard and rocky, it's true, and you have to be careful not to slip. It's also true that the map indicates a sharp decline – *bajada pronunciada* – between Manjarín and El Acebo (nothing more than a few houses and a *refugio)* but the view is great and we're in fine fettle going down the winding track and an hour or two later are sitting outside in the sun in Molinaseca – Noreen and myself – having a coffee when Rien, the Dutchman, swings round the corner, *Whoooa,* trying to hold his trolley back like a runaway horse.

I run into Rien for the first time on a drizzly morning in Los Arcos, a day's walk from Puente La Reina), nearly three weeks ago. Then again in Fromista (about 60 km before Sahagún) where he asks me to take a photo of his trolley placed against the statue of Santiago across from the café where I'm sitting with Muldoon. He was a butcher, has recently retired at sixty and has been walking for over two months since he left Rotterdam with his wife, pushing his deluxe two wheel trolley in front of him, loaded with over forty kilos of stuff. After a month his wife went back and he continued on his own, twenty kilos lighter. In material baggage, that is. It gets a bit lonely, he says. A trolley is a great idea if you have lots of baggage but useless for walking along and chatting to someone.

Lorna and wee Claire have vanished. Unless they appear soon we will assume their spirits have become one with the spirits of the mountain. As Rien passes the cafe. I wave. Is he going to stop and have a drink? But the road falls steeply over the cobblestones through the village. His face is tense and he straining to contain the forward movement of the trolley. The forces of nature in these parts are strong and have their own designs. He can't stop even if he wanted to.

"Tot ziens" I call out as he passes. *See you.*

"Zie je in de hemel," he says. *See you in heaven.* He waves, briefly raising a hand before seizing the trolley handle again.

"Tot ziens," I say.

"Zie je in de hemel," he insists and I laugh and say,

"Zie je in de hemel."

17
A Walk in the Sun into Galicia

Cacabelos is a nice place with a river running through it. The hostel is on the outskirts: an old baroque church surrounded by a high stone wall lined on one side by a long continuous row of what looks like wooden chalets. The Cajun says it used to be a stable and maybe he is right. The chalets are like pens with half doors, the kind you see horses gaping out of, wondering how the humans keep tricking them. There is a single bed in each cubicle which is separated by a partition from the next. You leave your boots outside. Most of the doors are left open or half open in the night because of the heat.

A grizzly bear snoring next door wakes me up in the night. It's like lying in a bear cave next to another, snoring bear, the partition is so thin. I get up for a pee in the dark, mistake the number on the door coming back and just about sit on the guy's face. Fortunately he gives a shudder just on time as a message from the other world sends him a danger alert, but not sufficiently strong to wake him up, thank goodness, allowing me to back out on tip toe.

In the morning I head out. The Cajuns, the two Canadian women, the two French women and the Portuguese woman who shared a bottle or two of wine the night before, are long gone. The cleaner is busy. The cubicle doors have all been opened. The horses have fled. The plastic beakers on the tables from last night still have to be cleared.

Head up the hill looking for a place to get a coffee, leaving the town behind me where I swam in the river in the late afternoon sun, watched the canoeists paddling their yellow canoes, lay on the grass next to the bridge that Sir John Moore passed over in his retreat to A Coruña in 1809 and had a run-in with the French.

Nothing after Cacabelos till I come to a little place called Pietro, not more than a row of houses. A sign on a board by the side of the road says 'breakfast – coffee, juice, bread and butter and jam' – so I head downhill to a little old farm house about 50 metres from the road. Two puppy dogs are rolling about on the ground. One comes up and gives me a lick, sinks its little teeth, in the way puppy dogs do, into the flesh of my hand, God bless the little bugger. Go up the steps inside and sit behind the big wooden table and have a chat with Lourdes who is in the kitchen and has to lower her head to talk to me from the other side of the pass-through. The place has a nice smell to it so you know the breakfast is going to be good. Big slices of bread cut from a rustic loaf toasted on the grill. And jam too. And tea. And coffee. Ham and eggs, if you like. Lourdes is very chatty. She'll be in her mid-forties. She has a very good friend from Glasgow, she says, who plays the bagpipes with a band in Galicia and speaks Galician, Spanish and Portuguese, so well you can't tell the difference. And she loves the place madly. Where in Galicia is she and what's the name of the band? Because I think I might just look her up. But Lourdes doesn't know. She's got an address somewhere but can't find it. The Celtic connection gets me a bowl of cherries, ripe on the trees down this way now, big juicy and very red.

Lourdes' place is nice and cosy. It's an old farmhouse. And there's a notice on the wall. By the door. They're looking for someone to help out. So we talk about that. It's an idea and it's no problem for Lourdes. Yes, she would love to have me, she says. There's always plenty to do. So I tell her: a bit of painting and plastering? I'm your man. Gardens? No problem. Kitchen too. Help out. Do a nice apple tart. And quiche. Chili con Carne, oh yes!

Oh, my dear brothers and sisters, I am warming to this idea. It is sorely tempting. I could stop here forever and help Lourdes clean out the rooms in the morning and make the breakfast in the kitchen, feed the pilgrims and sit out later on the stone steps and watch the dogs lying in the sun. They'd love me. Oh yes they would, a little pat here, a little tickle behind the ears there. Get the hand licked. And I'd love them back, the little devils, and we'd go for walks together in the late afternoons, hunt for rabbits, though they're still a bit young for that, but no matter. And I could paint a new sign – the sign needs fixing, I tell Lourdes. And with the lovely new sign I' d painted and stuck on a pole up on the road, pilgrims wouldn't be able to resist the place, would come down and book in, stay for weeks at a time, stay there forever. Oh, it is so tempting. But then I think: It's still only early July. If it had been later in the summer. August or even September, say....

Then I'm on the road again, going down a rocky path, the vineyards stretching away on either side, rolling green with the landscape. Rabbits scarper into bushes. A donkey lies flat out on the grass in a meadow snoring in donkey heaven. Then into Villafranca de Bierzo, a lovely little town set in the valley, past the first of the churches and head downhill to the square where I have a *café con leche* and some *churros*, you know, the dough fingers they fry in oil and put castor sugar you lick from your fingers. Head out of town.

There's a big street market going on where I run into Paul and his wife Maureen, an Irish couple who manage a private school in the West of Ireland and have only a couple of weeks holiday. They try to do part of the route every year. There are two routes out of town. An easy route and a difficult route. They go into discussion about the alternative route up into the hills. They don't want to take the route along the main road because they think it will be busy, and have had experience of that in the past. I tell them I am taking the easy route on doctor's orders, and they grin knowingly. It is getting after eleven and the sun is starting to beat down.

Nothing to report at the next watering hole, the name of which is not in the Michelin, apart from Lorna and Claire who have not gone to heaven after all but have descended from the mountain to alight on a broken slate stone wall in front of a little shop in a broken down village, Lorna puffing, red cheeked and swollen faced, at a fag, Claire with a can of lemonade in her hand, glowing with pure satisfaction at finding she is still of this world. Good old flabby Lorna and dear little Claire of the pretty little, shining, empty face.

I stop and have a word with them and an Irish-American they have picked up along the way, an ex-marine, John McLaughlin who introduces me to his classification of Spanish towns and villages. Not one horse towns, he says correcting me, but one-donkey towns, one-chicken towns and two-fly towns.

Before I hit the open country, I pass through more broken down hamlets, places so dismal, desolate and forlorn, even the flies have deserted them and out of commiseration I dispense a *buenos días* occasionally to the odd oldie left behind on a bench contemplating the abyss or hobbling, shoulders hunched, like a lost soul, amid the stones and the rubble.

Thankfully I get on the main road ten minutes later. A cyclist whizzes past. *Buen camino,* he calls as he passes. *Buen camino,* I call after him with gratitude, uttering the words of greeting that brings us all together. Then the vineyard country folds open like the pages of an ancient book and the Galician language starts to appear on the signposts.

Portuguese is derived from Galician, it is said. For some reason the lines of a Brazilian poem come to mind, the most popular poem in the language apparently. 'Canção do Exílio' (Song of Exile) it is called:

Minha terra tem palmeiras,	My land has palm-trees,
Onde canta o Sabiá;	Where the thrush sings;
As aves, que aqui gorjeiam,	The birds that warble here,
Não gorjeiam como lá.	Don't warble like over there.
Nosso céu tem mais estrelas,	Our skies have more stars,
Nossas várzeas têm mais flores,	Our fields have more flowers,
Nossos bosques têm mais vida,	Our woods have more life,
Nossa vida mais amores.	Our life has more loves.

                                        Antônio Gonçalves Dias, 1843

18
The Laughing Cows of Cold Fountain

Pass through O Cebreiro after a stiff climb; take a photo for two Canadian girls against the backdrop of the green landscape far below, the highest point on the route at 1330 metres according to the Michelin pocket map. Have a snack in the cafe.

Lovely place O Cebreiro, with little round stone cottages dating back to Celtic times, the style anyway. Think of staying the night, it's such a delight but walk another 12 kilometres to Fonfria. Fon is fountain and Fria is cold. Cold Fountain has a ring to it, so we'll call it Cold Fountain. Sounds nicer. Like some resort where you go skiing. Or dream about it. In the mountains somewhere. Italy. Maybe even Sun Valley, Idaho.

But let's not get carried away with the name. It's a collection of uneven stone dwellings, with two or three hens perched on crumbling oak wood balconies – put up when Columbus sailed for the Indies. That kind of place. God know what it's like in the winter and the mist. But the hostel looks nice and I'm not up to walking any further. You pay 20 euros and for that you get bed, dinner and breakfast. It's a pretty big place, owned and run by a Galician woman in her forties, part of the family farm not so long ago and maybe still too because there's a few of the big watery-eyed doleful ones hanging around in the fields outside.

"Cows are pretty stupid beasts," she says, "and pilgrims are more interesting."

It's a moot point. I am not a great cow man myself, I'll say that. I've tried my best with cows. I've studied one or two closely on the way down, looking into their big dumb watery blue eyes, at their slobbering pink tongues, their tails flicking the demon flies. Hanging over fences, chewing the cud flopped out on their big swollen bellies, condemned to chew grass all their life and churn it into milk for the humans as they waddle, flopping their udders, a day's work well done, back to the barn in the evening. I still can't make them out. But the farmers in these parts love them. Give them their own names: Linda,

Bonita, Paloma. Miss Fonfria's father even had one he called Teresa, after a favourite aunt. And they respond to them, she says. It is touching. They're a neglected species because of the slavering and the low cuddle content, it seems. I'll have to check to see if anyone has anything good to say about cows. Like Gerard's son, aka Erasmus of Rotterdam, the Prince of the Humanists, for example, who's always got something to say about animals.

"Cows never give their milk so readily as when they are stroked," he says.

Hmmm. Kindness works better than mistreatment, is the message.

That's something to go on, I suppose.

There's also The Laughing Cow – La Vache Qui Rit. Its face has been laughing at me for weeks from those packets of cheese wedges I've spread on the *panecillos* and *baguettes*. It has the consistency of whale blubber and taste about the same.

"Who thinks these things up?" I say to Noreen who honours the round box of cheese wedges with a disdainful glance and drops her eyes again to her *Practical & Mystical Manual for the Modern Day Pilgrim*. She doesn't do cheese on rolls, Noreen.

It seems the emblem was thought up during the First World War. To boost the morale of the French troops. The Germans had the Valkyries painted on the side of the wagons that brought supplies up to the troops in the trenches. The Valkyries, according to Norse legend, were a bunch of harpies with the power of life or death over the troops in battle. French high command had nothing on their wagons and after the necessary brainstorming at headquarters someone came up with the idea of starting a competition for the best emblem to put on the wagons of the Fresh Meat Supplies Regiment (Ravitaillement en Viande Fraiche) going up to the front with juicy *bistecs* for the *poilus* to give the *Boche* their comeuppance on a full belly.

A popular French illustrator Benjamin Rabatier, clearly a man with a feel for language, came up with the idea of the Vache Qui Rit which was a play on the word Valkyrie (va-ki-ri) the German's were using. French High Command, whatever its shortcomings, apparently had a sense of humour, liked the joke, especially at the expense of the *Boche*, and put the cow's face on the buses commandeered in Paris and on the trucks going up to the front.

The laughing cow was originally a brown coloured specimen looking stage right, and frankly not too pretty. Leon Bel, a processed cheese maker who had been with the Food Regiment during the war, bought the rights to the brown cow for a thousand francs from Rabatier after the war in 1921, but clueless as far as advertising was concerned, cheapskate Bel stuck legs on it. Everyone who saw the re-vamped acquisition agreed it looked downright awful. The master was called in again for a re-design. His wife took one look at the wretched cow and said it needed to be made more feminine. Rabatier then tarted it up by sticking two big earrings on it, one hanging from each pierced lug, so it ended up bearing an uncanny resemblance to Gypsy Rose Lee.

That would have been the end of the affair except that when the brown cow went to the printers, the treacherous printer turned it red, registered the rights to La Vache Rouge and held out his hand to Bel to stump up again. That's why the cow is red-faced, has got two big flashy earrings and is bursting fit to choke with laughter. The printer has just whispered in its ear how much he has squeezed out of Bel for the rights.

If you look closely at the bling-bling earrings that are like bottle tops, you'll see they've each got another – smaller obviously – laughing cow on them, exactly the same as big mamma. They're all looking stage left. There's enough happy cow happiness in that one picture to halt half a dozen wars.

On the subject of cows, Noreen later informs me she saw a big Cow Parade some years back in Dublin. The Parade travels all over the globe every year with local artists invited to paint life-size cows made of fiberglass. There's one dressed as Super Cow, I see, when I look them up, with a big "S" on its side and a neat little red cape round its neck. It's so endearing I fall in love immediately with cows. I am a changed person. From now on they can do no wrong. Regardless of the fact every company worth its salt these days has a cow somewhere in the company closet: McDonald's, Yellow Pages, Louis Vuitton, to name but a few. And now, come to think of it, wasn't

Clarabelle the Cow, one of Minnie Mouse's best friends? But 'Holy Cow' as Batman used to say, look at the time, they'll be serving dinner soon.

The hostel is run by emigrants from the Dominican Republic. There was a big influx of South Americans during the boom years especially from 2000 onwards. Argentineans, Peruvians, Chileans, Bolivians. But with economy on its uppers now after the financial crisis, many are returning home, ditching their Spanish nationality. Even Cubans are going back to Cuba, and that says something. The immigrants – what do you expect? – are mostly cheap labour, like elsewhere in Europe, doing jobs the locals no longer want to do: the men working in the construction industry, the women looking after the elderly and the infirm, taking the kids to school, looking after them while the parents are at work. Both Spanish parents now have to work to make ends meet because wages are so low – what is called in economic parlance 'squeezed' – so now they have to call in their mothers to take up the slack. Look after the kids while they're working all hours to pay the mortgage.

There was a big kick-up in the press not so long back about 'slave grannies.' The slave granny syndrome – *abuelas esclavas* – it was called, stressed out oldies looking after the stressed out children of their stressed out sons and daughters. The solution? Get yourself a cuddly little Dominican or a sweet *bonboncita* Bolivian. They're more patient than the home-bred mules, don't kick up a fuss, and apart from getting more miles to the gallon out of them, they're also sweeter. Not only that they're also pretty small, don't eat so much being used to starving up there on the Altiplano, so you can knock them about with impunity. It's a win-win deal for employers and well-heeled households.

This lot is one big family. There's about a dozen of the Dominicans looking after the place out here in the middle of nowhere. There's a few kids running about. The hostel is nice with a big lounge where you can watch TV, carpets on the floor. Quite luxurious and more like a small hotel. In the evening at seven they serve a meal in the spacious dining room with the Dominicans at attention, doing the tables.

Caldo Gallego (cabbage soup) is on the menu, followed by potatoes and meat and then a piece of tart. With wine and water to drink. There's about thirty of us on either side of the long table. Noreen is on my left and on my right a Dutch woman from Veldhoven in the south of Holland, who has been walking since 21st April, over two months ago. She did her leg in somewhere in France and had to rest up for a week. Across from us are two Japanese gentlemen with white hair who don't speak English or any other language but have nice bright eyes and enlightened Buddha smiles. They are kind enough to entertain us to the time-honoured slurping sounds of their ancestors as they spoon the slimy cabbage down their throats. I honour them with a deep bow of acknowledgement as demonstrated by the noble Samurai in *Seven Samurai*. The Kurosawa film, that is.

It's pretty chilly and cloudy outside when I leave next morning. Put on my jacket, and having caught a cold, wrap a towel round my neck and take the track between the straggling farm houses and dubious dwellings. I award Cold Fountain the one-chicken and four-fly classification in honour of John McGlauchlin. Great place to arrive. Great place to leave. Hit the road again, which according to the Michelin, drops over the next ten kilometres from about 145 kilometres from Fonfria to Triacastela and further down again to Samos and on to Sarria. Noreen has gone on ahead. I'll probably catch up with her later.

19
The World is a Wedding

The World is a Wedding. I read this sentence in an old book last week. I had to think for two days before I had any conception of what this sentence The World is a Wedding is supposed to mean. Does it mean anything? Yes and it means everything. For example it means that world is the wedding of God and Nature. This is the first of all the marriages.

Delmore Schwartz, *In Dreams Begin Responsibilities and Other Stories*

I am trying hard to love mankind, my dear brothers and sisters, I really am. But one is sorely tried at times and the Evil One never sleeps. It is no excuse of course, but when young Yamamoto pokes his nose through the door of the pension and asks how much it is and the lady who runs the place says eleven euros and he asks if he can use the kitchen, I am alerted. This sparse exchange is enough for me to decipher Yamamoto's hidden agenda. And since the Spanish lady's English is close to non-existent, I give it to young Yamamoto in nasal European continental cryptic: "You payee… you kaaahn…yoos."

Then I get back to the internet. There are two stations. The keyboard on mine is pretty useless as some of the letters are not working and the screen freezes regularly. I am waiting for the French lady next to me to vacate her seat because hers seems to be working. She does eventually and I settle down to doing what you always do on the internet which is read the newspapers and then your emails. Not the other way around if you have any sense.

Half an hour later young Yamamoto shows up again and sits at the dud station. When the lady owner of the pension comes in, he asks if the internet is free. He read it on a sign coming into town. I know that because I saw it too, which is why I'm here, though I have booked in. The lady says it is the custom to ask first. "You payee, you yoozee." I translate. But Tokyo Joe, impervious to words of the Lord's servant, takes possession of the empty chair and types with a vengeance into space on the splintered dud keyboard. It's going to be a contest to see who gives up first.

"And they're off and running now in the two thirty here at Triacastela… in this two horse race and its Wile E Scott up on Bob's Your Uncle, well in the lead with the young Yamamoto on Tokyo Joe trailing five or six lengths behind as they go into the straight in this five furlong handicap with Bob's Your Uncle, the odds-on favourite now passing the email marker, the poles are flashing by as Scot gives Bob's Your Uncle its head in the next long stretch past *The Guardian*, *The New York Times* and *La Vanguardia* banners with *El País* coming up next, he passes those easily and Tokyo Joe's moved up closing the distance slightly but not much as Yamamoto gives Tokyo Joe the button, but with sludge on the track from last night's rain and the going soft at this point Bob's Your Uncle is keeping to the inside, on the rail, and is going to wade through *The Mail* sludge stretch instead of taking to the outside to avoid it… And he's keeping to the rail as he ploughs through the green tabloid fungus that has formed on the water on this low lying stretch of the track, that's a notorious feature of the track, and never seems to go away… I have to say the rain these last few days has left it bogged down worse than ever, a recurrent problem for years now creating sludge backup caused by the poor drainage run-off on that side of the field…as I said just a moment ago I was talking to the course management about it, but they say they've tried everything… and the fetid green sludge is flying behind Bob's Your Uncle's flashing hooves now, splattering some race-goers too close to the rail there… not a pleasant sight… but Bob's Your Uncle's taking it well as I can see close up through the binoculars here in the Press Box and what a sight it is…but he's still firmly in the lead though Tokyo Joe has closed the gap some, helped no doubt by the fact he's wearing blinkers, and is now taking the outside, wisely avoiding the sludge as they go into the final two furlongs uphill with a furlong still to go, past financial world shenanigans, political venality, melting glaciers and gold mining in Greenland banners, heavy going even for a two year-old filly with Bob's Your Uncle's form, who's now visibly slacking with Tokyo Joe closing the gap and Yamamoto banging on the keys to egg him on… it's Bob's Your Uncle who's taken centre field, going all out, trying to maintain his lead, Scott glancing over his shoulder… and look, coming up fast on the inside lane now, lashing the dud keys for all he's worth it's Yamamoto on Tokyo Joe for Japan, the outsider. And yes, it's Tokyo Joe… Tokyo Joe all the way by a short head from Wile E Scott on Bob's Your Uncle as they flash past the winning post neck and neck in the two thirty here today at sunny Triacastela, a big surprise and a turn up for the bookies though with yesterday's rain keeping the punters away in the numbers we've come to expect at this great regional venue, they've started to trickle in since early afternoon and with the sun out now it's got all the makings of a great day as I can see now looking at the crowd…."

Later in the afternoon, I run into Danish Doll Birgit, and her Spanish Rastafarian friend Augustin on the main street and again in the bar opposite where's there's a better internet. They're trying to book a flight to Copenhagen. Which he has to pay for, it seems, from the gist of the conversation. He's a pretty nice guy who has no money and she is a pretty nice, older, laid-back lady who has a bit money and a nice thing about her: she thinks she's still sweet sixteen. Sweet she is but not sixteen. But there you go, if you bet the fillies and have to choose between sweet and sixteen, take it from me, pal, put your money on sweet every time. There's about thirty years' difference between them and they seem a nice couple. But the money? Yes Augustin told me he had come down the Camino so far, over six hundred kilometres, for less than a hundred euros, which says everything. She has a house somewhere on the coast, down south, so she's not poor. As I say, a nice, if unlikely couple, two sweeties.

Next morning it's drizzling as I head out of town. I have to put on my rain jacket soon after I leave Triacastela but not my rain trousers as I think the drizzle isn't too bad. I calculate about two and half hours to do the nine kilometres detour it says on the signboard to Samos to see the monastery, and that's how it turns out, up over the hills and down into the valleys, stopping on the wooden bridges over the fast flowing streams to spy for trout. Till you come down the hill and there between the trees is the huge Benedictine monastery of San Julian y Santa Basilisa, dating back to the seventh century, the biggest in Spain.

Saint Julian and Saint Basilisa, usually portrayed together, were very popular as a couple in the Middle Ages, for reasons few would understand in these horny toad days. Julian was forced by his family in fourth century Antioch to marry and choose Basilisa for his bride. Both of them took a vow of chastity and set up a monastery together of over a thousand monks and nuns. Basilisa died a natural death but Julian was decapitated in the Christian persecutions during the reign of the emperor Diocletian.

Lodging for pilgrims at the monastery is free. The two institutionalized extra-terrestrials I meet at the desk are like those obsequious servants who welcome the visitor on a stormy night to the castle of Count Dracula in Transylvania where the Count is lying downstairs in the vaults in a red-velvet padded coffin because the daylight hurts his eyes. I suppress a shiver and, in the parlance of *News of the World* press sleuths in the old days, "make my excuses and leave."

I choose to stay instead at the Val de Samos hostel down the road. It has a nice modern kitchen with electronic hot plates. I put the beer in the fridge and fry the leg of chicken I bought from the little supermarket coming down the hill into town. I fry the chicken and when it is ready I break it up with my hands and drop it into the canned tomatoes mixed with chicken stock and when the soup is ready I sprinkle it with basil leaves. Basil in Spanish (Castilian that is) is *albahaca*. Words beginning with al in Spanish are usually of Arabic origin. Albahaca comes from *al-habaqa* in Arabic. Al is equivalent to the definite article el or la in Spanish. The H in Spanish is redundant. It is not sounded in any of the Romance languages. It comes from somewhere else. Basil is also what the French call it, possibly because it entered English via French. The Dutch call it basilicum and the Germans call it basilikum. But for me it is always *albahaca*, sweet smelling albahaca. And that is what I tell my little basil leaves as I stir them in the pot.

It's Saturday today and I need another T-shirt as my clothes were soaked when I stopped at a hotel coming into town. Later, after three, I go round to the monastery to do the guided tour. It is a memorable. The gardens, the long corridors, upstairs and downstairs, the countless rooms, the silence, the beautiful murals that cover the spacious corridors, long and endless as airport gateways, the plaque commemorating *Generalissimo* Franco who gave them the money to restore it after it burned down in 1951. Ah yes, General Franco. Who helped find the funds for the restoration that started in 1952. It took 5,000 reinforced concrete beams, 630 windows and 430 doors, without counting the furniture before the *Generalissimo* came to open it in 1960. And now in May 2013, the plaque dedicated to Franco's 'crusade' against the infidels in the Spanish Civil War is being covered up following a complaint. It contravenes the Law of Historic Memory (*La Ley de Memoria Historica*). In other words it is an insult to history. An offense to the perception of those who know better.

"On the 26th day of August in the year 1943," the plaque says, "Francisco Franco, Caudillo of Spain, victor in the crusade against communism, accompanied by his wife and daughter, a civil and military entourage, visited this monastery of the abbot Mauro."

Abbot Mauro was the main force behind the restoration that the leading Falangists, looking at the immensity of the task, suggested be abandoned and the monks move to other monasteries.

Back at the Val de Samos pension, I exchange tales of the Orient with the girl who runs the place. Just in case I have been maligning our Oriental brothers.

"One day, when I came in, we had these Koreans staying here, maybe three or four of them, and they were cooking in the kitchen. And I thought how they can possibly be cooking so much for three people. There were all these pots on the stove. And then when I looked later the kitchen was full of people. What they had done was, there were all these other Koreans staying at the monastery where there's no kitchen but where you don't have to pay. And they all got together to eat here."

I tell her she has the sympathies of the HON man. That I already met a few Korean locusts in a few places further back down the line. Up in Logroño, they were stripping the kitchen bare of leftovers. Not a crust even for the mice when they were gone. God knows what Coelho says in that book of his about the Camino that's got them going. It became a bestseller in Korea. Maybe they have all been looking for their swords in the kitchens, getting chased by wild dogs and having secret cabalistic meetings with Korean demons migrated over this way for the tourist season. Who knows? And another thing, maybe I have been maligning the Japanese. Young Yamamoto might just have been Korean. They seem to have a reputation for bad manners.

Today is Saturday and there's a wedding at the monastery. Along the otherwise deserted main street that runs through the town, a crowd of people are heading up to the monastery. They're dressed in the kind of clothes you see in *Four Weddings and a Funeral*, the film, although there are no top hats and kilts among them.

Later in the evening I follow the road round the bend to the outskirts of town to the hotel where the wedding party is holding the reception, have a glass of white wine in the lounge and enjoy the noise and the bustle of happiness made by people of all ages rustling new suits and gowns in the scent of freshly cut flowers. And just as I was thinking the world was a Grand National Steeplechase with Oriental Freeloaders making all the running, turns out the World is a Wedding. That's one for the book. Pretty good result for the day. No? Sometimes you're holding a winning ticket and don't realize it.

20
Last Chance Sarria

Sarria is a pretty little place and one of the nicest little towns a person would wish to visit in this life. I'm sitting outside a little guest house at the edge of town called La Pedra, talking to Luis. Luis is maybe in his mid-thirties. I detect a touch of Catalan in his Castilian accent and ask him if he is from Catalunya (Cataluña). Yes, he's from Barcelona, he says. So we get to talking. It's one of those days you can sit happily outside in the sun and watch the occasional townie pass on the other side of the road and find it enormously interesting. Especially, as happens once or twice, Luis recognizes a mate and waves.

Luis is sitting on a chair outside in the sun, smoking. He looks after the pension during the main pilgrim season which runs from about March to October. After that it gets colder as the year goes into winter and the pilgrims get scarcer till you're into December or January and there's snow on the hills and it is bitter cold. Or the rain comes lashing down. But really that's when you want to go. That's when you want to be coming down the Camino. Not like now when the traffic is building up daily as the year moves into mid-July when the sun can get very hot and temperatures rise above 35° C.

For the last few days the pilgrim traffic has been building up, and the road is starting to get that crowded feeling. So now instead of being carried along in a trickling stream of pilgrims you suddenly find yourself on a moving escalator flushing groups of superfluous school kids and superannuated, no-budget tourists on the last one hundred kilometres to Santiago de Compostela to get their *Compostela*. About three million people visited the Cathedral last year and another 192,000 were registered as pilgrims. Equally they could have registered as fish.

Sarria is the last place you can start from to qualify for the *Compostela*. On the Camino Frances, the French route or the French Road, in any case. So it's time for a break. I've been on the road for nearly a month now, passing through village after village, town after town. And in each one I ask myself the same question, though on reflection it has no real meaning. And the question is this. Would I like to live here? And Sarria, as I'll soon learn, has that subtle perfume. Because, make no mistake about it, a good town, like a good woman or a good man is waiting for you to arrive. Waiting to tell you it loves you. Has a bed prepared for you. And when you get that feeling, your life becomes enhanced. Your perception changes. And when your perception changes, your mood changes. And when your mood changes you meet only angels. And all the demons – the humanoids, the sawn-off runts, the mountebanks, the untermenschen, the subhumans, you take them all in your stride and greet them with a smile and they vanish in a puff of smoke. That's the kind of place Sarria is. That's why I decide to hole up here for a few days and get my breath back. Take in the sun and lay on the deck chairs in the garden behind the house, eat with the Argentineans, share their barbecued roast and their Rioja wine or chat with Axel the retired German with a busted knee, bald as a coot, in his sixties.

But we're not there yet. I'm still here and I've come home. Just like Paul, the Englishman who fusses about behind the bar or in the kitchen helping the girls prepare the evening meal. He came down the Camino some years back, having walked all the way from Nottingham and decided to go no further. He found a home, coming into town.

"Didn't you see it?" Marina says from behind the counter in the bar.

"The house? The big house with the blue shutters?"

That was what Paul bought. He sold up everything and left England. You can't blame him. On the bar there's an old English tabloid newspaper, probably left by some Brit. Certainly not a Spaniard. They haven't been trained to get their daily press fix by buying a newspaper. And even if they could. Even if they could be trained to be tabloid readers, it would take decades for the needle of their moral compass to point so far south. God bless Britain's popular press, there's nothing like it. The nation's mind – and God forbid that such a thing actually exists – must be a sewer of toxic sludge.

The headline in the paper on the bar says: 'Wannabee Model Gets 36 DD Boobs Courtesy of the Taxpayer.' What do you say? Brits have been brainwashed for decades into their daily fix of the Seven Deadly Sins: Wrath, Sloth, Gluttony, Anger, Lust, Pride, Envy. Abroad they yearn for Heinz Beans and PG tips, poor things and their Daily Mauls. And nothing is more certain to get their attention than big tits, cleavages, bums, thighs and ankles, how much the house of the guy living on benefit with a dysfunctional family of goblins costs and who sired the frog-eyed creatures staring at you from a living room in Bradford or Leeds or some other post-industrial hen-run, designed by the Devil on one of the many days God was sleeping from exhaustion trying to keep the whole wretched show on the road.

Luis, is a nice, normal guy, fortunately. He takes off in the winter, closes shop and heads off somewhere.

"Where to?"

"Africa," he says. He's been to Madagascar, Sierra Leone. Spaniards, like the French, go to different parts of Africa from the Brits. He's going back to Sierra Leone for a couple of months.

"You've got a great life," I tell him.

"The women are very beautiful there," he says out of the blue. He doesn't quite sigh, I'm not suggesting that. He says it as an afterthought.

Like you'd say, "They've got these lovely trees there, called …"

Yes, Sarria is a lovely place. If you ever come down the Camino, stop in Sarria. It's only 125 kilometres from Santiago and the last place you can start from to get your little certificate, the *Compostela*, saying you walked the walk. The one you can get framed and can hang on the living room wall or balance on the sideboard between the family photos and the birthday greeting cards. To tell everyone who comes in, including the plumber, you did something more with your time last year than visit the supermarket a couple of thousand times to raid the shelves and take advantage of two-for-one cut-price offers and discounts. That you're better blotting out like a trauma in case you remember how you spent it.

But, my dear brothers and sisters, we are innocent only when we dream. Happiness is short-lived in this Vale of Tears. Be ever vigilant for the snares and iniquities of evil men. In the afternoon – it's a Sunday – I go and look for a place to eat. Pick a pretty looking little place on the corner at the top of the hill in the old town. The food is lousy. As is the service. First the waiter, a *Sud Americano*, addresses me as *amigo* after he has ripped his velcroed shoulder from the doorpost of the cantina and comes to the table to take the order.

"Hola, amigo" he says "Qué toma?"

Now that's a bad start. That's a very bad start. And if my little ant antenna had been functioning properly and passed the message immediately to my little ant brain, my little ant legs would have scuttled me out of there naked as a polite smile. First of all, I'm not your fucking amigo, pal, I don't know you from Adam. But that's just the start. The *macarrones*, when they come eventually – and I've done half the wine by then, chilled fortunately – are cold.

I call Speedy Gonzalez over again and ask him to heat them up. He brings them back, or rather the girl brings them back – another *Sud Americana* – but they're still cold. Call my friend the waiter again and say:

"Look I don't want to go on about this, amigo, but this is cold and I told you twice and I'm not here to be insulted."

Just at that moment the girl comes out with the cod and chips, which is the second course and I say to her,

"I'm not finished the first dish so what do I want the second one for?"

She's from the Dominican Republic, she says when I ask. Then this busy little Spanish guy, this little *Ferengi*, this little *sinverguenza* with burning, red hot chili-pepper, greedy charcoal *Ferengi* eyes, a sure fire sign of the demon, appears and I say to him are you the owner? And he says *Sí*. So I say yes, well I've got quite a few complaints to make and am about to fire the first salvo when his shifty eyes are caught by an eager party of young Italians who have just arrived and are looking for seats. I am on the point of telling the Italians this is the worst possible place on earth to eat and they best go elsewhere because the food is lousy, but the little demon shoots off in flappy, flurry helpful mode, grabbing chairs and going all obsequious, seating the Italians and abandons me to the worst crap I've had the misfortune to stare at on my plate this side of the Pyrenees since I arrived.

We're all patsies, big fat stupid hens waiting to get our feathers plucked and it's the *Ferengi's* job to run about the hen house waving his arms to distract us and get us all clucking and screeching and fretting and flapping on our perches, fucking feathers flying over the shit heap, while he's off with the eggs, the little bastard, like Reynard the fucking Fox, his fucking sneaky little, red, demon eyes glowing in the fucking moonlight as he hightails it with the fucking goodies.

21

Singing Italian Dwarves High on Exodus

Dwarves! It's like the Italians have been parachuted in an hour or two ago. It's early morning. I've just left Sarria and have been eying a few places where I might stop for the obligatory morning coffee. I always have a morning coffee in a bar along the road, usually by nine, but am programmed to stop before ten o'clock no matter what. So far today I've had no luck. I pass a couple of places but there are too many people sitting outside. And if there are so many sitting outside what does that say about inside? I'm not looking for an empty café but one with few people. I'm on the road not to meet people, but to get away from them.

So sometime after ten on the cracked face of my wristwatch, I climb a slope past the shell of a crumbling stone farmhouse and take a rocky path running slightly downhill between the trees. Some Italians guys are gambolling like bunny rabbits between the trees beside the path, bent over with their snouts in the verdant grass looking for mushrooms, their tails in the air, calling out. The rest of the group, the girls and the women, ignoring them, descend the path singing their little hearts out like Vestal Virgins lauding the glory of the rising sun.

How do I know they're Italian? I know they're Italian because they're shouting in Italian, things like *eccola*, and *questo qui*. That's how I know they're Italian. But even if I didn't, even if I could only distinguish between *cappuccino* and *espresso*, even if I turned off the interplanetary buzz or went permanently deaf it would make no difference, I'd still recognize them. Italians are the only people on earth who can carry on a conversation with half a dozen other Italians simultaneously all holding forth at the same time on a subject of interest only to themselves. The words dialogue or monologue have no relevance to Italians, only multilogue. If everyone is not talking at the same time, they cannot communicate. That is also illustrated by the fact in the present case, that while the guys are shouting to the girls, waving the occasional mushroom, and calling them to come and have a look, the girls, singing with a gusto Joshua himself would have envied before the Walls of Jericho, listen but do not hear, blithely ignore them, and launch into a louder chorus, obliging the guys to shout more often and more loudly.

Now, apart from the fact that I have now established their nationality, the next thing I ask myself is why are they looking so eagerly for mushrooms and leaping around among the upcoming bluebells and shouting like they've just picked up a hash trail scattered by the Papal Hash Hound Harriers on secret paths all the way to Santiago. Because if you've been walking for months, weeks, or even just days, the contents of a woodland are about as interesting as your boot laces.

On the scant evidence I have of their behaviour, I deduce the men are mushroom worshippers, the girls are Vestal Virgins singing to the rising sun and that they all landed on the other side of the hill only a moment ago by helicopter or plane from Rome and are concentrating on the only other piece of advice given to them before they left Italy which is to follow the yellow arrows.

When I catch up with the singing troupe and fall into line, my Italian lady companion, who speaks some Spanish, tells me they are a choir going to sing in the cathedral at Santiago de Compostela and are practicing the hymns they are going to sing when they arrive.

This news is distressing since I will not be able to sing along with them. The fact that I do not know what they are singing is not a stumbling block. So imagining that we are no better than Snow White and the Seven Dwarves, minus Snow White, winding through the woodland paths on the way to the mines in Santiago, I hum an improvised version of the Dwarf song.

"Hi, Ho, Hi Ho, it's off to Church we go, We sin all day and we've lost the way. Hi, Ho. Hi Ho. Hi Ho."

But I can't quite get it to rhyme and my heart is not in it because they're singing so beautifully. I give the girl beside me a charming, irresistible smile and they all continue chanting away, penetrating deeper into the wood like a party of hobgoblins looking for a stream to cross so they can turn into fairies.

When we come out of the woods again there are hundreds of people up ahead on the road, cycling or walking. To qualify for the *Compostela* certificate you need to present your *credencial,* duly stamped, at the Pilgrim Office in Santiago. Sarria is the last place you can start from. About 77 per cent of the *pilgrims* doing the Camino Frances, leave from there, arriving by plane, coach or train to nearby towns. So much for *pilgrimage.*

On this last stretch of the Camino, the hikers, lone cyclists and groups of cyclists, backpackers and, for want of a better word, newly-arrived tourists, pop up all day long like squirrels with their tails on fire, bounding into cafes, restaurants, souvenir shops, roadside hippy shacks, God knows what not, anywhere where there's somebody with a little rubber stamp in one hand and an ink pad in the other ready and waiting to press the coat-of-arms of their noble establishment in blue or black ink on the eager pilgrim's card.

We have been warned that we'll find Santiago a bit of an anti-climax. Numbed by the gloomy portends, we plod on as one, a mindless column of ants snaking across the landscape drawn by the subliminal buzz of insects coming from the great ant hill of St James that is waiting to consume us.

22

Is Paul Coelho a Flash Harry?

Little Jack Horner
Sat in the corner,
Eating a Christmas pie;
He put in his thumb,
And pulled out a plum,
And said, "What a good boy am I!"

Nursery rhyme

Chancer is a lovely word. My father invented it. He always maintained, like the Greek Cynics, that dogs were wiser than men but got no credit for it. "See that yin," he'd say loudly in the pub, with undisguised scorn, pointing or nodding his head in the direction of some formless being in the gloom further down the bar or at one of the tables. "Nothing but a chancer." Another term from his philosophical lexicon was "no-user," as in "He's no use to man or beast." By a simple process of deduction, it is clear that whatever chancers are up to cannot be worth talking about since it is of no use. So I never asked him what they'd done to blot their copy books. And he never told me. It was of no further interest. My early training in the Wisdom of Dogs was only a start.

One day he took me to the local Roxy Cinema – it was part of the training – where I discovered Flash Harry. Flash Harry opened up a whole new world of philosophical enquiry to a young and eager dog.

I first saw Flash Harry in his pin-striped suit in *The Bells of St Trinian's*. It was a black and white film about naughty doings at a girls' public (private to you) school in England. The girls all had lovely legs and cute little short skirts and were clearly above the age of consent. They were being trained to be 'ladies.' Flash Harry, played by George Cole, had all sorts of dodgy deals going with the headmaster of the school, Alistair Sim.

Americans had their own version. Most famous of all being Milo Minderbender in Joseph Heller's great novel of the Second World War: *Catch*

22. Minderbender raised Flash Harryism to new heights. He buys up all the Egyptian cotton in existence, can't offload it except to others who buy it from him and sell it back to him. But since he owns all the cotton and can't do anything with it, he ends up coating it with chocolate and serving it to the men in the mess. "You eat candy floss," he says, "so why not chocolate-covered cotton." Critical students of economic theory will recognize the paradigm.

But Flash Harries aren't confined to the material kingdom. They move on the waters too. A few pit-stops back in Sahagún, I was nosing through some books on the Way of St James in a little supermarket. There was one by Shirley MacLaine and another by Paul Coelho. I bought the Coelho book entitled *The Pilgrimage* and have been reading it since. The problem is, having walked over 500 kilometres down the Camino, I hardly recognize the landscape Coelho describes and have my doubts whether he actually covered the route at all. It bears no relation to my experience however far I stretch the imagination. Fair enough, it takes place in another dimension where he is attacked by strange devils in the form of dogs, gets whisked off to secret meetings with *illuminati* who've got the gen on the lost secrets of the universe from the Templars who got it from Adam in the Garden of Eden and sound like a cross between the Masonic Lodge and the Ancient Order of Muffins.

Now that I have finished the book I'm none the wiser about who has nicked his sword or whether that's dipshit code for his dick. I look at the back cover of the book, same as you do when you finish your dinner and sit staring at the empty plate in a state of shocked disbelief, wondering what that was all about. Did you actually eat what was on the plate in front of you? Or was it somebody else ate whatever it was and not you? And what was it you ate anyway because you can't remember? Or is the plate empty because they're about to serve dinner and a nice big juicy steak will appear presently on your plate which you will presently devour and which will presently make you happy and fulfilled?

But it's the back cover of the book that reveals all. Not the message. On the back cover of the book, he's staring out at you like a Cheshire cat that's just swallowed the pelican that ate all the herring in the ocean from the Bay of Biscay to the coast of Brazil. That's when you know he's a flimflam Flash Harry artist. Because he's not looking down at the plate in front of him, the plate he's just served you. He's not looking down at the plate because he knows it's a plate of chips he's served up and doesn't want you to look down. Flimflam men always look you in the eye especially when they've put chips on your plate when you thought you were getting steak. They're addicted to chips. Love chips. Can serve up chips till the cows come home, want everyone to eat chips.

Now I'm not talking about those lovely crispy *Patatas Fritas*, *Patatas Bravas*, *Vlaamse Frites*, *French Fries* or any other version of the nobly cut and fried *batata*, which may rise to the challenge occasionally, but those plain old greasy old chips you get from the fish and chip shop, served up wilting, greasy and half-baked in a clump of soggy newspaper stained with printers ink, a diet of which will clog up the arteries to your heart and your brain with sludge in a matter of days.

I mention this to Sophia. Now Sophia is a lovely girl of about twenty three I've just met in this fly blown place called Airexe. She's in the bunk above mine in the hostel. She's Brazilian too, like Paul Coelho. Sophia's doing the *Camino* because she's faced with a difficult decision. Whether to continue her studies at the university in the U.S. or get a job. Her English is perfect and she's also read Paul Coelho.

Now why would the fates, chance, God's plan for the Universe, aliens from outer space, probability theory, the horoscope in the Daily Record or anything else conspire to present me with a Brazilian who has read, of all people, the work of another Brazilian, Paul Coelho, when I am reading his book, *The Pilgrimage* about the walk along the Camino Frances to Santiago de Compostela while I am actually doing it? See what I'm getting at? And how come out of the over 150 million people who have reportedly read his books there's only one person I can find on the internet who thinks he's a load of hogwash.

And how come I've had to walk all this way, to this fly blown place to run into Sophia, who has also got him sussed? How about that? Got to mean I'm in somebody's plan out there. No? And don't give me that coincidence crap. What does that mean anyway? Coincidence?

I show Sophia the preening face of Coelho on the back cover. "He absolutely oozes vanity" she says. "And another thing he doesn't explain anything.

All that stuff about looking for his sword."

"Yeah, his sword. He loses it at the border or something. How come he doesn't get arrested for carrying an offensive weapon? Or as a terrorist? I reckon he did the walk in a taxi. Or a chauffeur driven car. Stayed at a lot of posh hotels if you read between the lines. But how can you claim to be a spiritual person and ooze all that vanity? You don't get Christ or the Buddha with a smirk on their face, giving you the thumbs up: Look at me, Little Jack Horner."

"No way," says Sophia, and she puts the book under her pillow. Next day when I awake, Sophia is gone. I'm sitting on the veranda of the hostel about to leave. There's a hush in the air and the morning is deathly still. The hostel has closed and everyone is gone. Something catches my eye. It is the book. The Paul Coelho book of *The Pilgrimage*. Sophia must have left it there for me. Or maybe she dropped it. It is lying in the middle of the lawn in front of the hostel. I have a strange sensation. Something is about to happen. I get up from the porch and cross the grass to retrieve it but as I do so the book bursts into flames. A sudden gust of wind whips it into the air and scatters the flaming pages across the sky. A deathly hush fills the air.

"The crow, the crow," I hear my own master, Don Juan the Yaqui desert Indian, whisper, "When evil comes, take to the sky."

Now that I've turned into a crow and am sitting on the branch of a tree overlooking the path, a voice in my crow ear says,

"Check out the servant of the master in Amsterdam, your philosopher friend clap-for-the-wolfman, Wolfgang B., aka Erasmus P. Hegel, and consult him before going any further. Things are not what they seem."

Now I have become one with the landscape of rolling corn fields all the way to the hills, I will hunger no more. Most of the morning I sit on the branch, squawking till I finally fall silent and out of the dead bone membrane of my crow skull, I hear the voice of the Master's assistant, Erasmus P., from the Hegel Room of Magic Spells and Potions in Amsterdam.

"Snoepjes," he says

"Snoopies? Like Snoop Dog?"

"Neen, snoepjes," he says, making a smacking sound.

"Ah! Sweets? Like Jelly Beans?"

"Ja," he says.

And since everything is coincidental in crow's world, crow hops from the branch onto the path where a pilgrim on his way to Santiago has carelessly dropped a little plastic bag. Crow hops along the path in the time honoured way of crows till he gets to the pack. It is a pack of Jelly Beans. Crow, who is of an inquisitive nature, pecks at the cellophane wrapper till it bursts open. Then he pecks at a nice big green Jelly Bean. *Mmmm.* Yes, it is quite soft inside and quite delicious as Erasmus P. Hegel implies.

Crow has another peck but this time the Jelly Bean sticks to his beak and he can't get it off. He thrashes the Jelly Bean this way and that against the stones but can't dislodge it. Quite distraught, he flies swiftly back to his perch on the tree overlooking the rolling landscape rolling between the trees and the fields. If any of his fellow crows see him he will be outcast as a fool.

A fool crow.

But crow is wise. Crow is always wise. He jams the Jelly Bean between his crow claws, tugs it off and emits one big loud squawk of crow joy and flaps away over the fields towards the hills to see if he can catch a glimpse of little Sophia down on the path below winding across the winding landscape. When he catches sight of her, he will descend from the sky, hop along behind her. And so as not to alarm her, he will wait for an opportune moment before adopting a semblance of human form.

Presently he will appear from behind a tree, a bush, a wall, a house or some other obstruction of which many have been placed in this world, visible or invisible or somewhere between the two, because she does not know I am coming, that I am on my way, because she knows but does not know she is thinking of me, her heart will fill, will fill fully with the joy that is waiting to fill it when I appear and she will say to me: "Oh, what a coincidence! Fancy meeting you here, where have you been?"

23
Melide Ma Home

It is not far from Airexe to Palas de Rei: only five kilometres. I catch up with Sophia on the way. It is drizzling as we come into Palas de Rei. She'd best buy a good cape, I tell her when we pass the sports shop, but she says she doesn't need it. The leg injury she got soon after she arrived is bothering her. She can't walk much further. From Palas de Rei she wants to get a bus to Santiago. That is a shame. To come all that way and you have only just got here, I say. I think of going with her on the bus.

We run into Danish Delight and Rastafarian Augustin on the main street in Palas de Rei within minutes of coming into town. They are also taking the bus. But something has happened between them. Something bad. They are miles apart, silent, sullen and unable to look at each other. I have a chat with Augustin. About the road ahead, where we stayed last night, that sort of thing. He is pleased to see me and I am pleased to see him, though we have only spoken briefly a few times. And as we are chatting I look across to Sophia who is chatting to Danish Delight. They are only about ten metres away but it is an enormous distance. Sophia does not know Danish Delight.

She is meeting her for the first time.

It must be the money. I remember both of them sitting right next to me in the bar in Triacastela. On the internet. Trying to book a flight. To Copenhagen, I think it was. She asked him twice if he had the money for the ticket and he said he had. But he did not want to go and he probably did not have the money. That was my impression. They were sitting next to me. On the internet. In the bar. Across from the guest house. The tone of his voice, hers. Their faces. So it has come to this. An older woman with money and a young man without money. And after paying for him coming down the road, or from wherever they met up, now she feels she is being used. Now she feels he does not love her. Does not love her for herself, loves her for her money. And because he cannot pay the entrance fee to her world, they have had words. And when the bus for Santiago de Compostela comes, they will sit alone, as far apart as possible and watch the raindrops course down the misty windows and see their own reflection in the glass.

And Sophia will get on the bus too. Likely as not she and Danish Delight will sit chatting all the way, because they are two women together who have just met and women always have things to tell each other even though they have never met before. But I have to go. I have to leave them. Getting the bus is not a bad option. It is only 65 kilometres to Santiago and I have walked most of the way so there is no dishonour. And it is raining, raining hard, there's that too. But I have to go. I take Sophia's hand – there's that at least – and say goodbye. And say goodbye to Danish Delight too. And give a last wave to Augustin further up on the pavement before turning my back on them but still thinking of Sophia as I cross the road and head downhill between the dismal grey buildings out of town.

The rain is lashing down even harder so it looks like Melide for the night. And that is how it works out. A walk in the rain downhill through forgettable pit-stops like Casanova, Laboreiro, Furelos and then uphill to Melide, a decent sized town 12 kilometres from Palas de Rei where the rain is lashing down when I arrive.

Yes Mel-EE-day Ma Home. That is where the Primitivo comes down from the north and meets the Camino Frances. And to get on to the Primitivo you can also come along the northern route, the Camino del Norte, and cut down to Oviedo. So it's a sort of crossroads. And probably why there are so many people lined up outside the hostel in the pouring rain waiting for it to open, including two jolly, giggling American college students of about eighteen. One big. One small. From North Carolina. They make up a comedy team. Bit like Laurel and Hardy. I've run into them several times in the last week and no matter what, they're always in a jolly mood. What it is they say to each other, I don't know but I would love to have some of it. The small one says something to the big one and the big one doubles up with laughter. Then the big one says something to the small one as they walk along, and the small one doubles up with laughter. And when they are doing this, they don't look at each other. They sort of speak out of the side of their mouths and take in the earth and the sky. And that's some way to get along, going down the road, giggling and laughing, shaking with laughter and I mean real down-home, beanbag shaking, honey, *nuff-tamake-ya-flesh-tremle* laughter.

Soon as I can, I'm off to that Big Rock Candy Mountain out there in North Carolina where they hail from, sing them my version of *West Virginia Ma Home,* which is what I do waiting for the doors of the hostel to open. We're all pressed up tightly together on the porch and practically nose to nose, Miss Tall Carolina and Miss Small Carolina and myself. And when Miss Tall Carolina tells me she's from North Carolina, this news activates the break-into-song switch in my head and since I am two inches from Miss Tall Carolina's ear I break into *West Virginia Ma Home.* I can't help masel. I hev tu. Go,

"West Virginia Ma Home, West Virginia where ah belong…in the dead of the night an eh still en ah quiet ah slip away like a burd in flight…to the fiels en eh plaice thet ei call haum…" Wailing like an ol' prairie dog, dog-gone it, and Miss Tall North Carolina, suh, she say,

"Thet wus ma grendeddies feyvrut sung. Used ta sing it alla time."

And that, as they as say, makes my day, or the rest of it, all the way down to the *pulperia* where I celebrate with a bowl of juicy red octopus, tentacles thick as your lower arm, ripped straight out of the sea that very same day, baby, with a bottle of white wine in a green bottle, unlabelled otherwise I'd slip you the name. Packed to the gunnels the place, two hundred people stuffing themselves with *pulpo* and sea foods, the front of the place open to the street, more a huge shed than a restaurant, the rain lashing down. Galician rain.

It's still raining next morning when we head off on the next 15 or so kilometres stretch to Arzua – Yolande and I (Mrs. French to you). I have run into Yolande a few times in the past weeks and have just met her again here in Melide.

Spend the night in Arzua with Yolande, another place to quickly forget. From Arzua to O Pedrouzo we walk in the pouring rain and the mud. Despite the raincoat and trousers my clothes are soaked and I have to change into my spare clothes in a cafe out in the woods. When we get to the hostel which is packed, the young bucks and the school kids have commandeered the washing machines and the spin dryers which are all rattling like the clappers of a corn thresher at harvest time.

Fortunately the Prague Five who have been pulling a kid in a wheelchair all the way from southern Czechoslovakia, have turned up so we have a drink of wine with them in the spacious kitchen while the threshers work their way through another container load of wet clothes.

It is still drizzling on and off but things are going fine next morning when we leave O Pedrouzo. I start to recall how to decline French verbs again and toss the occasional English bone to Yolande to get her teeth into and halt the non-stop monologue of French – the only language she speaks – for an instant. Bones or not, the landscape and the houses start to repeat themselves. It is beginning to look like Groundhog Day in which I am doomed to wake up each morning next to Yolande babbling in French saying the same things she said yesterday and today, looking at her map and assuring me over and again, "Ah, non," we haven't been here before, as we go round in circles.

24
French for Lost and Bed Bugs

Today we take the wrong turning, the first time it's happened since I started around June seventh, nearly a month ago. I put it down either to long-term mental fatigue or getting distracted listening to Yolande rabbit away in French from dawn to dusk. We take the wrong turning and end up on the highway. But that's for cars. Not for us. There's no other choice so we plod on to the ends of the bald tarmac, gleaming in the morning drizzle, past the café on the corner where we had a sandwich earlier in the morning till we spot a little yellow scallop sign pointing into the woods and take the rocky path between the trees. And that's for a while. Except, what's this? That looks familiar. That church blocking the path. Is this a flashback or what? And that garden next to it? With the knobbly cement hobbits and knobbly dragons together with a knobbly character on a pedestal that could be a knobbly knight or a knobbly avenging angel, brandishing a huge knobbly cement sword? Or rather the hilt and a bit of the blade because the rest of the blade has weathered or dropped off because the goblin artist scrimped on the cement when he made it all those pockmarked years ago or maybe just fell off out of sheer embarrassment?

"Ooo-la-la, that looks familiar" I remark to Yolande.

"Zut alors," or words to that effect she says and we continue on round to the right of the pockmarked angel instead of the left. Again. Repeating the error. Compounding the mystery as Yolande continues the running commentary on her life.

Logically, if you've never been to a place before, nothing along the way will be familiar. Everything will be new in other words. And things will always be new provided you don't see them again. But if you see them again they will not be new. They will be familiar. That's what you would expect. And as a way of reasoning, it seems pretty sound. Indisputable, you might say. Not open to discussion. Only thing is it doesn't apply in Yolande's case. Passing a pretty little house with a lovely garden and hedges over which the flowers are hanging, and which we are passing for the third time, I say to her, "Look there's that lovely little house with the flowers. We passed that already." I say to her, passing the pretty little house with a lovely garden and hedges over which the flowers are hanging, which we passed about an hour ago, and which I remember because it's a lovely little house with flowers and hedges and a lovely garden with flowers hanging over the hedge.

The remark falls on deaf ears. On the other side of the road there's nothing but bushes. A long line of boring bushes with an occasional gap where you get a glimpse of the fields before you pass more boring bushes and boring trees before coming to another gap in the boring bushes and the boring trees. From this I conclude that Yolande, due to some visual quirk – she's wearing rimless glasses – either sees everything on the right hand side of the path and nothing on the left. And since the bushes and the trees on the other side all look the same, she can't be blamed for thinking she's never been here before.

"Regarde, Yolande, there's that little café we stopped to have a coffee and sandwich. You remember where we ate the sandwiches sitting outside in the rain?"

And Yolande, God bless her, as she usually does when interrupted and has to think about something other than the time of the bus or the train or the plane that is going to get her, has got to get her, back to France before the 14th of July, stops talking, wrinkles her nose like a cat sniffing sardines on the breeze, peers through her glasses, tucks the stick under her arm and rummages in the breast pocket of her red anorak.

"Ah Oui," she says, squinting at the map.

But I'm not sure what she's saying "yes" to. Or if we've agreed anything. Yolande has her ways. Because when we eventually find the yellow arrow on the post indicating the direction of the Camino we take a path between the trees and after a few kilometres pass through Labacola, a one chicken place with a line of half a dozen pretty houses with gardens.

Put it this way. If you think that's an unfair or an unkind description of this pretty spot, just remember, if you break down the word Labacola into constituent parts *laba* and *cola* it means either wash-cabbage or wash-neck. The *Codex Calixtinus* says it's called that because it is a place where pilgrims could wash their necks before reaching Santiago. Why their necks and not the rest of their carcasses, it does not explain. My own preference is for the cabbage link. But I keep these considerations to myself and say nothing to Yolande. We don't want to complicate matters now, do we? Instead I say:

"Regarde, les mêmes maisons." But it falls on deaf ears.

Now to give Yolande her due, it's too much to expect her to see the same things as me, never mind the same houses. That is if she saw anything when we passed through the village the last time, with its notably pretty flowers hanging over the hedgerows. Maybe she saw nothing. Maybe she was looking at the sky or listening to the birds chirping in the trees on the other side of the road or listening to Plastic Bertrand on her mobile singing Ça Plane Pour Moi (Jet Boy-Jet Girl) or worrying about where she could fill up her water bottle.

When the penny finally drops that we've been going round in circles for three hours, and it's time for the obligatory lunch of a *baguette* and a slice of ham, we're in Monte do Gozo, about five kilometres from the centre of Santiago in a Polish Hostel, something to do with Pope John Paul. It's free but you can put a donation in the box on the table as you sign in. We make a donation. The dormitory is empty. Yolande investigates the beds. Spots something on the mattress. Gets down on her knees for a closer look. Gets out the flea killer.

"Ooo la la…" *Hiss. Hiss.* Shakes the canister a few times and sprays again, says: "Oh voila je le vois."

How big the flea is I can only guess. I am staying well clear.

Miss Polish who is in charge of the hostel informs us there's free soup at eight thirty but the restaurant is closed. Times are hard. It's Sunday and reserves are low. There's nothing in the bag but a tin of sardines and a hard lump of *baguette* that even a starving bird won't touch. I archive the cabbage soup. I'll give it a sniff later as there's nothing much to eat in chicken town. No restaurants. But there's a bar, we discover when we have a closer look. Where we get a big hamburger with everything on it and everything turns out hunky-dory as we sit outside at the table next to the local young bloods doing the things that local young bloods do, which is talking about girls, cars and work. And hightailing it out of there first chance they get, if some honey doesn't get her claws into them first. In Galician. Which sounds now and then like Italian and now and then like Portuguese.

When we get back, Axel of all people has turned up. You remember Axel, the German I met in La Pedra in Sarria? Well he's on the internet in a corner of the spacious recreation room, which is otherwise empty. We exchange battle plans and I go back down the stairs when I hear the sound of the Internationale being sung in the dining room, which is also spacious. In fact everything about the place is spacious. It's got a huge garden, that's spacious too and it's got three or four long lines of chalets and they have spacious rooms. The design is unmistakably Soviet.

A bus load of Poles has arrived. They've commandeered the dining room. The dining room has a long table. Or they've put about a dozen tables together and made them into one long table, unified by the white table cloth and on either side of the table, thirty or forty, maybe more, Poles are lined up. Men and women. Mostly in the fifties and above and they are singing the Internationale. On the wall behind them is a huge crucifix, also of unmistakably tortured Polish design, from which a suffering Christ looks down.

Looking in through the glass door I cannot determine if they have the fists of their left hands clenched and raised, which would be a nice touch for a Catholic hostel. But it's the Internationale, they're singing, alright. And nobody with half an antenna in their head can mistake the melody. I can't join in because I don't know the words. Only the melody, which, like the Marseillaise, is the unmistakable cry of rage and protest of the suffering and the exploited of the earth.

Luckily Pope John Paul II, the Polish pope (in case you don't get the reference) isn't around any longer to hear them. He hated the Communist system. With lyrics like these it's better if you're French. The French at least had a proper revolution and a mind-set to take things to their logical conclusion also known as the guillotine. They don't work in English. Maybe that's because the Brits have been trained by their masters not to get too upset about things and reach for the rope. Or maybe it's just the lyrics, because they are pretty awful in French too now, never mind the English translation. Let's just put that down to the century they were written in. But here they are in any case. The lyrics. For the record. And unless you want to give the French lyrics a re-write, you're probably better humming the melody to get into revolutionary mode.

Stand up, damned of the Earth
Stand up, prisoners of starvation
Reason thunders in its volcano
This is the eruption of the end
Of the past let us make a clean slate
Enslaved masses, stand up, stand up
The world is about to change its foundation
We are nothing, let us be all
This is the final struggle
Let us group together, and tomorrow
The Internationale will be the human race.

25

The Man who Stole the *Codex Calixtinus*

Then things start to fall into place. The theft of the *Codex Calixtinus* has been front page news for the past month, building up all the time I've been trudging down the Camino Frances in search of salvation and is now reaching culmination. I haven't reached Santiago yet but I'm close. And they've found the Codex. Can you believe that for a gift from the gods? It's in all the papers and it's on TV. They've got it! The nation is agog. The nation, or half of it, is crying with relief, the other half are doubled up with laughter. You pays your money and you makes your choice. The police are crying, the bishop is crying, the prime minister himself is crying. Almost a year to the day since it disappeared, the priceless *Codex Calixtinus* has turned up in a garage in a small town six kilometres from Santiago de Compostela. In a garage owned by an electrician who worked in the cathedral. Whose face will appear soon in the papers, soon as the press wolfhounds sniff him out, the ratbag.

Mariano Rajoy, prime minister of Spain, is among the first to elbow his way in front of the cameras. A Galician himself, born, would you believe, in Santiago de Compostela, he's flown in specially from Madrid and is now holding the Sacred Book of St James in his hands, in an over-familiar way, akin to astonishment, like it was his or his grandmother's beloved, lost breviary or that reports have reached him El Cid is approaching the capital on horseback with proof one of his ancestors wrote it. He's nearly in tears.

As is the bishop who hands it to him.

But look, Rajoy the No-No! He's not wearing gloves. Nor is the bishop. What a twat! Where are the latex gloves, screams the press? Only goes to show, the voters on the wrong side of the fence say, that Rajoy is not only a puppet of the dark forces behind the Popular Party but a dimwit to boot.

The thief meanwhile is in the cell. Jose Manuel Fernandez Castineiros, under suspicion from day one. The cathedral's dirty linen pantry is about to open. And when it does the moth-fleas will escape, morph into demon bugs and descend like the legions of Beelzebub on the cathedral and into the pants of the worthy prelates. Or the bum-boys among them. Or not. The thief's an electrician. Has been working for the Cathedral for 25 years until they fired him. Has a close relationship with the 80 year-old dean, whatever that means.

But read on, you slavering dimwits: He's got *carte blanche* to the cathedral; keys to the sacred places. He's even got a little room where he keeps stuff. The police have had the markers on him from the beginning. Nearly a year ago. But he isn't croaking. Not even about the 1.2 million euros found in the family home or the 30,000 dollars in cash. Dollars mark you, not euros. Could he be in the money laundering game? On the side? He's also bought himself a flat six months ago. Paid cash and getting ready to buy another one. But still he has his lips sealed tight as a St James scallop deep on the ocean floor. Here! What a bummer! Then his wife Remedios and his son Jesus – get the name, another Jesus? – who cracks first, telling the police there's also a garage 200 metres from the family home where he keeps more stuff. What Jesus' girlfriend thinks about it all – and dig this, she's called Maria Jesus – is not revealed.

When the police open the garage and search the place, there it is, or there they are, because there are a couple more books including the *Codex Calixtinus* among the pile of dirty bags, wrapped in newspapers and dumped on top of a cardboard box. In a garage containing beer crates piled up on the shelves and on the floor, breach blocks, more shelves of household junk, a beaten-up bedstead against one wall and a beaten-up bed frame against another. And when the investigating magistrate opens up the white plastic bag on top of the heap and takes out the *Codex*, he too has to suppress a tear.

The policemen have lumps in their throats when they leave the garage. And as they drive out onto the village main street, the crowd in a rare show of public appreciation for a job well done, is cheering like mad and clapping their hands. And right next to the camera – because it's a police video – the policeman invokes the sacred host "Ostia," he says, which although blasphemous, means diddly squat when you're pissed off or harassed.

But wait a *segundo.* What's all this? An extortionist pops up in the wash and the whole show gets sidetracked for a bit as the press release their best tracker dogs. And before you know it they're sniffing up the skirts of Baronesa Thyssen-Bornemisza, millionairess, philanthropist and art collector of worldwide fame. She's being blackmailed (or her daughter-in-law is) by a guy called Fernando Sieira Maneiro, arrested and released 16 times for fraud, blackmail and extortion. Who, as will be revealed, is also trying to blackmail the dean, Jose Maria Diaz, a dear old soul now in his eighties. He'll retire soon but before he does, now the *Codex, gracias a Dios,* is to be handed back to the proper authorities, he's got something to get off his chest. He's been the victim more than anyone of the whole affair, he says.

Wazzatmean? And waz Maneiro trying to blackmail the old bugger for? When the press finally squeezes the facts out its mindless butt, they're about as easy to read as chicken shit for Julius Caesar on the Ides of March. Maneiro specializes in videos. He's a sharp operator. There are hints of sexual abuse. But who? By whom and of whom? *Hola* and *Interviú* magazines have got an even bigger story. The blackmailer is having a go at Baroness Thyssen's daughter-in-law peachy: big booby Blanca Cuesta. There's bad blood between her and the Baronesa. The question that torments the Baronesa (or so the press claims) is whether her son is the father of the daughter that peachy, booby Blanca has brought into this miserable, sinful place they call the world. That's the big question for the Baronesa.

But fine. Okay. This Blanca, a serious looker ten years younger than the son, this TV presenter – photographed in one of the glossies in a couple of pieces of string astride a hard black gleaming Yamaha water scooter with her cute little bum in the air – has been doing naughty things, according to the blackmailer. Could it be true all that stuff about gang bangs with guys on the yacht? Read on, baby. The police arrange a drop off to wolf trap Maneiro and as always – you've seen enough Hollywood movies by now – they screw up and the blackmailer hot foots it with the 18,000 euros and disappears from the front page.

So it's refocus time again for the national psyche and back to the cathedral. José, the electrician is on his knees. He's down but not out, folks. Not by a long shot. So *sniff, sniff* he gets some smelling salts up the snifter from his trainer after the first round, taps his gloves together and…

"Boing! There's the bell for the second round and it's Sticky Fingers José, the challenger out of his corner faster than an electric hare and swinging *de puta madre* at The Hooded Phantom of Rome, the champ. Dancing rings round him, ladies and gentlemen, firing off quotes no doubt from the 15 page dossier he's drawn up alleging all sorts of shenanigans in the Cathedral. From pats on the bum – *palmaditos en el culo* – in the sacristy to some of the clergy going off with the best wines and hams brought in by the poor gullible faithful in baskets and silver platters as offerings to the saint.

"And look there! With a ringside seat, in the front row, ladies and gentlemen. Yes, it's poor old José Maria Diaz, choking on camera in mid-sentence trying to express the humiliation and calumny he's been subjected to. But he's clearly not your man if it's a good headline quote you're looking for.

"Boing! And there's the bell for the end of the second round. And back in his corner, The Hooded Phantom of Rome whispers to his trainer in the cassock to get someone else fast. Another dean. Good for quotable one liners. Not just any old thing. But quotes that are *de puta madre*, finger-licking good...."

So they dig up a new dean. "It's like the squid squirting black ink when it's cornered," he informs the nation in regard to the electrician's threatened revelations. *Olé*. All is well. *Todo España* throws its hat in the air, has another glass of wine, a bite of *chorizo*, picks its teeth and goes back to sleep again and sleeps the sleep of the innocent.

But new brooms sweep clean, even if they don't know it. Maybe the new dean's onto something. Former colleagues say Sticky Fingers José is off his rocker.

Then the only press sleuth in *todo España* left with a modicum of horse sense gets to thinking it might be a bright idea to talk to people who know the electrician and hightails it down to the village where he comes from. Down to O Miladoiro and talks to the villagers. You remember? The ones who were on the street that day cheering when the police cars drove off with the *Codex*? That's when some common sense gets injected into the whole business and we start getting some insight into the workings of the ratbag's mind and his motivations. He was like his old man, the villagers say. Also called José. Wandered around praising the Lord and snatching whatever he could get his sticky fingers on. Even built a shed out of corrugated old iron and tin cans to put the junk he collected in. Ring a bell?

And then the mother, Lola, a clean hard-working woman who was the family support. Who went around Santiago de Compostela selling milk door-to-door. And one day knocked on the door of the Archbishop's Palace and asked if they had a job for her twit of a son. And that's how he got a job. They took him on as an odd-job man. And where it all went wrong. When he got fired and the Cabildo – the Cathedral council – refused to pay him the 40,000 euros he claimed in severance pay. You can't pilfer for two and a half decades and nobody notices. Then he was out for revenge. His honour had been im-pugned. His honour? God, some people.

So maybe a few bums got squeezed in the inner reaches of the temple. With so much hanky-panky among the Catholic clergy these last years, they might as well add bum patting to the ritual. Remember the opera? The Hunch-back of Notre Dame? Forget it. Now it's going to be Sticky Fingers José, the Sparks of Santiago. Somebody somewhere is writing the script for the screen and stage at this very moment. It's rumoured they might make it into a musical. Just picture it: José the loopy electrician with a candle in his hand wandering the cathedral vaults in the pitch black, filching the poor boxes, pocketing sacred manuscripts and high up, under the roof, poor old Santiago shrouded in dark-ness, tears rolling down his cheeks at the whole wretched affair. The proposal a few years back to stop pilgrims from kissing him for fear of spreading a viru-lent strain of influenza was bad enough. But this? This is a real bummer!

So the next time you're in Santiago, wayfaring stranger, and have done the pilgrimage and made your peace with God, as you see it, go and have a coffee in La Quintana. It's across the square from the main cathedral entrance. That's where the electrician used to whine about the 40,000 euros the Cabildo owed him and have his morning coffee. And pseudo speculate about who stole the Codex – serves them right, wasn't properly guarded, he'd say, illuminated by his visit to early morning mass and filled with the Holy Spirit.

La Quintana is open till the wee hours. There's a sort of disco downstairs and it can get pretty crowded with young bloods at the weekend. Sodom and

Gomorra it's not, but it will put a different complexion on things when you visit the cathedral. When you go in, make sure you climb the narrow stairway behind the altar and give San Tiago a hug. God only knows he's had enough to put up with over the centuries with these *sinverguenza* pilgrims and these *sinverguenza* priests. So don't you go making things worse for him, you hear? You might think twice about dropping something in the poor box. That's fair enough, given what we know now. But don't let this cautionary tale dismay you. Keep the faith. As a general rule, it's always better to give than to receive. Plug that in your ears and keep it there!

26
The Nature of Ants

But ask the animals and they will teach you, or the birds of the air, and they will tell you; or speak to the earth and it will tell you, or let the fish of the sea inform you. Which of all these does not know that the hand of God has done this? In his hand is the life of every creature and the breath of all mankind.

Job 12: 7-10

The ant has three characteristics. The first is that they march in line, each one carrying a grain of corn in its mouth. Those who have none do not say to the others: "Give us some of your grain," but follow the tracks of those who first went out to the place where they find the corn and carry it off to their nest. Let this description serve to signify sensible men, who, like the ants, act in unity, as a result of which they will be rewarded in the future.

The ant's second characteristic is that when it stores grain in its nest, it divides its supply in two, lest by chance it should be soaked in the winter rains, the seed germinates and the ant dies of hunger. In the same way, you, O man, should keep separate the words of the Old and the New Testament, that is, distinguish between the spiritual and the carnal, lest the law interpreted literally should kill you, for the law is a spiritual thing, as the Apostle says: "For the letter killeth, but the spirit giveth life" (2 Corinthians, 3:6). For the Jews, who paid attention only to the letter of the law and scorned its spiritual interpretation, have died of hunger.

The ant's third characteristic is that at harvest time it walks through the crop and finds out by nibbling the ears whether it is barley or wheat. If the crop is barley, the ant goes to another ear and sniffs it, and if it smells wheat, it climbs to the top of the ear and carries off the grain to its nest. For barley is food for beasts.

The Aberdeen Bestiary

27

The Ants Arrive at Last

Last night I had a dream. And in the dream I saw a great Ant Hill. And the Ant Hill was replete with buzzing, busy ants, millions upon millions of them, a black burning mass, fixated, each one for itself on pushing away the grain of sand, big as a rock that blocks the hole and prevents us entering into the burning light of the inner kingdom before it is too late. Before we burst into flying insects, wasps, sprout wings, rise into the sky, block out the sun and descend mercilessly on the cattle in the fields, on the horses, pigs, birds, on every living creature, and inject them with our poisonous, pestiferous barb. But I am not afraid; it is only another bad dream. Because when we enter the Cathedral, there are horses and pigs and donkeys aplenty wandering around gaping in awe at the golden throne of St James and the Doleful One on the crucifix, his Holy Mother, the holy pictures hanging in the chapels, the statues of the Saints, St James on high above the altar, the crown of thorns, all gazing in wonderment, in adoring silence with their big watery eyes.

Parrots, doves and small birds alight from high above the altar. The true form of the pilgrim is revealed. The sky opens up and from a hole in the roof a beam of light falls onto the altar. A little church mouse appears by my side. The ceremony of the *Botafumeiro* is about to begin.

The *Botafumeiro* is an incense-burner which expels incense, the mouse explains. And since the church mouse senses my interest in the origin of the word, he explains that *bota* in Galician has various meanings. One of them is to throw. As in throw a ball. *Fumeiro* is less complicated. It comes from the word for smoke. So a *fumeiro* can be a brazier or a smokehouse.

"We still have fairs for smoked meats in Galicia," he whispers. "And they are called *fumeiros*. So the *Botafumeiro* is something that expels smoke. In this case incense. Its use was popular in the Middle Ages because the pilgrims slept on the floor of the Cathedral. There were no pews then. And not having washed unless they'd fallen into a stream or got soaked along the way they stunk to the high heavens. The incense killed the smell."

The censor is attached by a rope to the ceiling of the Cathedral about 20 metres higher. It is now swinging to and fro. From left to right, disappearing behind the pillars as it swings ever higher.

"It weighs over 60 kilos," the mouse whispers, "and they shovel in forty kilos of incense, sometimes twice that amount, on top of twenty kilos of burning charcoal. And swing it back and forth at speeds of over 60 kilometres an hour."

Then he says, "But you have come here for a purpose. There is something you wanted to ask?"

Perhaps the sensation of the inevitability of disaster is more present in the ant race than in any other species. Arguably it can be traced to the sudden footfall of The Feet, crossing our paths, trampling our caravans. Or to the vehicles and contraptions of The Feet. The bikes, cars, motorcycles, all the constructions that litter the landscape and wipe out millions of our nation daily. From this we have learned one simple truth. That the machines and artefacts of The Feet are subject to self-destruction. Sooner or later something goes wrong with them. It is part of the nature of objects. Disaster is built into them. Everywhere we see evidence of this. Tangled rusting metal objects along the wayside, buildings that collapse, canyons in the footpaths and highways not made by the weather.

So the Botafumeiro must have crashed too. That is the simple conclusion I am inspired to draw from the movements the pullers force it to execute: Sending it roaring up to the roof and letting it fall again at the end of the ropes with the speed of a meteorite. No object can be moved indefinitely against its will without impunity in my humble assessment.

So when I ask the mouse if it has ever crashed, logically, I already know the answer. But why I ask the question is something even I do not understand. And it is only when I receive the answer, I realize why I, out of all the ants in the world, am compelled to enquire about the Botafumeiro.

"The Botafumeiro has come crashing down three times," says the mouse, "but the only occasion of concern to you is the first time. That was in 1499. It was in July, on the feast day of St James, the 25th when Catherine of Aragon was present. She was only thirteen at the time. She'd left the Alhambra Palace on 21st May accompanied by 65 ladies-in-waiting and servants, together with an escort of knights and archers to protect her. And a group of nobles, clerics and scholars to advise her. They were on their way up to La Coruña on the coast to get the boat to take her to England to marry Edward, Prince of Wales, eldest son of Henry VII of England who was nearly the same age. Perhaps the archbishop suggested they make a detour and visit Santiago de Compostela, who knows? But with the Saint's feast day approaching it was a logical choice. And having been underway two months already a detour of a few days more was not going to make much difference.

She arrived a day or two before the feast day and is reported as praying in the chapel the night before. Next day they brought the *Botafumeiro* out as usual to celebrate the Saint's birthday. As they had been doing each 25th of July for centuries. But with the young princess present, the day was more special than ever. Perhaps it was the solemnity of the occasion, the great expectations for Catherine's marriage to Edward. Perhaps it was the hand of God. But in full swing the ropes of the *Botafumeiro* broke and the censor, the weight and size of a small donkey went hurtling down the aisle to the right to smash against the door of *La Plateria*. Some say it went right through the door or the window and killed some horses in the square where the *platters,* the silversmiths, were working, but that is not so sure. Not that it matters. More important was its significance. It was a portend. And like those comets that flash across the sky portending the collapse of civilizations or the end of time, this one was hailing not only the Reformation but the death of the Scottish nation. Some say the cannonball that hit the *Plateria* door did not stop there but crossed the sea to England where it went into orbit round Catherine's head till she was regent and married to Henry VIII, Edward's younger brother. Or maybe it lodged like a cancer inside her. Whatever the case, when Henry went off to fight the French, she sent the English army to meet the Scottish King James IV at Flodden Field. And that was where the Flower of Scotland were wiped out in 1513. The king, the nobility and over 10,000 men. The sad thing is, under other circumstances, Catherine might well have married James. The Spanish ambassador in Scotland was working on that. Or so he gave James to believe. And that is what you came here to learn. Whether you know it or not. You have been sent here to bear witness. To what I don't know. That is a question only you can answer."

Then he asks if there are further questions troubling me.

"The origin of the name Tiago. Why does Tiago mean James?"

"For that you'll have to consult the dog that guards the door outside," he says, nodding behind him. And without another word, he sneaks off in the direction of the altar in search of some morsel or other, perhaps even a crumb of the Holy Host fallen from the chalice during communion so that he too can go to paradise when his time comes, the other paradise, the paradise reserved for the beasts of the fields and the fowl of the air.

The dog that guards the door of the Cathedral is called Cipio. Or that is how he introduces himself. He is a big, russet-coated, curly haired Spanish water-dog.

"Glad you asked that, Cipio says, "because it was left out of Cervantes' 'Dialogue of the Dogs.'"

"Who?"

"Cervantes, everyone knows Cervantes. Wrote *Don Quixote*. You remember? Also wrote the *Dialogue of the Dogs* about two dogs chatting with each other. His dog book is the Bible for us dogs. Has been passed down to us for generations."

I hold my peace out of shame. I dare not tell him the ants in my country are an ignorant lot and few have heard of the illustrious Cervantes. Fortunately he is immediately off on another track.

"Did you know we water dogs were trained to retrieve the arrows of the hunters when they went to the marshes hunting for ducks and wild fowl? We'd dive into the water, bring back the catch in our mouths and lay it on the bank at the feet of the hunters. Then we'd dive in again and go looking for the arrows. Oh, it was great fun, I can tell you."

"Very interesting" I say changing the subject fast as I can. "But what I want to ask is how the name James became Tiago?"

"Best to start from the beginning on that one," he says, peering out from under the curls covering his eyes. "We have to start with Iacobus in Latin. That changes in time to the shorter version of Yaco which you can also write as Iago. That was then lengthened to Tiago, possibly because it is easier to pronounce with a T at the beginning..."

I am lost by this time so I say "But what about Jaime? That's also James in Spanish?"

"Glad you asked. Starting with Iacobus again in Latin we get, Jaco, Yago, Jaime, Santiago, some more popular than others depending in which part of Spain you come from."

"Yes, yes, but what about James in English?"

Well, the nearest to that is Gemmes which is what they call James in French, although you also have Jacques. Gemmes is Norman French and that is possibly how it got to Scotland and became James. A popular name with the Scottish kings. And then there was the Jacobites ...."

To prevent him going on forever I interrupt again to say "there are many people called James in Scotland: Jamie, Jim, Jimmy, Seamus. And also lots of dogs, many running wild."

Cipio pricks up his ears at this intelligence. "Dogs you say?"

"Lots of wild and savage dogs. Running about loose," I tell him, warming to the subject. Before I know it, I am rambling on about Scots terriers and collies and even Black Bob before I notice his eyes darting in his head. So I quickly drop that line, do a little back-peddling and tell him none of the dogs up in that savage land have the skills of the noble Spanish waterdogs and none are as learned as he. He smiles, shows his teeth and wags his tail. He thanks me for the compliment, asks me to convey his regards to the Scottish dogs, and fixing his eye again on the pilgrim on the other side of the square feeding the pigeons, lopes off to investigate.

Listening to the mouse and the dog telling me all that stuff I begin to feel maybe being an ant is not so bad after all. There are many misconceptions about us ants. That we love toiling from sunup to sundown. Nothing could be farther from the truth. We simply don't know any better. Without rhyme or reason we chase about all day, running up and down the line, lugging all sorts of stuff to the ant hill. All sorts of trash: injured flies, struggling, dying beetles, wings of moths, even the mangled corpses of our own brothers and sisters trampled by *The Feet*. And when we have delivered this debris to the hole, we hurry back down the line to start all over again, picking up twigs big as trees, pieces of vine leaves the size of barn-doors.

It is only at night when the deep darkness falls and the light on earth disappears that we are still. That we lie side by side in the deep dark, dead as stones. That we dream. Sometimes I dream I am a fish deep in the ocean or bird high in the sky only to find I have been deceived by these promises from the dark when I wake up and see that nothing has changed and my hard shell still keeps me prisoner. But I do not care. And though I realize we are blessed only when we accept the limitations of our humble ant station and our imprisonment in this armour, I refuse to betray my desire to become a bird someday.

I thought briefly of becoming a mouse, because the church mouse was very interesting and knew much, but later when I was in the sacristy exploring to see where the thief had stolen the Sacred Manuscript of St James, I came across a tatty half-nibbled volume of the writings of Erasmus of Rotterdam in which he says mice are mean, despicable creatures with nothing else on their minds but fornicating and gobbling corn. So I will have to give the question some more thought.

El Camino de Fisterra

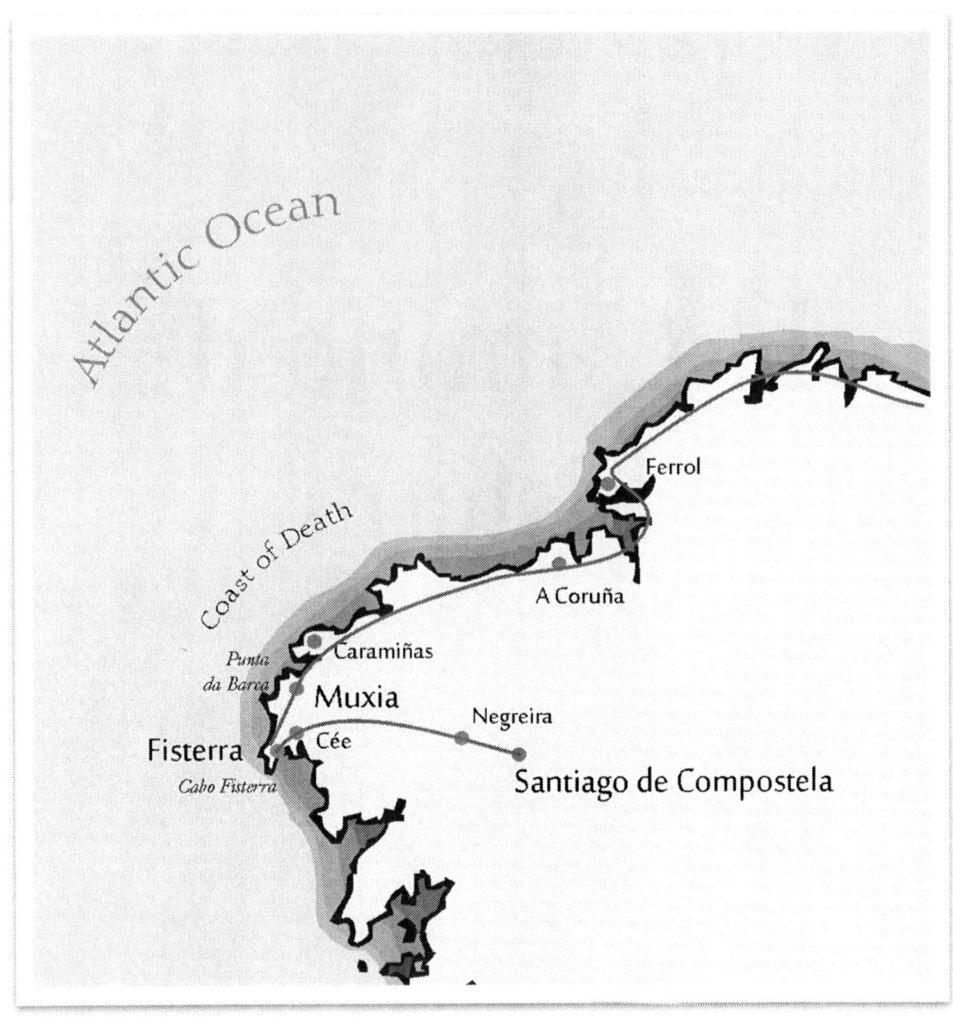

Camino de Fisterra: from Santiago de Compostela to Fisterra

28
West Coast Run

It's a stiff climb up the hill to the huge monastery of San Martin Pinario over-looking the city. Hundreds of beds spread over several floors. Have a celebra-tory meal in an Italian restaurant, stay the night and leave again in the morning for Fisterra. It is about 15 minutes' walk to the bus station. Santiago de Com-postela is a pretty big city.

So good to go by bus for a change. Beautiful big new scenic buses where you can sit upstairs. An absolute delight after over a month of having to leave the hostel before dawn and hitting the road. Yolande has to be back in Santiago by the 13th of July to get the bus back to Bordeaux on the 14th. She's been busy with the arrangements for the last two weeks and not a day goes by but she rambles on about how to go. By bus? Train? Plane? I can't remember how many tourists' offices we've checked out to get the combination right. One way she ends up in Bordeaux in the middle of the night and someone has to come and pick her up in his car, but she doesn't want to put him out. Her daughter's husband? And the train doesn't stop at the right places. Then she can't get a bus ticket with Eurolines beyond the Spanish border so that's another X-the-unknown factor. In the end so many possible combinations have been re-viewed you could patent the search process – she's now decided it's the bus – and sell it as a sure-fire way to pick winning lottery numbers or help teachers draw up school timetables.

Get into Finisterra this morning after eleven after taking the bus at nine from Santiago. It's a beautiful drive along the coast and the scenery is wonder-ful, passing through several small villages looking onto the water. Mrs French, who is on an even tighter budget than me, wants to book into the municipal hostel which is five euros a day. It does not open till 2:00 pm.

I leave her to her devices and head through the narrow streets looking for some place to stay, call in at an interesting looking bar where they give me the address of the La Paz Hostel at the other end of town. A nice friendly place but with just about no cooking facilities to speak of, for 10 euros a night.

Go and lie on the little beach for an hour, head back into the centre which is about ten minutes' walk. If you can call it a centre, more the entrance to Finisterra where the bus comes in and where the municipal hostel is. Pick up Yolande who has been refused entry to the hostel because she didn't walk from Santiago but took the bus. Through the narrow streets. Where we run into Cajun Daniel, grinning like a loon as always, with the bearded mountain men.

Leave it to Yolande to chat with the Cajun as we walk along. In Cajun French, though on second thoughts that's not possible because Yolande only has one version of French, the French she speaks to the neighbour next door and that ergo is the only acceptable language in existence. Ergo they must be talking two different languages or versions of them: Cajun French and Bordeaux French which is approximately where Yolande comes from. Ergo they only half understand what the other is talking about. Ergo it makes no difference because they always talk like that.

Finisterra is a lovely town and has a nice atmosphere, the sort of feeling you only get when you're close to the ocean. There's great sea food in the restaurants and it is reasonably priced. There's an open market on the quay where you can buy fresh fish, clothes, fruit, that sort of thing. On Friday and Saturday.

Buy two cheap T-shirts. Maybe burn the white one I have been wearing for over a month up at the lighthouse, which is what you're supposed to do when you finish the walk. Burn all your stuff. If I do that I'll be naked. Got hardly anything with me. Period. Mind you, washing those two T-shirts every second day, they deserve to get burned. Sick looking at them.

To make Yolande feel better – after all we don't want to make her feel guilty about something she has been doing all her life – I tell her the English are even worse than she is when it comes to foreign languages. She was married for 40 years to a guy who gave her two kids. Pregnant when they got married at 18. Or was it 22? Forty years. She in one room, he in another. Came occasionally and lay with her. All her life waiting for a sign of love. Waiting for someone to love her. Maybe even just kindness. But not even that. No, right to the end. Nothing. Resents him like hell. Hates him. Her life gone like that.

Wasted. That's what she feels, although she doesn't say it. Forget it, I tell her. Forgive him. That's the only way you can get something unclean out of your system. But what is that? Forgiveness? It's easy to say but how do you get something like that out of your system? Forty years. I don't know how that works either. What do you say? You can't reduce a life to a couple of phrases. Yours or anyone else's. Such a lovely joyful person. Who should have spent her life with a lovely joyful man. Abuse, I say. Emotional abuse. You've been emotionally abused. All your life, I tell her. Maybe he was too. But she hates him. She wants to go on hating him. Does not want to stop hating him just as she could not stop waiting for his love. Now I know these things, now she's told me, I put my arm round her now and then or squeeze her arm when she speaks. It is never too late to be kind. I don't know what to say. Will miss her when she goes though I'll also be glad to see the back of her. There's nothing you can do. It's all gone now. It's over.

Run into the Czechs later on the other side of town. The Prague Five. Call them that though they don't come from Prague. Down in the south of the country somewhere. I'm lying sunning on the beach on the outskirts of Finisterra. Big wide beach. Between a couple of small fishing boats to break the slight breeze blowing. Stand up, see Janz. The father. Of all people. Heading for the beach restaurant but don't see the pushchair. Where's the pushchair? They must have arrived in Santiago, having pushed and pulled the wheelchair with Janz's spastic son all the way from southern Czechoslovakia. Straps tied to the chair and over their shoulders. Pulling it up the hills. Holding it back when they go downhill. Can still see them. On that long stretch of highway in the drizzling rain. And another time, going up the crest of the hill and then over it. The son, about sixteen, in the chair. The wheelchair. His head dangling on one side. Don't see the pushchair, don't see the rest of them. The young physiotherapist that plays the guitar and the other guy, the oriental-looking one. Must be Vietnamese. They're the third largest immigrant group in the country after Slovaks and Romani. Thought there were five. Must have got it wrong. Maybe only four, counting the boy. Maybe they're inside. Inside the restaurant. I wave. Janz stops and I cross the sand. It is good to see him. He fills me with joy. He's just come in a taxi with his wife, he says. She's flown into Santiago. What a good, noble man. I feel humbled in his presence. The sun is out. Lie on the wide beach next to the boats to shelter from the breeze. It's about a hundred metres to the water. To the sea. Too cold to swim much. May dive in for two seconds and back out again later.

29
Nearly the Big Sleep

I that in heill wes and gladnes,
Am trublit now with gret seiknes,
And feblit with infermite:
Timor mortis conturbat me.

William Dunbar, *Lament for the Makaris*

It's been raining today. It was raining yesterday when we arrived. But the two days after that were very good and yesterday especially was hot and sunny and I had a dip in the sea. I have been in Finisterra – Fisterra in Galician – these last three nights and tonight again after which I leave for Muxia, a nice little place on the coast north of here. After that it's on to La Coruña – A Coruña in Galician.

Finisterra is a lively place with a nice atmosphere. Yesterday I took a walk uphill, out to the lighthouse on Cape Finisterra where you have spectacular views of the coast line on both sides terminating and running into the ocean. But I didn't burn any clothes like you're supposed to. I had nothing to burn.

The night before we go with Armando, the little Madrileño who looks after the hostel – 450 euros a month they pay him, he says: it would make you weep. Armando is the Good Samaritan. He's a good-hearted guy who has walked the Camino himself and gets a kick out of doing good. Looking after pilgrims wandering mindlessly on God's earth below – excuse the flowery parlance – and lending a helping hand to miserable mortals. He is the kindest person I have met in a long time.

On Friday night we follow him – with Yolande and a friendly Bulgarian couple – uphill through the winding streets to get to the beach to see the sun sink into the ocean.

Armando's got his guitar stuck into his backpack and he's smoking a joint. There are a few people on the beach. Some of them Americans. Voices.

The beach is wide and long. A wobbly looking character, naked apart from a pair of dustbin shorts, pissed or stoned, or both, is trying to piss into the ocean, but the horizon is rocking like a ship in a storm, so, shit man, he's pissing more on his feet than in the ocean by now and still the fucker won't stand still. Shit! It's as well the ocean is in a good mood. It could be dangerous if aroused.

At the moment the waves are lapping the beach like puppy dogs in a long line down the sand about as far as you can see to where the beach meets the rocks. Armando throws up his arms and waddles across the sand like a turtle come to lay its eggs and embraces a sheep. That's what the bundle looks like. On closer inspection it turns out to be a long dark-haired crone wrapped in an Astrakhan coat and a blanket. A kindred spirit by the looks of it because before you know it, and after an obviously most welcome embracing session, Armando is sitting cross-legged beside his Crow squaw like a Crow Indian chief outside the wigwam with his squaw deep in some happy-family-matters conversation, which for all I know might be a continuation of yesterday's when he also went to see the sun sink into the ocean, something he does just about every weekend when the weather is right and the sun, the ocean and the world are all in a co-operative mood. To be joined by other sunset worshipers and toasted with hit of dope and a gurgle of red wine swigged straight from the bottle like the young American is doing now in front of me. Before he turns round and sees the goat. The goat? Yes, the goat. Next he's on his knees in the sand a few feet away communicating with the goat. And to show he's a serious knower of goats, he presses his forehead against the goat's – a young, white goat. Kid goats, I believe the human creatures call them. Its owner, a big bearded Spanish wild man who looks like an old straw mattress turned inside out, has it on a leash. And since the American kid, like any normal person, can only make a mental connection between leashes and dogs, and not goats, he's now talking about the dog he has back home. Wooffy, we'll call it. And he goes on at great length about Wooffy. Not to the Spaniard. Because after congratulating the *barbudo* for being so clever as to go wandering the world with a goat on a rope, inquiring solicitously about its eating habits, its mother and father, because it's a young goat, pulling its lips apart to study its teeth, and making other diplomatic inquiries, he stretches out on his side on the sand again with the other

American kid, and by the look of things they are both soon deep into Wooffy matters.

So that's the setting. Some fires are lit in the shelter of the rocks. The huge ball of the sun starts to sink down towards the sea. It's a nice feeling. And no two ways about it, it's special when you let everything go and feel yourself going with it.

It must have been like that too for primitive man. For the cave dwellers who tracked across a landscape with no human settlements, with names only for the rocks and the rivers and the fish and the birds and the animals. To the ends of the earth. To see the resurrection. To see the sun die and be reborn next day.

That's what will happen to Armando. Because really that's why he's come: to be reborn. But as the sun sinks into the ocean and the light fades, we leave him, Yolande and I – the Bulgarians have already gone up the long zigzag boardwalk before us in the fading light with darkness coming on fast. But if Armando sees the rebirth of the sun the next morning, I certainly don't. I get woken up a few times in the night by the guy sleeping in the bunk above me. The Italian, Sergio, thrashing and turning and jumping up and down like a pine marten on a bed of burning hot pine cones. And I'm thinking what's wrong with this swine that is disturbing my sleep and should I get up and prod him in the ribs and wake him up? However being a gentleman by nature, I press the ear plugs deeper into my ears and continue to snore away to my heart's content.

But I have the poor guy fingered. And when I go down to the bus stop at the other end of town to see off Yolande who is finally headed back to France, off to Bordeaux, Armando is also there. With Sergio. There are about ten people getting on the bus. And when it gets to the Italian, he's looking pale and sick. Sick as in deathly pale. Yolande climbs aboard and takes a seat at the rear. Armando says something to the driver and the driver gets down and they get into discussion. The driver says they need to get Sergio to a doctor immediately.

The bus is about to leave. Armando tells the driver to deposit poor Sergio at the hospital in Cée, the next outpost down the trail on the way back to Santiago de Compostela. The driver climbs behind the steering wheel and starts the engine and the bus heads up the hill.

I hear later from Armando that Sergio has had some sort of a heart attack. No wonder he lay thrashing two nights in a row in the bunk above me. The Big Sleep had come to check him out. But I feel bad about it all the same. Not so much because of the Big Sleep. I'd never wish the Big Sleep on Sergio or anyone else. And Sergio has escaped its claws anyway. For the time being. No I just feel bad about misreading the signs and bearing him ill will.

The Galician rain is pissing down when I wake up in the morning and it's pissing down too on my clothes hanging on the washing line. My green shirt, my blue T-shirt bought in the market on Saturday, my khaki shorts, my pathetic only towel looking more like the beard of an old grey Scots Terrier, they're all dripping wet on the clothes line outside the window. But as we Camino revellers like to say, all you need to keep you going; apart from a *baguette*, a banana and a wedge of Laughing Cow, *Vache Qui Rit* cheese, is a bottle of wine in the evening.

I'm with Axel my bald German mate, who turned up in these parts two days ago. We walk in the pouring rain to find this very good, fresh fish, highly recommended restaurant Armando wrote the name of on the piece of paper I have in my hand. I order *pulpo* with white beans and Axel has some grilled hake. We have white wine. It's not very good. Maybe we're spoiled but it's not a great meal.

"Even a monkey can grill a fish," Axel says.

And that's our final word on Spanish cooking after seven hundred kilometres. You can take that as gospel, not matter what others tell you, and do whatever you have to do with your time for the rest of the day knowing it's not been wasted with this practical piece of information.

30
The Grim Reaper in German

"I've lost my hat," she says. "I must get it" and she hurries on past the cafe where we're sitting, like the Mad Hatter in Alice in Wonderland, an Australian flag-handkerchief hanging behind from the belt of her khaki shorts. She'll be somewhere in her mid-fifties. She's over here with Ryanair via Dublin, her grandparents, O'Connor, being Irish, she'll tell us presently when she calms down.

"Let it go." Axel says

"No I've got to get it back. Somebody's stolen it."

"Who'd steal a hat like that?" I say.

"I've had it since Le Puy."

She's been walking for over three months, she says.

"Look at it this way," I say. "You haven't lost your hat. Your hat has left you. He doesn't want to continue. He's happy here. Because this is the end of the line."

"No, I've got to find it."

"She hasn't learned anything," Axel says, his feet up on the chair in front of him, outside the Don Quixote bar-restaurant. Behind him the sunshade has been folded down and tied tight to stop it flapping. There's a slight breeze blowing. He's referring to O'Connor. What he means is she's been like that all her life. Has been repeating herself over and over. And she can't do anything about it. She's caught in a loop. He knows his women, does Axel.

Soon the fishing boats will come into the harbour. Down from Camariñas, the fishing village on the other side of the bay. You can't see it from the Don Quixote but if you walk over to the quay and look towards the lighthouse across the water, you can just about imagine it. If you come back in an hour or so you'll hear the hooting of the boats before you see them. Before you see the flotilla of fishing boats and sailing boats and dinghies, their bunting and flags flapping in the breeze. And the hooters sounding and the rubber dinghies bouncing and rocking as they zigzag between the fishing boats. And if you follow them back to where they came from, right across the bay, that's Camariñas. They have an English cemetery there. That's where the 172 members of the crew of HMS *Serpent* are buried. A British cruiser that went down in 1872 after it broke up on the rocks off Punta da Boi over there. The seas off the Costa da Morte are lethal.

It's Monday and the feast day of the Virgen del Carmen, the patron saint of fishermen. It's held on the 16th of July here, which is a few days later than the rest of Spain, according to *La Voz de Galicia*. It doesn't say why. The Virgin Mary was brought here in a stone boat with stone sails so heavy a team of oxen couldn't shift it, the plaque on the esplanade says. It lies at the bottom of the sea, out there, beyond the church, but so light you can move it with your finger.

"The boats will come in soon. After two," Angel says at the reception desk when we're back at the Bella Muxia, the new hostel just opened in June.

We go and sit in the sparkling new, gleaming kitchen.

"I got married every seven years," Axel says over a glass of wine.

"Every seven?"

"No, there were seven years between each of my marriages."

"Seven is a lucky number, they say."

"I never use it in casinos."

"Maybe the seven lucky years was the bit between year one and year seven?" I say and he laughs. "And when the seven ended that was when your bad luck started."

But Axel is a believer. He believes in love. "Maybe you should go down and see her. Get her email." I'm referring to Caroline, the charming Canadian woman we met a few days before. She's gone down to Finisterra.

Angel comes into the kitchen. A party of Catalan school kids has arrived and is doing a ten-day tour from Barcelona to La Coruña. The long kitchen table is piled with sandwiches: *jamon York*. They smell delicious. Axel has a little Canadian flag lapel pin he got from Caroline, the Canadian honey.

"He got one too. A little flag," I say pointing to the handsome young Swiss blade at the end of the long table. Caroline's husband died three years ago. She is a remarkably beautiful woman and she's got class. Come to think of it, she's the first woman with class I've seen since Betty Grable. On screen, of course. They always look different on screen.

Earlier, O'Connor, coming up the street, distraught and still looking for her hat, says to me, "Who you with?"

"Axel."

"Oh Axel, you know Caroline?"

"Caroline?"

"The Canadian. Met her at the pub."

"The pub?"

"Only place between Fisterra and Muxia," she says.

Later in the Don Quixote I mention it to Axel.

"Did Angel get her email address?" he says.

"Don't think so."

"You think I should go down? Down to Fisterra. Get a taxi?"

"If you were twenty-five it's the kind of thing you'd do. But you'd have some future. Some hope. And what would you do anyway? Start all over again?" I don't mention his three previous marriages. Hope springs eternal while the Grim Reaper lurks in the wings.

"What do you call the Grim Reaper in German?" Maybe it's Axel's *seven years* that inspire the question. Or maybe it's his shiny shaven head that inspires the thought. He looks at me.

"The Grim…" and I stand up, pull my lips back and make a sweeping movement with my two hands close together in imitation of a reaper swinging the scythe as reaps the corn. "The Grim Reaper?"

"Gevätter Todes."

"Vader Todes?" because that's what I think he says. Father Death.

"Gevätter Todes." he says and writes it down in my notebook with a pencil. He laughs and I smile broadly. I pick up the newspaper from the table. The headline on the front page of *La Voz de Galicia* says: 'Subsidy for unemployed will be below the 426 euros minimal for survival.'

I put down the newspaper and pick up the book I've been reading: *Waiting for the Barbarians*, it's called. By J. M. Coetzee, the South Africa writer. I found it in the hostel kitchen yesterday. It's only about 150 pages long so I should get through it soon. Then I can ditch it. You don't want to be carrying any extra weight do you? It's a shame though because it's a good book. Coetzee says, "Why pretend? We all know all old men seek is to recover their youth in the arms of young women."

So that was it. It was curtains for both of us. Nothing to do but wait for the Grim Reaper or Gevätter Todes to come for us.

I picture him as the hooded figure in the long cloak in *Seventh Seal*, the film directed by Ingmar Bergman, set in Sweden during the Black Death in which a medieval knight plays chess with a hooded figure who has come to take him to the other side. The Seventh Seal is from the Book of Revelation. It says, "When the Lamb had opened up the seventh seal, there was silence in heaven for the space of half an hour."

Yes, the meaning of life was waiting to be revealed to all of us. But there is little point in waiting for an answer when we know already. As Coetzee says, "… every moment life is telling you who you are, and where you are going. It is known. It is known to you. It is written in God's hand. But there is little you can do about it except acknowledge it and pass on like a donkey drinking from the trough, that only looks up to shake the flies from around its eyes. Everything is known."

31
The Legend of the Stone Boat

7th and 8th century documents...refer to the belief that James spent a number of years preaching in Spain before returning to Jerusalem and martyrdom. His followers are believed to have carried his body down to the coast and put it into a stone boat, which was carried by angels and the wind beyond the Pillars of Hercules (the Straits of Gibraltar), to land near Finisterra, at Padrón, on the Atlantic coast of northern Spain.

Confraternity of St James

Most people who visit the site where the Stone Boat lies on the Punta de la Barca, about two kilometres outside Muxia, clamber over the huge boulders that lie on the headland. They are like great, soft sea-beasts delivered up by the sea. These huge rocks or boulders are the sail, the rudder and the hull of the Stone Boat. Under one boulder you can crawl to cure ailments. Another supposedly has properties for lovers guaranteeing eternal love. And when you have exhausted those possibilities, you can walk up to the church overlooking the site and, if you know where, tug at the rope on the wall outside and try to ring the bell in the tower.

I've been down there three or four times these last days and usually run into Axel who is also having a break before moving on. There's a nice walk along the headland down a sparkling, fresh grit road that never sees a car. Or you can take the footpaths between the rocks and the high grass past the conger eels drying on racks in the sun. In the afternoon heat, it is so still you can almost hear the big coloured butterflies flutter their wings in the summer peace.

Time is what it's all about here on the Coast of Death. It is written in the stones. From the no-time of Neolithic man who came here first, before the Celts. When there was only sun, moon and star time. Then the time of St James who came next. Roman time. Conquest time. The time from the founding of the City of Rome. In Roman time. That became Christian time, Anno Domine time. Invented by a monk in the seventh century. Then Modern time, electronic time. And then there's climatic time, more temperamental and treacherous than all the rest put together.

But before I tell you about the Stone Boat, I have to tell you about the sea and then the Celts and then the Romans. Because the sea was here first, then the Celts, then the Romans. And when I have told you about that I can tell you about the Stone Boat. Otherwise you will not understand the Legend of the Stone Boat shipwrecked on this rocky coast where the land ends and falls into the sea. Where the warm waters of the Gulf of Mexico meet the cold waters of the North Atlantic and two climatic zones clash giving rise to hurricane winds and 20 metres high waves and it becomes a graveyard of ships. Thousands have gone down over the centuries.

In 1890 HMS *Serpent*, a 1770-tonne cruiser ran into the rocks off Carominas with the loss of all but three of its 175 crew. In 1846, the *SS Great Liverpool*, and in 1870, HMS *Captain* went down. Most notable disaster in the new millennium was the sinking of the Greek oil tanker *Prestige* in November 2002 giving rise to one of the greatest ecological disasters. Thousands of Spaniards were bussed from all over Spain to scrape the black rubbery *chapapote* off the rocks with spoons and knifes.

But those are all minor compared with the sinking of nearly half a fleet of Spanish ships in 1596. The fleet, of some 84 vessels including 24 galleons under the command of Martin de Padilla y Manrique, commander of the Ocean Fleet, was headed for Ireland to raise the Irish in rebellion against Elizabeth I of England in the Spanish-English wars of the period. It was planned to join up with more vessels and troops on the north-west coast ports of La Coruña and Ferrol. But after sailing nearly 160 sea miles along the Atlantic coast of Spain from the deep water port of Lisbon it ran into hurricane winds and 15 metre-high waves off Finisterra where many ships with over 1,700 men on board went down on the reefs at the entrance to the river Corcubión. Months later when the papal nuncio submitted his report on the disaster, he listed 30 vessels sunk and the loss of 3,000 Portuguese nobles, or *gentlemen adventurers* as the English were pleased to call the freebooters they sent in similar fleets to Spain.

But the accounts of these disasters are as nothing compared to that of the Stone Boat. The *Serpent*, the *Great Liverpool*, the *forgotten armada* of Martin de Padilla, were all real ships with real men on board that sank in real time, in historical time, in recorded time. The Stone Boat had no men on board. It was piloted by angels with the Queen of Heaven, Star of the Sea, on board and if it can imagined as moving, moved in no-time, in another dimension, in mythical time. And when it appeared off the coast to Santiago, St James, around 44 AD, the event went unnoticed by the Celts of Galicia, till it surfaced nearly 1200 years later in the form of a Christian myth, fabricated in a monastery for the propagation of the faith.

Not that it would have made much difference to the stone worshipping Celts of the time. Their collective memory would start to dissipate under the heel of the Roman occupier. Four hundred years later, by the time the Roman Empire fell apart, all traces of the Celtic languages spoken in Spain would be lost and the only indigenous language still spoken would be Basque.

The Romanisation of the Celtic regions of Spain began when Roman legions under Decimus Junius Brutus Callaica (the Galician) arrived in 137 BC and fought the Celts on the River Douro, grandsons of the men who had fought for Hannibal in the Punic Wars (264-241 BC between Rome and Carthage), killing 60,000 of them. Two years before, in a first campaign, the gods of the Celts were still on their side and came to their aid. Junius Brutus was halted at the river Limia (running 108 kilometres from the Talarino Mountains near Ourense in Galicia to the Atlantic at Viano do Castelo in Portugal). The legionaries took the river for the mythical river Lethe, one of the five rivers of Hades and refused to cross in case they lost their memories and no longer knew who they were. To show them they had nothing to fear, Junius Brutus crossed to the other side, called out his men's names and waved.

The Romans were no doubt the butt of a few jokes for while up in the Celtic hill forts, in the *castro* of Santiago too, when they heard the story, the Druids acclaiming the strength and protection of the gods of their rivers, the half-men, half-fish who had so terrified the Romans. But by the time the Romans came to the second river, the mighty Mino (Minho) 310 kilometres long and the longest in Galicia, the foot soldiers and auxiliaries crossed without a whimper advancing closer to the Celtic heartland, deaf to the calls from Hades, leaving the Galicians laughing on the other side of their face. It may be coincidental, but there are also two rivers up in El Padrón: the Ulla and the Arousa, a pretty spot where St James preached.

The local legend has it that when James died his followers carried his body down to the coast and put it on a stone boat that was carried by angels and the wind beyond the Pillars of Hercules to land at Finisterra.

Another version of the story has it that St James arrived in a stone boat in El Padrón and moored it to the great stone post (Pedrón) there, a piece of a menhir which still stands in the local church.

Yet another version down Muxia way is that St James, despondent about the success of his missionary efforts, goes to the coast to pray. Soon a mysterious vessel made of stone, piloted by two angels appears with the Virgin Mary on board. The Virgin tells James his preaching has been a success and he is to return to Jerusalem. She then gives him a figurine of herself and the Apostle builds an altar beneath the stones which the present church on the headland stems from.

Anyone, it seems, is entitled to invent a version of The Legend of the Stone Boat, provided they include the basic puzzle pieces: St James, the Blessed Virgin, two angels, a stone boat with hull, sail and rudder. Mention is best omitted of where it came from and where it is going as that only gives rise to further geographical confusion. Proving the boat actually existed is no problem; you need only go to the headland outside Muxia and point to the hull, the sail and the rudder.

Until such times as *the competent authorities* come up with a better version of the myth, and so that you may all sleep peacefully abed of a night untroubled by historical howlers, I herewith present for your delectation and edification, the official version of The Legend of the Stone Boat. And it is this.

When the languages of all the peoples of Hispania are dead by the time Roman rule ends in 460 AD, all except that of the Basques who side with the Romans against the Celtiberians and the Galician Celts can no longer recall who they are or where they come from and the Latin tongue is thick on their tongues, in a little house on the Coast of Death, hundreds of years later, in

Muxia or Fisterra or some other settlement, a little girl has a dream one stormy night when hurricane winds are howling and the wild-horse waves are galloping out on the black raging sea and she sees a radiant figure approach in the darkness of night in a great Stone Boat driven by a huge stone sail and piloted by two angels. And when she wakes up suddenly from the dream she tells her mother she has seen the Virgin Mary. And days later, when the wind has lain down like a lamb, and the sea is calm, she and her mother together with some neighbours hurry out to the headland and contemplate the remains of the boat: the upturned hull, the sail and the rudder, and are filled with wonder. And the faithful understand the dream of the child has been a visitation, a sign from the Lord, and tell the abbot of the nearby Benedictine Monastery of San Xulian de Moraine, four kilometres outside Muxia looking onto the sea. And when the abbot hears the story from the lips of the little girl, he summons his chief scribe and tells him to get his quill and ink ready because he has a tale to tell that must be committed urgently to parchment for the propagation of the faith and the greater glory of Christ our Saviour.

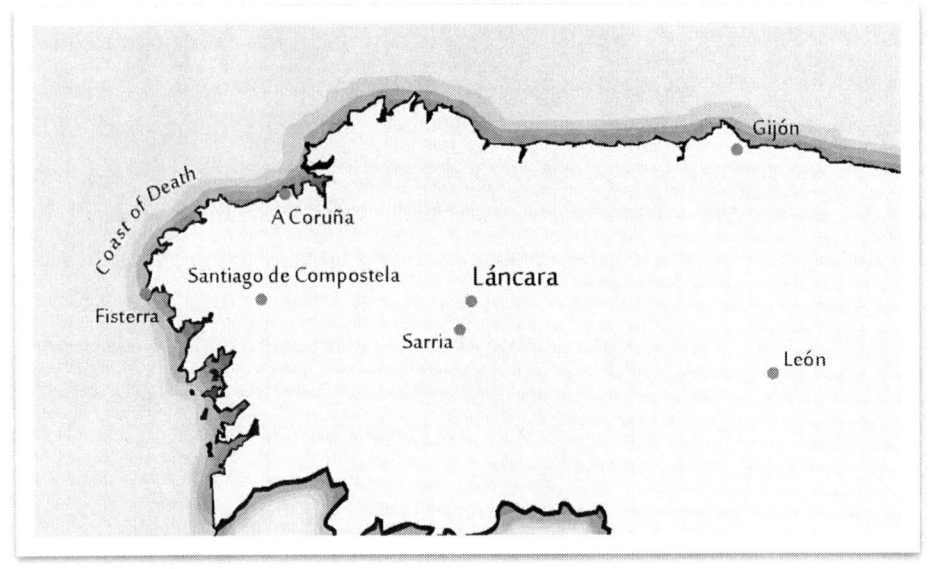

Láncara: Where the Castros Originate

32
All the Castros

I never do manage to get up to Láncara in the end. To see the house where Fidel Castro's father was born. I'm on my way up to La Coruña and Ferrol by then. But I'll tell you about it anyway from the bits and pieces I've cobbled together. Since I've crossed into Galicia, that green rolling country that reminds you of Ireland and parts of Scotland and all those places with rolling hills and trees, the name Castro is everywhere: on boards, on a little roadside café, on sign posts. Only a craven fame worshipper would imagine they are a tribute to Fidel or his father, Angel. Castro is a popular name here. There are over 200,000 people named Castro in Spain and over half of them are in Galicia. A *castro* is also a hill fort in Galician. A Celtic hill fort.

Fidel Castro's father came from Láncara which is not far from Santiago de Compostela, but nearer to Lugo. It is off the beaten track. A village of 222 people. More a collection of houses. There's a good article about his father Angel in the *La Vanguardia* magazine I'm reading. With photos. Of Angel Maria Bautista Castro Argiz to give him his full name. He has big ears, a hard mouth, and a bald pate that makes him look like Pablo Picasso, the painter, in later years. Though the face isn't quite as ugly as that ugly mush of Picasso's. In later years, is all I'm saying. I'm not saying Picasso didn't maybe look like a little angel in his mother's arms. Just that I've never seen a photo. Only that ugly mush. Same goes for Angel. As a baby, I mean.

The house will be a monument someday. Fidel came over once. Just that one time in 1992. There's a photo of the occasion in the magazine. A crowd of three or four hundred people is squeezed between the stone houses with *el barbudo*, the bearded one, in the middle in his olive green battledress. The photo has been shot from above so you're looking onto the heads of the crowd. You need to look hard to see Fidel, crushed tightly between two stone cottages by the mob. Of admirers, one presumes. As always he has that look of permanent astonishment on his face. As if the man next to him has just whispered in his ear a secret recipe, lost for centuries, for cooking *pulpo* in the Galician manner.

Then there's a photo of his father. He's with a young woman. It could be his daughter but more likely it's his young wife. He's on the right and she's on the left. He looks pretty worn but she looks alright. They've got their elbows on a small stand, one of those long-legged stands you sit plants on. The stand is just that bit too high so they have to raise their elbows. Uncomfortably high by the looks of it. There's a big vase on the plant-stand too. There's a plant in the vase. The leaves of the plant are striped and look like the extended wings of butterflies but you can't see any flower petals. The photographer probably took the portrait in his studio in Santiago de Cuba. That would be the nearest big town. But in a hole like that in the east of Cuba? In Biran?

There are a few anecdotes about him. About the father. That he left Láncara after a card game in which he won a house and a man's wife with it but declined the offer and took off for Cuba in a steamer from La or A Coruña. There's another anecdote tells how Angel comes back to Galicia to see how his old paramour is. But she's got someone else by then and he heads back to Cuba. Back to Biran where he has the house. Built in the same style he had known in Galicia. Made of stone in Galicia but of timber in Cuba.

He takes his house with him. He takes the animals too because when he gets to Cuba they are the same animals: the cows and goats that keep the family warm in the winter on the ground floor in Láncara, Galicia, fret in the heat in Biran, Cuba.

In a sense he never leaves home. He takes his body with him, but not his mind. That's where he starts building up his little empire. Out in Biran. On the north-east coast of Cuba, about 90 kilometres from the provincial capital of Santiago de Cuba. It's near Alto Cedro (High Cedar) and Mayari. It's unlikely you'll ever visit the place, or even want to. But if you want to get the feel of it, because it's quite special, go and listen to Compay Segundo on his seven string guitar sing "Chan Chan":

De Alto Cedro voy para Marcane	From High Cedar, head for Marcane
Llego a Cueto, voy a Mayari	Get to Cueto, go to Mayari

You can practically smell the cedars and the pines and at the tempo it is sung in, feel the weight of the sky and the heat, listen to the donkey tip-toe under the shadows, careful not to wake the ghosts of the trees and the bushes slumbering in the sweltering midday sun or the three chickens and the goat lying in the dust by the fountain where the donkey dips its head in the water and the rider rubs his hand with the scented limes he picked from the trees coming into Alto Cedro. Well that's near where Angel had the farm and where Fidel and his brother Raul were brought up. A world of lost time with no clocks on the walls and the next village an important place to go. Angel was an astute man, by all accounts, carving out a niche in greedy times. He sold lemonade to the field hands from barrels on a donkey's back, worked in a sugar mill, ran a cheap restaurant called El Progresso (Progress) and co-owned a mine called El Desirio (Desire) and bought a fourteen-acre logging company before moving on to consolidate his little empire. He is said to have had an amazing memory, learning to read just by looking to see how others did it.

Angel Castro was an opportunist, an organizer and a disciplinarian. He has been accused of moving the boundary posts on his land in Biran under cover of night to extend his landholding. But since that seems to have been a Galician custom, he doesn't lose too many points on that no matter what the historians say.

The subsequent Castro family, his sons and daughter, are a colourful bunch. It's a pity *Hola* magazine didn't follow them from the 1960s on. It would have made great reading. And great viewing. More a Dallas than a Sopranos soap opera. Or a great big fruit and nut cake that close friend and writer Gabriel Garcia Marquez could have made into a Cuban *Hundred Years of Solitude*. About a hard working peasant whose son organizes the farm labourers to strike against the lousy conditions his hard-nut, exploitative father makes them slave under. Who later starts a revolution. Becomes a dictator. Whose only suit is a green battledress and who has never been known to shave in God knows how many years is it? – fifty now? – so no one has ever seen the dimple on his chin, or can even dispute that he has one. Except for those few who have seen faded photos of the horse, *el Caballo,* in his university days or sniffed in his wallet.

And then the brother who follows him and takes over the tacky old moth-eaten throne of the dictator: Raul. Soon too to retire. When is it? In 2018? The usual family dramas. Alina the rebellious illegitimate daughter who makes a living badmouthing her old man, Fidel, for a buck and cracking jokes about him on the lecture circuit in the U.S. Alina, the ballet dancer. Alina Fernandez who worked as a model for a Havana fashion house and now works in Miami pharmacy, who put the old boy to rights in an entertaining autobiography in which she says she was closer to Raul than to Fidel and, reading between the lines, damaged emotionally by his lack of fatherly love and attention: he was too busy putting Humpty-Dumpty land together again.

So you've got the picture. That's where Fidel's father comes from: Láncara. It's 127 kilometres from A Coruña from where his father departed in 1898. On a boat for Cuba. To fight in the War of Liberation, the war the *gringos* like to call the Spanish-American war. Further up the coast is Ferrol where The English Way (Camino Inglés) to Santiago starts. So-called because pilgrims travelling to Santiago de Compostela and coming from the north, from the British Isles, sailed there directly in medieval times. It is also the town where that other Spanish dictator comes from: Franco. In Franco's time it was called El Ferrol del Cuadillo (leader) to remind everyone where the generalissimo came from. Francisco Paulino Hermenegildo Teopulla Franco y Bahamonde, the little general whose countenance is more at home on a bench of the Tribunal of the Holy Office of the Inquisition, touched as he was by the dank breath of those dolorous Spanish saints you see in the churches telling you that life is unspeakable pain and suffering and people best get it over quick as they can and go to heaven.

Castro. Yes, think too of the hill forts. They too are *castros*: made of stone, one piled on the other to form a series of circle shapes. They date back to before the Romans invaded. To the Celtiberians times which is why they have an affinity with the mounds in Scotland. After the fall of the Roman Empire in the fourth century AD, the German tribes made their way through Spain. The Goths settled in the north and the Suevi, the biggest tribe of Germans, here in Galicia. But the Celts were here before them and they're still here. They play the bagpipes in the streets of the towns in Galicia, and the Galician language, for some unknown reason, is one of the official languages of the European Union.

El Camino del Norte

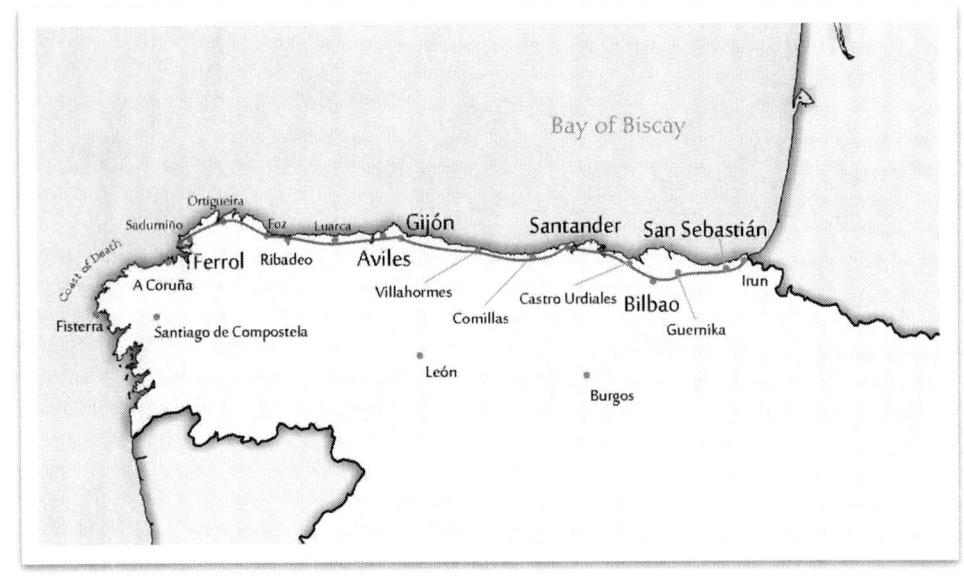

Camino del Norte from Ferrol to Irun

33
Waiting on the FEVE

Ferrol, Ribadeo, Tapia de Casariego, Navia, Luarca, Soto de Luiña, Cudillero, San Esteban, Aviles, Gijón, Villaviciosa, Lastres, Colunga, Ribadesella, Llanes, (Picos de Europa), San Vicente de La Barquera, la Isla,
Comillas, Santillana del Mar, Santander, Santoña, Laredo, Castro Urdiales, Bilbao, Guernika, Lekeitio, Deba, Zumaia, Zarautz, San Sebastian.

The little FEVE trains run along the north coast of Spain from Ferrol on the
north-west coast to Bilbao on the north coast, a distance of about 550 kilometres with another 120 kilometres to Irun on the border with France. The FEVE
initials stand for Narrow-Gauge Rail Company (Ferrocarriles de Via Estrecha).
I pick it up in Ferrol where it starts and have a meal in the station restaurant,
empty except for another couple, before heading north along the coast. Gaps
in the trees reveal small beaches between the coves, people sprinkled here and
there sunning or bathing in the sea. Places few people, apart from the locals,
will have heard of. Names like Atjos, Cedeira, Origuera on the headland,
twenty three in total along the line, although the train only stops at some.

Then it's another long run, passing through another 27 places, some bigger than others, but not much. Lovely little coastal towns like Cervo, Buekla
and Foz. So by the time I get out at Ribadeo the train has passed through about
50 places in total, motivation enough for a strenuous walk from the station to
the other side of town looking for the hostel, which it turns out, is full-up about
five o'clock in the afternoon since it's only got about a dozen beds so I have to
walk back into town and look for a *pensión*.

A few days later, with some hiking in between, I am sitting with a
Frenchman from Normandy waiting for the FEVE again. That's where I discover that waiting on the FEVE is even nicer than getting on it.

There is nothing so wonderful in all the world as killing time waiting for
the FEVE at a rusted table and watching a car speed past on the bald two lane

Nacional headed for God knows where. And when the car has passed out of earshot, feel the silence fall like the dull toll of the bell in the midday heat and turn your attention to the catch of the day: what's left on the shelves of a little shop in a one-cat village: a pot of *paté de canard,* a can of San Miguel beer, a tub of chocolate and cream goo, and one of the last, tired oranges from the broken crate at the entrance. And with great consideration, thankful the broken red plastic chair you're sitting on hasn't collapsed so far, examine each of the objects in turn before plucking the ring of the beer can and giving a gasp of relief.

What's happening to the train is what the half-dozen travellers are discussing further down the road at the station on the other side of the road at this very moment. The train is over an hour late and nobody knows what's happening. Maybe it's got stuck somewhere coming down from Oviedo or coming up from Ferrol. The trains have got to get to a station where they can pass as there's only one track. And they can't pass here. And you can't ask anyone about the delay because most of the FEVE stations are automated. You buy your ticket from the machine and to find out what's happening with the trains you have to phone the information line on your mobile.

We've done some great walking these seven or eight days since we left Luarca, the Frenchman and I, nearly 200 kilometres. Glorious walking when it's on little paths along the coast, the mountains on one side, big rollers flopping on deserted beaches on the other, or even through the hills and the woods.

It's been a pretty good day today since we left the lovely holiday resort of Ribadesella with its beaches and boats. But now we've hit this Dead-Eye Dick place called Villahormes (209 inhabitants) and since we can't find any of the little yellow arrows painted on walls, trees, on the road at our feet, or the yellow scallops on tiles pointing the direction of the Camino, the asphalt is getting tiresome.

Along the northern route (Camino del Norte) many, if not most, of the old paths have disappeared under highways and flyovers. There are beautiful walks for days on end on paths bordering the sea and apart from one or two industrial areas, you're never far from the sea. There's some great hiking all the way to Santander passing through lovely coastal resorts like Ribadesella, Llanes and San Vicente de la Barquera and on to Santoña, Castro Urdiales and Santillana del Mar. After Guernika it's through the woods and the hills of the Basque country before you break out again on to the sea at Deba. Then it's along the coast again for some of the loveliest beaches in Spain at Zumaia and Zarautz with kilometres-long lines of the little blue-striped bathing tents that give it a 19th century allure. But whenever you hit an industrial area as you do around Aviles, Gijón and Bilbao you may have to take a bus or the train when the road lets you down. As we are doing here in this flea-bite village of Villahormes.

Finally the FEVE comes in at five to one, half an hour or so later. The delay has shone the light on the lame and injured. There's a French woman, a Belgian and a Dutch girl and all three of them are injured in some way or another. A busted knee here, a twisted ankle or an arm in a sling there, standard for the entire route. We climb aboard and head for Guernika.

Among the highlights of the northern route is taking a little ferry across the bay of Santander and walking to Laredo across the beach of Somo – five or six kilometres but endless in the blazing sun, across a kilometre wide beach with the tide out. Then there are meetings with cousins you didn't know you had. Asturians and Cantabrians who tell you they're Celts like the Scots and you're their *primo* (cousin). The Cantabrian pipers playing the bagpipes in a little village on the coast, high above the Playa de Silencio (Beach of Silence). And even meeting one who told me the Cantabrian Celts had helped build Hadrian's Wall. Coming through the pine woods in the Basque country after a stiff climb for hours on end to finding a lovely little stone cottage where they serve homemade Basque blood sausage (Buzkantzak), before continuing on till the horizon opens up and the sea is before us and we're walking along the beach at Deba. And of course meeting up again with Axel, who has taken the bus up to Irun and started to hike down the northern route. We finally connect in a holiday village high above Castro Urdiales in some musty caravans looking onto the sea.

But the FEVE is special. And even if you're not waiting for it, you can always walk along the railway line looking for the next village if you lose the way. As happens once. And when we arrive at the station after walking for about an hour along the railway track, we can't get out since we don't have a ticket to put in the machine and the exits are barred. The only remedy is to rattle on the locked gate like a couple of apes at the zoo to attract attention. Fortunately there's a guy in the kitchen of the bar on the other side who eventually comes and unlocks the iron gate. Then we're having a beer in the garden at the side of the station, trading stories with a young Belgian couple headed south. It's a lovely warm sunny day and you can smell the grass and the flowers. It's Sunday. Maybe the FEVE doesn't run or runs less frequently on a Sunday, because in all that time, we haven't heard it. But who cares. At the moment we don't miss it.

34
Flies, Squids and Fulgencio Batista

I'll be in that fly-infested hostel soon. Where the flies are stuck flat dead or hanging from the ceiling big as gobstoppers. Soon as I get my bearings. If I can find someone to show me the way first. Because coming up from the port, there's nobody out here in this wasteland of scattered urban houses and fields and, far beyond that, the hills. Climbing and climbing a one-in-two gradient, and walking and walking. I've been walking uphill from the port of Luarca for what seems like an hour and I still can't find the pilgrim hostel. The reason, I'll soon learn, is the hostel isn't in Luarca, it's in Almuña, a few kilometres outside. And as I'm about to learn, it's the worst pilgrim hostel in Spain.

But as the Yorkshire man said to the dead haddock, "Where there's muck there's brass." The hardy rise to the challenge. Look at it this way. If I wasn't walking backwards like a hillbilly goon in a William Faulkner novel, I'd never meet the most intelligent flies in Asturias, see the biggest squids in the ocean, or peruse a newspaper clipping on the wall of the Mesón de la Mar restaurant on the waterfront, saying that Cuban dictator Fulgencio Batista passed that way once with his wife and went fishing.

But I'm not there yet. I ask about half a dozen people on the way up, knock on the doors of houses, see a man approach in the distance and wait till he arrives, accompanied by his little son of five or so. But no, he doesn't know either. But I'm getting close. I call into a roadside café and they say:

"Sí."

"Up there? That way?"

"Sí. That way"

Yes that way. And I have a cold beer in the garden and scan the country-side, the hills and the trees. Then when I get going again and can see the hostel in the distance, I have a chat with an old guy on the deserted road, who tells me he's been to Scotland.

"Edinburgh," he says.

And the weather was great. Five or six day's sun. You're never far from home. Yes but sun? That must have been in another century. "When the sun shines it's lovely," I say, as if I'm quoting from *Paradise Lost* or working for the Scottish Tourist Board. Or both.

But look ayonder, wayfaring stranger: That must be it. That blue painted bungalow sitting by itself out in the country. With a narrow road curving beyond it between the trees and up into the hills. The road I would be coming down this minute if I was coming down the Camino del Norte the proper way, from the north and heading for Santiago de Compostela instead of going backwards along the coast towards France.

And how am I going to get something to eat out here in the sticks? With no shops or cafes in sight. But things are under control. I've got an ace up my sleeve. Half a pack of instant *tagliatelle* in my bag and a fresh *baguette*. For times of emergency, a trick I learned from Mrs. French, little Yolande.

I'm about the first in the hostel. Fernando the warden books me in, stamps my pilgrim card and puts the money in a tin. I've got a feeling about this place. It's not just Fernando. There's something not quite right about it.

"The kitchen?" And Fernando gestures over his shoulder behind him.

Did he say kitchen? So first I take the bag through to the dormitory and place it on a bed near the door just in case I have to bail out quickly. That's when I see the flies on the ceiling. I get the *tagliatelle* out and the bread and go through to the kitchen.

"Do you have a smaller pot? Or a microwave?" I ask Fernando, looking at the only pot, a big ten litre job sitting on a hot plate. "Or a microwave?" But did I say kitchen? Did he say kitchen? It's not a kitchen anyone in his right mind would recognize as such. You can put a notice on a tree and say it's Frank Sinatra but that doesn't mean it can croon. A tree's a tree and a kitchen's a kitchen and this is no kitchen.

"Yes," he says and disappears through a door marked 'privado.' He comes back with a microwave oven and puts it on the shaky table on top of a primitive electric hotplate. That's just the start. The extension cable unit is plugged into the mains supply near the floor and the unit into which you want to plug the microwave is fixed to the wall with staples, about a metre and a half off the floor. I have never seen an electric extension cable and unit tacked to the wall before in such a position. It's a Mr Bean situation. You're standing with a plug in your hand and you can't plug it in because the cable is too short. You can't move the table closer to the wall because the table is blocked by something else. You can put the micro-oven on top of the electric plate to get it a bit closer. But it's still too short. Into the bargain it's dangerous like that. You could even try putting the micro-oven on the floor and plugging it in from there. That would probably work but then you would have to get down on your hands and knees to open the door and stick your head in the oven.

You're probably lost by now. I am too. Cut to the chase. The unit has been stapled to the wall by a lunatic and the only way I can solve the problem is by ripping the extension cable off the wall, wrapping it round Fernando's neck and strangling the bastard to death. I don't want to get into trouble so I abandon the idea, cook half a packet of *tagliatelle* on the hot plate, pluck a few leaves off a solitary basil plant sitting in a pot on the table, scoff that and go wash my shirt, trousers, T-shirt and a pair of socks in the outdoor sink, which, lo and behold, also offers a bar of half-melted soap, and hang them up on the clothes line to dry with two pegs between them. It's five euros by taxi from town back to the hostel, Fernando says, and the buses don't run till after five and then every half hour. A few more people book into the hostel, Spaniards mostly, and they all get the same information, plus the fact that there's a supermarket down there, yes to the right at the crossroads across from the petrol station. So I head down towards Luarca, with my shorts still damp. It's nearly three kilometres to Luarca, two according to the next signpost but only one according to Fernando. The view of the port is great, a lovely little place about 400 metres below. I head down stairs, stairs and more stairs, that tells you how high up you are, till I wind down into the port and stop at the Mesón de la Mar which specializes in fish. On the quay, on the Paseo de Muelle, you can have a *parillada* of fish or two *langostinas* for 90 euros. It says so on the board outside.

But having had the delicious *tagliatelle* already, my stomach is in no mood and I am not going to tempt fate so I order a *café Americano* and study the boats in the harbour.

I'm feeling pretty knocked out by this time, and need a siesta so I head round the corner to the end of the quay and stretch out on a stone bench outside the giant squid museum. Despite the fact that there's a slight breeze blowing, I fall asleep for about half an hour, wake up refreshed from the sugar in the *café Americano* to see a young fisherman squeezing his wife's bum fifty metres away as they push the pram. This sign of parental affection gives a little peck on the cheek to the morale and boosts the energy levels prompting me to call into the museum to see the biggest squids in the universe floating in perspex cases. Eight of them, the largest nearly 14 metres long. Then, refreshed, I call into the Mesón de la Mar for a cognac on the way back. The staff, about half a dozen of them, Ecuadorians by the South-American look of them and the accents, are scoffing the *crème de la crème* of the menu, spread out on an amply filled table. They've got that cagey look about them like cats with cream, anxious a sudden hand is going to whip the saucer away from under their nose.

I'm feeling ravenous by then but pesky clients aren't on the menu. "No kitchen closed," the Ecuadorian says when I ask if I can order something.

That's downstairs code for 'Closed to you, sonny boy.' And they get their snouts back into the fest, which by the look of it must represent half of annual turnover, crabs, *langostas, ensalada,* washed down with lashings of wine. No wonder the clients have to pay those inflated prices.

On the wall there's a newspaper clipping that says local boy Severo Ochoa, one of the great pioneers of molecular biology, was awarded the Nobel Prize for physiology in 1959. Ochoa has never blipped on my radar. But next to that there's a news piece about Batista. He has. Fulgencio Batista, president of Cuba till Castro chased him out in 1959 with the gold reserves. He came that year, 1941, the paper says, to fish in Luarca, accompanied by his wife. Batista was a Tano Indian. Or descended from them. They said the Tano Indians were all wiped out in Columbus' time. But I never believed that. It is illogical, doesn't make sense. And so you thread the strands of history together as if things are connected. Or the things that interest you. And they are too, though you have to work on the connections till they reveal their meaning.

It's a long walk back. There's a big bearded guy with a smile on his face, on his mobile in front of the hostel. Along with two or three others wandering about with their heads down, talking to themselves like patients in *One Flew*

Over the Cuckoo's Nest.

When I booked in, Fernando the warden said you have to be out of the hostel by seven in the morning, so there's that to look forward to.

Tomorrow I have to start walking backwards up the Camino del Norte to its beginning, which is becoming difficult. There are no signs and I may be forced to follow the highway. We will see. At worst I can get on a little FEVE train again. If I can find a station. Or maybe a bus. If I can find one. And head along the coast to Oviedo, Santander and Bilbao and San Sebastian. Up that way. And maybe across the French border after that. After that? Maybe I'll do a Forrest Gump and keep walking forever.

Next morning I get up early and head off. After about a kilometre or two along the provincial road, I run into a big bear of a Frenchman. Guillaume he's called. He's loaded up like a truck. He's heading back along the coastal route to France. He speaks no English which is fine. After the nearly two week refresher course at the Yolande School of French for Travellers, my ears are better attuned to the language.

35
Breton for MacDuff

It takes us three days, walking along the coast, passing through Soto de Luiña, Cudillero and Sant Esteban, wandering inland, up and down steep hills like mountain goats for hours because we can't find the place. In and out again. Through woods. Up and down more hills to where we are now on this dead-end spot on the road maybe 20 kilometres from Aviles, a big industrial city. Maybe less. We can't smell it fully yet but there's a faint sulphurous whiff in the air. The cars and the buses race hell bent to God knows where. Maybe the airport – I saw an Easyjet flying in earlier – so maybe that's where the traffic is headed this early in the morning. That or Aviles.

But now the pavement has run out. "I'm going no further," I tell Guillaume. This is industrial wasteland. We've still got a long way to go to Gijón then on to Santander before we reach Bilbao. We head on a bit further along the road till we get to the barriers that swing round to the left back onto the highway to San Esteban or to the right for Aviles. But you have to walk close to the hip-high metal barrier with traffic passing less than a metre away at your side. Less maybe if a big truck comes.

Guillaume is determined. He's a purist, does things by the book. And if his French guide says there's a pavement here to walk on, there's a pavement here. The fact that you can't see it has nothing to do with it. So we continue on the non-pavement for a bit, coasting the barriers till a truck comes by hooting and brushes our backpacks. Logic prevails. *Cogito ergo sum*, as Descartes said.

So I say to Guillaume "That's it. I'm going no further. I'm not risking my life on this stretch." And we head back down the road and sit on the pavement in front of the little bus shelter.

I get up half a dozen times to try to decipher the bus timetable but with scant success. I don't recognize the names of the places. And there seems to be more than one bus company. The only thing that's sure is the buses don't pass this way very often. Further down the road in the direction we came from, is a sign indicating a FEVE train station. That's an option. But Guillaume only does train options with a gun to his head.

Now, maybe it's because we've got time on our hands, or we've hit a brick wall and become rattled but this word Gijón is becoming an issue. "There's nothing else for it," I say running a finger up and down the timetables, "We'll have to get the bus to Gijón."

"Ah, Oui, Shishong," the big Palooka says, or something of the kind. This isn't the first time he's played that card. He's been waiting for me to say it. For the last three days, whenever the word Gijón falls, he says "Shishong." I don't know what the hell he's talking about. He might as well say Paris or Montpellier. It's got nothing to do with any place in Spain that I recognize. How many times have I told him that you don't pronounce a Spanish place beginning with G at the beginning as "Sh"?

"Look Guillaume," I say to him. The G in Gijon is the same as the G in Guillaume. You can say your own name, can't you? Guillaume? Gijón, Guillaume?"

"Shishong," he says giving it his best try, a grin splitting his face. So we sit on the pavement and eye the roundabout further down the road where the buses will come up from San Esteban. Presently a lost soul wanders into view on the other side of the road, limping along with a stick on a pavement that hasn't been trod by more than one or two hundred feet since after the end of the First World War.

I cross the road to get the gen first hand from the horse's mouth. The old guy is going to a hospital, he says, down there in the industrial hen-run. And you go that way to Gijón. And he points again. But he doesn't know when the bus comes. So I cross the road again and sit in the bus shelter with my legs stretched out and my back against the bag and take out the Michelin guide which gives you the distance between the hostels on the Camino Frances but is as useful as a map of Inner Mongolia here.

A young girl appears. I cross the road. She's about eighteen, has caps on her teeth and of an age that knows nothing except the times of the buses going to the disco and back.

Half an hour later another bus approaches heading into town. It stops and I cross the road to ask the driver. It's an Alsa bus, we want he says, a little grey bus that goes to Gijón. So I cross the road back to the shelter where Guillaume has his nose in the French guide book wondering how his wise French compatriots have bamboozled him. I do a few exercises. Limber up. Touch my toes; bend my knees, that sort of thing. The bus finally comes into sight, swinging round the roundabout, and we climb on board. It's going to Gijón, the driver says.

"Shishong?" the French fool says as he steps aboard. Bruce Springsteen is singing "Born in the USA," on the piped radio.

"What day is it Guillaume?" He looks at me.

"Quoi?"

So I repeat the question. He looks at me. But I'm not really interested in an answer. The bus gets into Gijón. We get out and have a coffee and *croissant* under the parasol outside on the pavement and get chatting to a pleasant French lady in her fifties who is waiting for a bus to take her to Santiago. Vivienne is her name. She's a Breton, comes from Brittany, next door to Normandy where Guillaume comes from. Her surname is le Duff. "Le Doof? Really? My antennae, the most sensitive organ we ants possess, shoot up straight. "How do you spell it?"

"Le and Duff," she says.

"We've got MacDuffs in Scotland," I tell her, "You must be related."

And Vivienne Le Duff smiles charmingly as if she understands what I am on about. "Macbeth, one of the great Scottish kings married a Duff and was killed by a Duff."

Duff or Dhuibh in Gaelic, is a person of dark complexion and dark hair, though Vivienne, alas for that part of the theory, is more your fair-haired type, though then again there's a streak of red in it.

"Mikdif?"

"MacDuff. Macbeth, the play by Shakespeare. MacDuff kills him."

"Eshekesper?"

A thought occurs to me. "Where do you come from in Brittany?"

"Finisterre."

"Finisterre?" Right on the coast. Land's End. So if the Le Duffs of Brittany and the Duffs of the north east coast of Scotland are the same family, they must have spoken the same language at one time and were probably connected by sea.

And that is about right, because the Breton language, understood by about 200,000 people today in Brittany and spoken daily by about 35,000, was brought here by Welsh and Cornish settlers who fled the Anglo-Saxon invasions in the fifth and sixth centuries. Whether it was the same language they spoke in the north east of Scotland is another question.

"You speak Breton?"

"Non."

Digging into the MacDuff connection later reveals some more surprises. The MacDuffs trace their ancestry to "The ancient German tribes who settled on the north and east of Scotland," a clan historian says. No doubt he got that from Roman authors like Caesar and Tacitus two thousand years later and decided Germans had a better pedigree than Scythians. What was wrong with the Scythians before that is a mystery. They were fine for the MacDuffs in the 13th century when the Declaration of Arbroath was written.

And they were fine too for Duncan MacDuff, 10th earl of Fife whose name is the first to appear on the letter to the Pope John XXII, accompanying the Declaration which says:

> Most Holy Father, we know and from the chronicles and books we find that among other great nations our own, the Scots, has been graced with widespread renown. It journeyed from Greater Scythia by way of the Tyrrhenian Sea and the Pillars of Hercules, and dwelt for a long course of time in Spain, among the most savage peoples, but nowhere could it be subdued by any people, however barbarous. Thence it came, twelve hundred years after the people of Israel crossed the Red Sea, to its home in the west where it still lives today. The Britons it first drove out, the Picts it utterly destroyed, and even though very often assailed by the Norwegians, the Danes and the English, it took possession of that home with many victories and untold efforts…

So there you had it. Sealed by a MacDuff. Of all people. What a bunch of numbskulls. It was bad enough being Scythians or one of the Lost Tribes of Israel. Now thanks to the MacDuffs the Scots were Germans.

"Quelle histoire," Vivienne says when I acquaint her with the gist of the story of the Bretons, the Scots and the Scythians. In much less detail than you are getting of course.

"Quelle histoire." she says. As you would say "That's quite a story, you couldn't make it up if you tried." And she's right, you couldn't. So there we are outside in the sun round the table, Scotland's gene pool in a nutshell. A Viking, a Scytho-Pict and a Lowland Scot cum Gael. Guillaume the Norman, namesake of William the Conqueror, the Norseman, the Viking. And Vivienne the Brythonic Celt with links, who knows, to the Scythians and the Picts and the Scots and now the German tribes, and myself the west coast Gael-lowlander. And just to check out what the Norman-French take on history is, I say to Guillaume,

"He was a Viking wasn't he, William the Conqueror?"

"Ah Oui. The French don't like fighting."

"So Robert the Bruce was basically a Viking since the family came from Normandy?"

"Robert le Bruce?"

"De Brus."

"Ah Oui," he says, but your big volunteer fireman doesn't know The Bruce from Larry the Lamb. No wonder. Later when I check out what the French called Robert the Bruce, I start to get some insight. Raibert Bruis in Norman French. Brix. Robert a Briuis in medieval Gaelic. Robert de Bruys, Robert de Bruys. It's hardly surprising he ended up being called "The" Bruce. The "de" was too difficult to pronounce for the locals and still is. But it's all a bit much really, these attempts to reconstruct ancient history from bits and pieces. What so-and-so said and whether he copied if from someone else. And we've only got the word of Greeks and Latins and all those writers who came after them and copied them. If they could speak Greek and Latin. Otherwise they copied each other.

All we can hope for is the resurrection of the dead. Have some of the kings of Scythia come back to life and give us the raw facts. See what Herodotus has to say for himself for missing bits out. What excuses he has for not doing a better job. Not like our modern historians. Not like the clan MacDuff historians. Pity Muldoon isn't here. He'd know the answer alright. He'd be the very man to ask.

36

The Vampires Suck Spain Dry

For the love of money is a root of all kinds of evil.

St Paul in his first letter to Timothy, ch. 6, v. 10

Spain is currently on its uppers. The front page of the *Nueva España* says the town hall in the last big place we passed through – Gijón – has received over 7,000 applicants for the 80 one-year jobs it has created to ease unemployment. Another headline says Spain is cornered by the financial markets and has banned short selling to prevent speculators driving the price of Spanish debt down and yields up. There's also there's an Interview with the Vampire by journalist Pedro de Silva. It goes like this:

> There's nothing personal about it, nor is he conspiring against Spain, nothing like that. Europe is the question. The man speaking isn't one of those men in black but a man in grey, obscured in that media cloud that goes under the name of 'investors.' His voice sounds metallic and betrays no emotion whatsoever so I ask him what he's got against Europe. Something against Europe? (Laughs). Nothing against Europe either. Europe's just there, with its enormous mass and its wealth and its terrible weakness. A big heavy lumbering dinosaur. Subject to the same things as any other beast in a living environment, the laws of survival in other words. If it's got lots of protein and doesn't know how to protect itself, the biological mass surrounding will go for it. Hatred, vengeance, getting your own back, are human passions. They don't exist in nature and that's what the laws of the market follow. Do you think piranhas have anything against the victims they devour?

Now, by the time I have completed this trip I will have passed through up to five hundred places: hamlets, villages, towns, cities, and from what I see Spain is a beautiful country where people seem to live well. Where there's lots of space with plenty of parks, where the motorways, the railways, the buses are all new or just about. The building boom of the last decade left behind over a million unsold houses and apartments, not including maybe nearly a million unfinished projects. Add those to the vacant second homes and redundant flats and you now have 3.4 million homes vacant in Spain.

You see the new projects wherever you go, outside the urban centres and on the Balearic islands too: huge villas often, spread over two floors with spacious rooms and set in ample gardens. What dreamweaving estate agents fondly call 'dream homes,' in their adverts. But in every dream home a heartache, as Bryan Ferry of Roxy Music sings.

A few days ago, somewhere out in the middle of nowhere we pass through a housing estate that looks like it has fallen from the sky. A bit like a set in a science fiction film waiting for the cameras to roll and the walking dead to come out and shamble between the concrete shells and the overhead lamps. With magnificent views over the rolling fields. And the houses are all the same. Poured from a mould. Hundreds of them. With roads and lanes linking and overhung by high street lamps from which a few electric wires are sticking, suggesting they haven't been connected to the electric grid and maybe never will be.

The overall impression is that Spain is complete. That everything that can be done has been done. And more than was needed since easy tourist money started to flow in from the late fifties and all the black money of the world followed it.

I passed through Barcelona for the first time about fifty years ago. If you took a train from the Estación de Francia to go up the coast, you could go to the rear of the coach and stand outside and lean against the rail and see the caves carved out of the sandstone embankment as you rattled past. People had lived in them till quite recently, I was told at the time, during the Civil War certainly. Coming up out of the metro, guys in shabby striped suits, left over from gypsy weddings, would offer you a single cigarette for sale.

I take out some postcards, half a dozen of them I bought about ten days ago and look at them, trying to figure out how I can get the address in. The postage stamps are pretty but they are huge and you need to put two stamps on each postcard to cover the 70 euro cents postage. But if you stick two of them on the postcard, there is no room left underneath for the address. I've tried about half a dozen *tabacaleras*. But no one has the small stamps. So I can't send a postcard. Maybe the postcards are telling me something. Because postcards too are made to spread feel-good *bonhomie*. They don't sell postcards of rubbish heaps or ghettos. The fact that I can't send them suggests something is wrong somewhere. Maybe it's the tip of the iceberg and there's a lot more wrong underneath than meets the eye.

The Four Horsemen of the Apocalypse haven't arrived yet but they'll be appearing soon on the horizon in their hoods and cloaks. So I spend the rest of the afternoon drawing up a list of who'll get it in the neck first. And whether it'll be hanging or the bullet. The day of reckoning is at hand. It'll be tricky though. Only a third of the world economy is in the hands of real criminals, the other two thirds is in the hands of unreal criminals that ride to their jobs every day on subways, trains, buses and taxis and even, a keep fit, healthy few, on bicycles, and pay the vampire his due, and their own selves by pressing the appropriate buttons all day long.

Before the Second World War and even up to the early sixties, Spain was a unique and special place where donkeys pulled carts out in the countryside. It still had one foot in the 19th century. Now it's like everywhere else in the world that's plugged into the global system, repeating the same mantras. Witnessing too much of the havoc wreaked by the mass tourism that started in the sixties, the construction boom of the last decade together with the blatant corruption, cronyism and mismanagement, can take away a person's will to live. About the only thing you can do in the circumstances is go sit under a tree and listen to the birds. A sparrow, a thrush, a finch, anything, it doesn't matter. Preferably one chirping its lungs out. Failing that you can look for a cat or a dog to cheer you up. They're either lounging about or strutting their stuff, ignorant of the affairs of men, heading off somewhere with gainful intent and true purpose.

37

The Mules Visit Bethlehem

And then, in the evening before the lights of the lamps are dimmed, the Angels of the Lord appear and whisper in the ears of our two pilgrims the whereabouts of the House of Bethlehem where goodly fare is to be had by one and all and a right warm welcome from your German hosts Manfred and Birgitta.

And so it comes to pass that our two travellers get their bits and pieces together in the early morning, stuff them into their bags and in keeping with the direction pointed out by the four angels disguised as three wise boys and one wise girl who share their cabin the night before, they depart from Deva, passing through many small hamlets with no names.

And as the sun rises, the day finds our two travellers sniffing the morning breeze, plodding ever onwards across the fields and through the woods being slowly transformed into beasts of burden. And beasts of burden their boots rise and fall slowly and relentlessly. And in the cadence of this rising and falling, they become one with the kingdom of the beasts, become mindless, become mules. And it is only when they stop at a fountain for a drink of water along the way that their big watery mule eyes take in the monastery between the trees without seeing it. And their big pointed mule ears catch the sound of the voices of the cooks and the noise of the clattering pans without hearing them.

And with no one to whack them on the rump with a stick all their big dull mule brains can register is a faint unease with the world of humans. But with their bellies now filled with water, they turn their big mule heads away. And keeping their big dull mule eyes lowered and unseeing, point their big shiny, wet mule muzzles to the path to re-join the mule train on towards Bethlehem, the big French mule leading the way with a map taped to the inside of one of its blinkers.

On and one they plod, hour after hour, between the trees, along the paths, looking at the signs with their big dumb unblinking mule eyes till they are quite close to Cuerres where the four angels have told them the wonderful

House of Bethlehem is to be found.

When they arrive in the village, they stick their muzzles into the only bar and hotel in the place, bray for directions and plod back down steps they have just come up, and go back through a tunnel they have just gone through, till they see the red van outside the white house exactly as whispered in their mule ears up at the hotel and see the little painted sign stuck between two boulders by the side of the path that says *Casa Belen* (Bethlehem).

And without further ado, our two mules tap on the door of the little house with their hooves. And since our French mule brays in no other language but French, it is left to our Scots mule to handle the discourse with the German proprietors of the inn.

Manfred, the innkeeper opens the door and Birgitta his wife invites the two mules in for lunch. Or to be more precise Birgitta invites to lunch the Scots mule since it has made braying sounds appropriate to her ears. The Scots mule declines the invitation, however. It is not hungry, it says. Our French mule, understanding nothing of the discourse or the lunch invitation, has parked its haunches on a slender seat placed at the front door and as its custom when it stops for the day, digs into its side saddle for a packet of Marlboro's.

The mule which has done all the braying, clumps upstairs and gets a couple of cans of beer from the fridge in keeping with Manfred's invitation, clumps back down again and hands a chilled can of beer to the other mule. Just at that moment two wayfarers, a young gentleman in khaki-coloured shorts and a young lady in a long white dress and heavy black boots, pass by. They glance across at the house, seeing but not seeing. And what they perceive is this. They perceive two scruffy looking mules. One, wearing a dark-coloured T-shirt, has a black beard and is almost bald despite its apparent youth. The other, a bit worse for wear, is wearing a long-sleeved shirt of a deep green colour and needs a shave. Both are tanned dark by the sun and are sitting in front of the little white house, one on each side of the door.

And the young gentleman takes all this in, seeing but not quite seeing, as explained. So why does he glance up towards the house a second time and look back? Is it because the two mules are drinking beer and smoking cigarettes?

Later in the evening Birgitta comes upstairs and asks the mules if they have eaten. She has prepared an evening meal. This time the mules cannot refuse. But since our young French mule is flat out on its back in a sleeping bag in the bunk next door and is dreaming its usual French mule dreams of absolute nothingness, it cannot be consulted. And since our Scots mule is famished it is now sitting in the kitchen eating its favourite meal of *baguette* and sardines washed down with cold red wine laced with *gaseosa* from the fridge. Together with the Knorr chicken soup it has prepared from a packet generously offered free, gratis and for nothing by the kitchen cupboard which carries an enticing little label in three languages saying: *Food, Essen and Manger.* Which explains why our Scots mule is now relaxing in the kitchen observing the humans who trickle in.

There's skinny Ivan, a Spaniard despite the name, who was doing his yoga stripped to the waist in the garden only a moment ago. And there's Miss Sinead O' Connor (not the singer) who lives in Hong Kong. Or is it Sydney? Because there are no jobs in Ireland. She enters with a young Finnish gentleman who pushes the kitchen chairs aside and starts doing exercises.

When Mr Finn has stretched his limbs this way and that and that way and this for five or ten minutes, he gets a little bag out with half a dozen lentils in it and pours them into the pot of water boiling on the stove. While Mr Finn is watching the half dozen lentils cook, Birgitta arrives with the real McCoy, real lentil soup in a huge pot and places it on the table. Ivan the mountain man, slurps his down with relish and between spoonfuls recounts his adventures climbing the *Picos de Europa.* Being one of nature's gentlemen, he offers what is left to Mr Finn of the little pony tail and to Miss Irish Sinead, who delight most happily in this unexpected treat.

Later when the sun is gone, the two mules meet again at the front door, smoke another cigarette and sniff the dank air of evening. Birgitta brings them out a piece of cake. It is Santiago's feast day she says, the 25th of July and she has baked a cake for the occasion. The Scots mule has never heard of anyone baking cakes for dead saints, let alone St James, and is truly impressed by the gesture. It makes a mental note to mention it to James when it gets to paradise with the beasts of the fields and the birds of the air. There is more to Birgitta than meets the eye. Presently she comes from behind the house with something wrapped in her apron. It is a goose. The goose is called Heidi. She says something to it in Spanish. Seeing one of its brother creatures so well treated, touches a soft spot in our Scots mule. Perhaps it is its heart. She should teach it German. German being her mother tongue, our Scots mule says. And that is the last word anyone utters that day for miles around.

The mules climb into their bunks, the lights go out, the globe turns and next day our two mules wander off down the garden path, followed at a distance by Heidi the goose. At the bottom of the garden, one of the mules turns to look back and failing to notice the little wooden, hand-painted sign stuck between the stones saying *Casa Belen*, knocks it over with its hoof. Dumb beasts of burden, they plod mindlessly along the path under the trees where the leaves drop their heavy shadows on them.

38
No Satisfaction

She's a dead ringer for Keef Richards of the Rolling Stones. She's got the bling-bling and the bangles all over the bod'. And if you could pick her up and shake her she'd rattle like one of those ghost chasers hanging from a hippy tent pole in the breeze. And yes, would you believe it, she's got those big gnarled, knobbly finger joints too. And big silver rings on her fingers and little delicate rings in her ears. And she's got those same sort of, sort of crazy sweet eyes. And, come to think of it, she must be about Keef's age too. Keef, the old Stoney himself, at his whacked out best. The parched weathered face, the skin wrinkled and rippled like a toffee-wrapper. And she's come all the way up the Silver Road, the Via de la Plata, from Seville. Over a thousand kilometres on foot, that's the thing. Over a period of two or three months, wintering in the mountains.

She is so Keef I could almost give her a big smack on the lips out of sheer delight. And she's French and since she's French, of the Frenchies that I meet or that meet me, that is, she speaks nary a word of English. I was going to say the Queen's but that's not exactly my version of English either. Maybe she speaks one or two words of English, let us not be unkind. So just to make sure I say to her:

"All the way from Seville?"

And she says, "Ah, Oui."

And I say, "Up over the mountains?"

"Ah... Oui." In that nice way the French have of leaving a tiny pause between the *Ah* and the *Oui* and giving a little shake of the head as though, goodness me, you've guessed the winning number in the French national lottery and by pure chance she's got it written in the palm of her hand and if you're nice she'll show it to you. But to make sure, because I am still thinking of that stretch from Seville, twelve hundred and fifty kilometres to be exact. Over the mountains. That I'd thought of taking till I read about the rain pissing down and the mist. That she has done. That little Keefie has done. I say since it hasn't quite sunk in yet, "Up over the mountains? "

And she goes, "Oui, Oui,"

Meeting the little French Stoney has clearly wired me into music land. "Yes, yes, my baby said yes yes, I'm glad she said yes yes, instead of no, no." I hear the words in my head but manage to suppress the compulsive tendency to burst into song.

I've been walking nearly a thousand kilometres and this is the first person I have met in over a month who has travelled the Via de La Plata, the old road that linked the south of Spain with the North in Roman times. We're in San Vicente de la Barquera, in a nice hostel called El Galeon. There's a big metal plaque of a three-sailed galleon on the wall, in case there is doubt about the meaning of the word. It's a strange sort of building. The hostel entrance is underneath the building with the Galleon sign outside on top. You could easily mistake it for a cave or a garage. Huge rocks outside make it seem like a cave but the entrance room is like a big concrete garage with wet clothes hanging up to dry, cluttered with bikes brought in from the rain. Beyond that, inside, there's a big dining room with a table that seats maybe twenty or thirty people for the evening meal they prepare in the kitchen. There's also a nice little relax corner with a couple of easy chairs to recline in, one of them currently occupied by Grandpa Arturo who hangs about the place in a cardigan and dispatches the occasional word of wisdom.

We're standing outside the entrance – I was about to say of the hostel, but since it is more like a cave I'll leave it at that. Guillaume and Nicole are smoking Guillaume's Marlboro's and I'm sitting on the barrel at the entrance looking up at them and watching the drizzle fall on the bridge and the estuary far below. There's a few fishing boats moored along the quay.

Beyond that the estuary widens into the open sea.

I say to Nicole, "You know Keef Richards?"

"Qui?"

"Keef ehhhh Rishaaard," I say, pronouncing the words very slowly to get the best French equivalent of the sound. "Of ze Rollin…K…estones,"

She looka me. So I try another code. "Ze RollinK…eh .. Estones," I say.

"Ah Oui," she says. But I'm not so sure the penny has dropped so I go…

"Doom doom do do dad da doom do do." That riff in *Can't Get No Satisfaction.*

And she goes "doom, doom, doom, doom, doom, do, do…"

Maybe she's just doing it to keep me happy and doesn't know Keefie from Adam. My rendition is also a bit off-tune so there's that as well. I make a mental note to work on it in case I meet more wandering Frenchies further down the road.

Nicole is from Paris where she has a daughter. No, she's not headed back there; she's taking her time, helping the other two ladies in the kitchen of the hostel, preparing the meals: breakfast in the morning and dinner in the evening round the big table. She is where she needs to be, it seems. And she's in a nice place. Sooner or later she'll move on. Further along the northern route, edging slowly back towards France.

All human beings are 99.9 per cent identical in their genetic makeup, I am told. Some people look like other people and there's a host of people trying their hardest and paying a lot of money to look like someone they saw in a glossy magazine. Then there's the Doppelganger syndrome of Subjective Doubles where you glimpse a stranger on the train or in the street and think it's yourself.

You don't want to suffer from that. Dante Gabriel Rossetti, the English Romantic artist, has a painting entitled *How They Met Themselves.* It shows a couple in the woods in medieval dress meeting their exact likeliness. And so that you know exactly which is the real couple, one of the women is depicted swooning in the arms of her companion.

But none of this is relevant to Nicole. She's in the kitchen now where I'm helping her clean the fish for dinner. There are all sorts of other explanations. That Keef has done a *Jumping Jack Flash* into the spiritual dimension and is scrubbing off the scales of a *dorado* next to me at the sink. That he's given slimey old Rubber Lips the finger and is hiding out in Spain pretending to be a French woman. That would explain the garb. No two people on the planet in their right mind could possibly peg the same crazy collection of gypsy bling-bling junk to their body. Yes it's Keefie alright. I've rumbled 'im, the cunning old fish. So I do the old *Can't Get No Satisfaction* routine, go "Doom, doom, do, do, da, da doom, do, do."

But he's having none of it. He's not letting on. That's how ya know, ennit? It's a dead giveaway. So I do it every time I see him after that. When he brings the food from the kitchen and lays it on the table at dinner. When he's standing outside late in the evening at the cave entrance smoking a last Marlboro with Guillaume, rattling his bangles and flashing his rings, that little French Keefie. Oh, he's trying his damn hardest to stay in there, pay no attention, the cunning little gypo. So I get right up close and go "Doom, doom, do, do, da, da, doom, do, do," in little Nicole's ear just to let them know I've got them rumbled, the two of them.

39
From Rags to Riches in Comillas

Early in the morning, I bid farewell and wish *bon voyage* to our volunteer fire-man, the young Norman, he of the black beard and the receding hairline, who, having studied his faithful French map for hours on end in his bunk last night, is convinced he knows how to find the paths along the coast to Santillana del Mar once he gets out of Comillas.

I'm sitting in a nice cozy little bar on the corner waiting for the bus to Santillana del Mar, having a *café au lait* and a *croissant* with a couple of pil-grims. She is Spanish and he is French. They endearingly give each other the occasional peck on the lips. These tender gestures spread such bonhomie and goodwill that our old Scots terrier is soon infected by the endearments to the extent he is silently reconsidering his options. Now that he is a free man again, in a manner of speaking. For if this jovial – also bearded – young Frenchman from Paris and the charming young Spanish lady have met – presumably – on the road, surely such a possibility must also be open to others on the road? To the Scotsman, for example? And in such a case the Scotsman would be a much happier little pilgrim with a nice young lady pilgrim by his side. Yes that is what the Scotsman will do. He will mentally re-attune and abandon contemplation of the universe at large for lower, earthlier things, tune his little ant antennae to charming female companion mode and the universe will comply with his desires. Sooner or later. For did not St Paul say "Seek and ye shall find. Ask and it shall be given?"

But just as our little Scotch terrier is wagging its curly little tail, this pleas-ing reverie and the accompanying scenario of felicity are abruptly and brutally crushed when the café door swings open and a giant blocks the bright light of day. It is our well-known, bearded Frenchman. The giant hesitates for a mo-ment in the doorway. Something is holding it back. It tugs.

And tugs again. The small boutique it carries on its back is blocked in the doorway. Twenty-three or so kilos of salami sausage, bread, assorted of tins of sardines, *pâté de foie*, packs of coffee and sugar and whatnot prevent its entry. The giant gives the great bear on its back one last tug and they both fall in through the doorway.

"Couldn't find the path?"

But our great woodsman, as is his wont, simply grins showing two rows of neat white teeth between the sprouting hairs of his bushy black beard. And when our woodsman gives the full frontal grin our Scots terrier has a flashback of a big wooden Golliwog it saw standing outside an antique shop in a little town back along the coast, the paint flaking off its face. Big rolling eyes, big as billiard balls. A toothy insane grin. Big perfect teeth clamped permanently together to keep the secrets of the universe locked inside its wooden skull. Then a little dog, ignorant of the affairs of men, comes along the street, lifts its leg and pisses on the Golliwog.

Now we're lying on the grass by the bus stop. The daily bus will be along just after midday and we'll head off to Santillana del Mar. Our bearded friend is studying the guide book and my broad green and white striped shirt is lying with its arms stretched out to dry on the grass while I ponder sweet nothing under a tree. Up on the crest of the hill behind us, up at the top of the rolling parkland is the palace of the Marquez de Comillas, the richest man in Spain at one time who bankrolled the king when the royal personage was on its uppers.

I visited it yesterday in the late afternoon. Around six, just before it closed. And did the guided tour, the last guided tour of the day. It was a surprise discovery, a family tale like something out of the Forsyth Saga, of how local poor boy Antonio Lopez Lopez goes from rags to riches to become Antonio Victor Lopez de Peliago y Lopez de Lainardid, names cobbled together from the humble places his humble parents came from but necessary to give him some sort of pedigree to go with the title of Marques de Comillas the king gave him in 1878 for providing the money to finance his wars in Cuba.

Comillas, the town between three hills, from a name the Celts had given it. Where his two brothers fished for the horse mackerel, conger eel, herring and *bonito* in nummer that they ate in the evening for dinner, with the *patatas*, *pimientos*, tomatoes and the broad white beans, the *alubias* they cultivated in the garden. Antonio, orphaned at two. Sent off to family in the South in Anda-lucía to work when they did not know what else to do with him. Who takes a boat from Cadiz for Havana when he is fourteen and for the next thirty years, dabbles in this and that, makes a killing on a flour shipment, moves to the east of the island to Santiago de Cuba, the old colonial capital, meets a rich Cuban Creole of Catalan descent who makes a gentleman of him, takes the *chulo* out, puts the *caballero* in and gives him four children.

And as the guide rolls out the details, a sense of doom and foreboding descends. Antonio the eldest son. Religious. Brooding. Who never married, another of the dark presences in the portraits hanging on the walls. Claudio, the youngest son who married a lady in waiting of Queen Vitoria Eugenia and became the next Marques of Comillas but left no children. And then Maria Luisa, the youngest daughter. She too married. But Oh, the waiting for an heir to the dynasty and the disappointment there too. Then the eldest daughter Luisa Isabel, bless her, who had ten children and more than made good the deficit induced by the two sons and the youngest daughter. But that is all look-ing back. Bankrolled by his in-laws since his marriage, he is now a rich *Indio*, moves back to a palace in Barcelona, sets up a shipping line and ships troops to Africa when the scramble for Africa starts in the later 19th century. And when the Cubans revolt against Spanish occupation in the first of the wars with Cuba, his vessels make over 100,000 trips between Spain and Cuba and back, loaded with troops.

The guide pauses in the grand salon and we gaze at the portraits on the wall. Thousands of feet have been treading these floors every year for many years, she says, as we admire the pristine condition of the hardwood parquet floor that came from the Indies too; that has weathered the assault of steel tipped high-heels for decades. Are there any questions? The usual. Does the family still live there? No, but some of them come for a few weeks in summer, she says, so everything has to be kept in mint condition. Then for some reason she mentions the chairs in the dining room. The high, straight backed leather-covered chairs of no particular beauty or interest. Every year some of the tacks disappear, she says. And we each study the chairs and sure enough there are gaps where the large square-headed copper tacks hold the leather to the wood, gaps like missing teeth. And this seems to me to be the most important thing the guide has said during the visit, though I do not know why.

"Some people are awful," someone in the group says.

And as we are leaving the salon the guide says, without looking back or turning round,

"Yes, I know, I caught someone peeing behind the door. A young man."

And saying this she continues on into the corridor, the crowd of twenty or so visitors trailing behind, her voice getting louder as it echoes in the long empty space and parts the still, dead air of the castle like a fish moving through stagnant water in a dream.

Last to leave the room, I glance at the wall. At the corner of the salon where the door is. Where the young guy peed. What to make of it all? The rags to riches? A Spanish 19th century Forsyth Saga, a tale of the great *noveau riche* dynasties created across Europe during the greatest period of capitalist expansion and exploitation known to man? When the history of the family is written will it include a footnote saying an unknown young man pissed in a corner of the salon of the Marquez of Comillas in the early years of the 21st century?

The family still comes up in summer and takes up residence in the palace, the guide says, mentioning a daughter, I suppose, of the current Marquez who lives in Madrid, the Marquez Alfonso Guëll y Martos. And the family still has some interests too in the town. But the image that lingers most strongly from the visit is not the portraits on the walls of the Marquez and his dysfunctional family, or even the desk behind which the workaholic toiled late into the night under one of the first electric lamps in Spain, touching his important papers and his important documents delicately with his fingers to assemble a vast mercantile empire. No it isn't that. It is the image of the guy pissing on the wallpapered wall in the corner of the salon, next to the door and the voice of the guide dwindling down the corridor after she said it. That and the salon with its high-backed, leather covered chairs where a ghost is trying to ease a copper tack off a dining chair. With a penknife or some of other sharp object. Some strange and alien implement that an unknown person might have in his jacket or trouser pocket. Or in her purse or her handbag. To fulfill some violent desire of possession, of revenge, of protest, whose impulse cannot easily be understood, let alone formulated.

The daughter of the current Marquez comes up to the palace in the summer and still has interests in the town, the guide says later to a further question about the family, but without elaborating.

At the bottom of the rolling park and across the street, are houses and shops, single storey mostly. Further along on a corner heading out of town, or coming in, depending on how you look at it, is a large, sumptuous, brightly-light tourist shop, offering all the delicacies of Cantabria, all the objects that its many merchandisers can conjure up to temp the tourist. It is an elaborate shop, primely positioned. A great deal of money has been invested in it, you can see that. It is highly organized and they know what they have to do to make money. That too is obvious. The question is, whose is it? But since nothing happens in these provincial towns in Spain without the approval of the powers that be, I have the strong feeling it is one of the 'interests' of the family, referred to by the guide. On display at the entrance are boxes of almond biscuits labeled Los Cojones del Anticristo or The Balls of the Antichrist.

If Lopez y Lopez was not above trading in slaves in the Caribbean before he was moved up the social ladder and got whitewashed into the nobility, for later generations of the family *tocando los cojones* or taking the piss with The Balls of the Antichrist must be child's play.

40
The Balls of the Antichrist

Fourteen years of the sixth millennium still remain; the sixth age will thus end in the era 838. What remains is uncertain for human inquiry; any question about this is vetoed by our Lord Jesus Christ in saying: it is not for you to determine whether the time or the occasion the Father has determined on his own authority ... and in truth in the year 6,000 the world will end.

Apocalyptic Vision of Beato de Liébana[4]

The Balls of the Antichrist are in my hands. I feel the weight of the box and think to myself: Do I want to be carrying the Balls of the Antichrist on my back all the way to the French border? Or should I send them to my philosopher friend Erasmus P. Hegel in Amsterdam by post. He'll be delighted with them and he and the Queen of Sheba can have them with a cup of coffee.

The Balls of the Antichrist are cookies, namely. Almond cookies. I can't tell you what they taste like because I don't get round to trying them. But you're buying them for the box and medieval illustrations of saints and angels. I'm in a shop in Comillas in Cantabria in the north of Spain, the loveliest and most interesting town in a nearly 2,000 kilometer trip.

Now the word Antichrist has a delightful ring to it. I haven't seen it mentioned for years. The last time, as far as I can remember, was when the Reverend Ian Paisley of Northern Ireland drowned out Pope John Paul II's speech to the EU from the back-benches with cries of: "I renounce you as the Antichrist."

I am filled with the joy of revelation. And come to think of it, I never thought I'd ever see eye-to-eye with Paisley. But given the perverts, sycophants and rapists lurking behind, if not peeping up the skirts of the Holy Mother Church in recent years, you almost wish for a return of those innocent days of yore when you could buy a plenary indulgence to get to heaven, and to coin a

---

[4]The beginning of the world was calculated at 5,200 years before the birth of Christ.

phrase, to hell with the sin. Maybe Paisley was onto something. But I digress. The blurb on the back of the packet, explains where the expression comes from.

"The Balls of the Antichrist," the label says, "is the insult directed by Saint Beato (Beatus) Abbot of Liébana at Elipandus the Archbishop of Toledo, as a result of his heretical belief in adoptionism, a 7th century heresy which Beato rejected."

On the shelves next to The Balls of the Antichrist, are some more naughty products: Shit-Hot Asparagus (Esparragos Cojonudos) and Orgasms in the Marc Cream Style (Orgasmos a la Crema de Oruja). Oruja is the name given to a strong local liqueur made from the skins of grapes after they've been pressed.

I'm about to plump for the orgasms but the small letters on the orgasms jar is a let-down. You've got to go elsewhere for the real thing, it seems.

"Only an orgasm is comparable to the satisfaction produced by these exquisite biscuits," the label says.

Heaven only knows what the Shit-Hot Asparagus do. They're in a tin and there are no further details of the delights in store for your woman or you. One can only speculate.

There's also a range of Liquors for the Shameless (Licores para Sinverguenzas) but again that's bottles and I don't want those in my bag, never mind the weight.

But to return to The Balls of the Antichrist. When Beato wrote his two volume *Apologeticum Adversus Elipandum* against the Archbishop of Toledo his beef was with adoptionism, the belief that Jesus was adopted as God's son either at baptism, his resurrection from the dead or his ascension into heaven because of his sinless devotion to the will of God. The error rose out of trying to understand the two natures of Christ: both God and man. It's not a polemic you need lose much sleep about today even if you do manage to understand it. But there was a lot more going on. At that point in time, around 776, most of the Iberian Peninsula had been occupied for over a century by the Umayyad Caliphate from Mecca, all except for Asturias in the north. Toledo was under Muslim control and its bishop under Muslim influence. Beato lived outside

Muslim territory in the small Christian Kingdom of Asturias in the mountainous north of Spain which the Moors had been unable to take. Apocalypse and the world's end were on everyone's lips. But before it happened God would separate the believers from the false prophets and the demons. Beato, best known for his commentary on the Apocalypse of John was particularly fond of quoting *Revelation*:

"And the fifth Angel sounded (his trumpet) And I saw a star fallen from the sky into the earth And to him was given the key of the bottomless pit."

Elipandus, feeling the heat, accused Beato and his disciple Bishop Etherius of being 'agents of the Antichrist. By way of reply, Beatus accused Elipandus of being 'the leader of the pack' that was taking sides with the unbelievers, reducing Christ the man to a secondary position relative to God the Father, thus attacking both Islam and the enemies within the church.

That's where the Ball or the Balls of the Antichrist comes in.

Firstly, the accusation was in Latin: Testiculum Antichristus was what he wrote. The Ball of the Antichrist. Did he only have one? Testiculum in Latin is testicle but it also appears to have a secondary meaning of the *leader* or *leader of the pack*. Beato in effect was accusing Elipandus of taking sides with the enemies within the Church as well as with Islam.

But to when it comes to balls we need to clarify a few things because they come in so many varieties.

"An example of the richness of Spanish (Castilian) is the number of meanings a simple word can have, especially one like that referring to the masculine attribute of balls (cojones)," is how one authority on Spanish slang puts it.

If the word is accompanied by a numeral, it has different meanings.

One ball signifies dear or expensive as in "It was worth piss-all" or "It was worth one ball" – valia un cojon. Two is admiration or surprise as in "He's got balls" or these days – lordy, lordy – "She's got balls" – *tiene cojones*. And then there are three balls. Three balls signify scorn or disdain. Not so popular maybe, but still a little treasure so listen up for as in "It doesn't matter three balls to me" – *no me importa tres cojones*. You could go on forever about balls, but to round off the topic, there are also multiple balls. And if you're wondering what you can do with those, what about pouring it all out, laying your cards on the table as in "He put his balls on the table" – *puso los cojones en la mesa.* Which is really what Beato did. But then you've only got my word for it and the blurb on the back of a packet of biscuits.

41
The Loveliest Village in Spain

Santillana del Mar is one of the loveliest little villages you could hope to visit in Spain. But I haven't come for that, or the fact, as I discover later, that French philosopher Jean Paul Sartre also called it "le plus joli village d'Éspagne," in *La Nausée.*

Now, nausea and loathing being two subjects I know a lot about, I am almost tempted to digress at this point out of respect for my dear traveling companion and fellow countryman of Sartre's and reveal my hidden agenda in coming to Santillana del Mar. My purpose in coming this way is to visit the caves of Altamira to see the drawings made on the walls over 30,000 years ago. The caves are about three kilometres out of town.

Now let me clarify that remark about the Frenchman. I am not saying I don't mention the caves to our Frenchman. I do. Granted I don't give the visit a hard sell as our Frenchman rarely shows any interest in sights of a touristic nature. I mention the caves in passing, assuming he is calculating the hours remaining of the day till he taps in the number of his girlfriend on the mobile, which is usually in the evening.

But at this moment we are headed down the main street of Santillana del Mar. We are looking for the pilgrim's hostel. The village is delightful. It has delightful streets. It has delightful ancient stones. It has delightful ancient monuments and delightful shops and restaurants and churches and it is slowly filling up at an alarming rate with delightful, alarmingly young tourists of every nationality, pretending to be pilgrims who are taking delightful photographs of the ancient, well-appointed delightful monuments and who knows, perhaps even of the delightful cobblestones trod on by that delightful rogue and rascal Gil Blas, anti-hero of half a dozen delightfully amusing picaresque novels.

A feeling of nausea begins to descend from all these delightful delights but is immediately stalled by a sign saying Museum of the Inquisition (Museo de La Inquisición) and below that in smaller letters, just in case there is any doubt about the meaning of the word Inquisition: Museum of Torture (Museo de la Tortura). Where the museum is, is anybody's guess because all you can see over the ancient crumbling stone wall with its interesting stones about two metres high, between what looks like two voluminous cedar trees, is a wooden scaffold. There are two poles with a bar on top. And hanging from the cross beam of the scaffold is an iron cage. It is too big to be a bird's cage, except maybe a giant parrot. Or a penguin. And there are no giant parrots or penguins around here, far as I know.

Beside the gateway to the garden is a gleaming suit of armour holding a broadsword between its mailed mitts. A notice on the wall on the other side of the doorway says the exhibition is a collection of such instruments as the guillotine, the iron maiden, the rack, garrottes and chastity belts used from the Middle Ages to the Industrial Age. Made by mankind, one presumes, and not aliens from outer space. The museum fortunately is closed for lunch.

This piece of good luck is such a delight, I take it as an indication of divine intervention. That's when I have my first vision of God. He is sort of Falstaffian character and he's lying on his back. He's got a jug of wine in one hand but looks like he's passed out. But he hasn't. He's shaking with laughter and big, round pearly tears are rolling down his rosy cheeks into his beard at the thought of the antics of the morons here below on earth. And then God opens one eye and I see what he's looking at. It's Sisyphus pushing the rock up the cobblestoned hill, a huge boulder, puffing and panting and when he's just about at the top, the weight is too much for him. He can't push it any further. And given the weight of the rock and the laws of gravity, the rock rolls back down the hill again. So Sisyphus has got to start all over again, condemned by the gods to a useless eternity of pushing a rock uphill.

Philosopher of the absurd, and friend of that other existentialist Jean Paul Sartre (at the beginning in any case), Albert Camus wrote a famous essay called *The Myth of Sisyphus*, named after a figure in Greek mythology condemned by the gods to repeat the useless task of pushing a huge rock uphill, so heavy it always rolls back down again. In the unintelligible modern world from which God is absent, man is condemned to the futile search for meaning, unity and understanding, life is absurd and the only real question of philosophy is that of suicide, Camus says. Best not to, he decides, we have to imagine Sisyphus as happy with his lot. The main difference between Sartre and Camus is Camus puts more emphasis on the physical than the intellectual in terms of existence. If hell was other people for Sartre, it was the absurdity and meaningless of existence without God, for Camus. Hence the idea of Sisyphus pushing the rock eternally uphill. In the end you get more laughs with Camus.

Existence is now in the shape of a few young bloods parked outside the hostel waiting for the doors to open at four and since we're now into August and the hordes are pouring down the highways and byways through France and into Spain, getting a bed for the night, a bunk rather, adds a touch of existential anxiety to the proceedings. So we wait in the wrong place for a while with the rest. We inspect the wrong entrance at one side of the building and the wrong entrance at the other. It is not clear which is which. The entrance is not marked. A cleaning lady opens the door and says the hostel does not open till four. She then disappears back inside. She omits to say to the half dozen or so young people in blonde hair and shorts plastered against the outside walls that they are waiting in the wrong place and that this is not the hostel.

Like the Holy Grail I discover the true hostel half an hour later when I see a backpacker go through a low gateway at the far end of the garden and disappear like Alice going through the looking glass to arrive in another wondrous world. And in this other wondrous world is a little courtyard, with a sort of garden in the middle and a stable for horses at the other end. Let me correct that. The hostel was once a stable for horses which belonged to the monastery. It has been restored, and as they say, renovated. And, as they also say, with all mod cons. It looks delightful. In fact it is a delightful little stable, sorry hostel.

I peer through the windows and count the number of bunks. Yes sixteen exactly, as Guillaume's guide book says. Sixteen. Then I count the number of assorted bodies lining the walls and clustered in the shed at the side of the stable with their legs stretched out in front of them in the well-known pose adopted by waiting pilgrims along the road or outside hostels, bottles of water by their side. Eighteen and rising as the weather forecast says. God knows what will happen when the door opens. We could be crushed to death in the rush. Some more Italian cyclists arrive, pushing their bikes through the secret gate.

Are Italians smarter than other mortals?

"Sardinas" I say when Pietro parks his bike and sits against the wall next to me, scratching his neck. I press my hands together like a concertina and nod towards the delightful stable-hostel.

"Sardinas," he says.

That is the beauty of the Romance languages. Sardines is just about the same in all of them. Even an English person can understand it. But that's because the English language is half French, so to speak. Since William the Conqueror brought it over and grafted it onto Anglo-Saxon along with the Norse.

Pietro has been adding two and two too. Within minutes, having consulted Guillaume's guide book for the nearest alternative, we are trudging up the cobblestones out of the prettiest village in Spain, past the delightful *posadas*, the inns, the delightful little medieval houses with their delightful flowers hanging from the exquisite, one assumes, oak wood balconies. Out onto the main road and two kilometres up the hill in the direction of Comillas to a bungalow park where we get a two bunk cabin for the night and later sit outside on the veranda, watch a group of mongols and other institutionalized persons singing in French with their guardians.

Singing childish sad songs that are faintly reminiscent.

Guillaume is training to be a psychiatric nurse for the institutionalized, the old cons, the old lags, those at the bottom of the feeding chain, the Humpty Dumpties that had a great fall and that all the king's horses and all the king's men couldn't put together again.

"They are happy" he says in response to these considerations. For which I am grateful. As I am grateful to the monitors of the group, if that's the word, for looking after the lost of this world. The little weedy looking guy with the razor moustache, the big fat black guy proudly clutching a ghetto blaster under his arm, a cigarette dangling from his lips. They're so real. So clear in these signs they give of their identity and their desires.

And all of them, the mongols apart, look like they've been flushed down this way in a sudden, violent midsummer flash flood when the plug was pulled on them in the night in some high rise suburb of Paris or Lyons or Marseilles, where people burn cars in the hot summer evenings to pass dead time and make offerings to heaven. The dispossessed peoples of North and Sub-Saharan Africa, the Roma, the Indians and Turks, all this surplus trash that God has sent the Good Shepherds to watch over. To hold them together in their loving care, unified in song. And lost, they find happiness together. The little mongols holding each other's chubby little hands, in the trustful care of their minders who possess the keys to the kingdom of this world.

Next door to us there's a French couple, in their late fifties. They're also happy. They met a few years back on the road and got married and now they do part of it every year when it's holiday time. We sit outside on the veranda at a little wooden table and trade remarks about this and that with another, young French couple who have just arrived and are headed south.

And drink more red wine.

I get a message later from Axel saying he's now in Irun and headed back down the Camino del Norte to Santiago. I told him over a week ago not to take the road backwards as we are doing because he'll never find the way. But we're heading for the exit and he is starting all over again, lost till time opens up and he can go to Berlin, back to the new flat he has rented to be near his son. But not yet. At the moment he's homeless. But homeless on a decent pension. Not homeless and hopeless. And he is starting all over again. Just like Sisyphus, pushing himself eternally down the road to Santiago, shortening the time that lies between him and the death that is hurrying to meet him.

A few drops of rain fall later in the evening and everyone disappears into their cabins. I lie in the top bunk and push the curtain aside and watch the fading light in the sky and the lights glowing in the cabins in the row next to us. There must be Spaniards there because the radio is on and it's playing a Celtic tune: bagpipes and accordion.

"Nothing happens while you live. The scenery changes, people come in and go out, that's all. There are no beginnings. Days are tacked to days without rhyme or reason, an interminable monotonous addition," Sartre says in *La Nausée*.

In the upper bunk, with the light almost gone outside, I pass the day in review: the Italians on their bikes, the long cobbled road into the village, the prettiest little village in Spain, Jean Paul Sartre and Albert Camus, the little mongols holding hands outside the cabins and singing the little songs they know word perfect and have been waiting all day to be asked to sing by the good shepherds who guard the flock.

Yes, Sartre and Camus. The nausea of the world. The nausea of existence among material objects. And thinking of Sartre, Camus *et al.*, I am thinking that thinking is not for the faint-hearted. True, I think, all thinking does is produce more thoughts. So I put my hands on my stomach, now well filled with a warm glow from the red wine, close my eyes and settle back on the pillow. Just before I exit into the next world I see God again. He's a big no-use chanty-wrastler in a long woolly robe. He's lying on his back, splay-legged. His hairy white legs are stuck into a pair of grungy, thonged leather sandals left behind by some old toerag, pot-smoking hippy at a midsummer solstice festival. He's lying on his back with a stupid grin on his face and he looks like he doesn't give a monkey's this side of paradise. And he's got a banjo parked on top of his big bloated belly, right on top of his navel. He's half gutted too, anybody can see that. And he's got a beard. A white beard streaked with grey. I can't see his hand when he starts tockling the banjo strings because the bum's got his hand on the other side of his body where I can't see it but I can hear a couple of riffs, like he's tuning up. Of course you don't know if we're going to get a tune because in the state he's in his hands just might drop off dead or freeze up. But the banjo picks up. It's not a fast number. One of those Celtic or bluegrass numbers you don't know which way will go, building up slowly and just might switch gear and take off like a runaway train. It could be McPherson's Lament, Going to Stornaway or maybe even a prelude, God forbid, to Foggy Mountain Breakdown. And then I see the long silvery, curly hair. Good God, look who it is! It's the Big Yin, that old hippy Billy Connolly and he's giving it laldy, bawling it all out, the tosser. And the last thing he says before I see a blinding white light and hear a great "whooooshhhhh" sound sucking my mind into the void, is Billy Connolly, aka God, gasping out in a barely audible whisper, one last time before he conks out for good, "Fuck off, wee thoughts, fuck off wee voices."

42

Caves, Sharks and Bankers

Nothing makes the heart of the seasoned cynic swell with greater joy than evidence that mankind is getting dumber every day. Evidence that prehistoric man, 36,000 years ago, had a higher IQ than the average *streber* these days, that he invented Celtic music and the blues, and round the cave fire in the evening, gnawing a bone, sat watching moving pictures, is enough to send the cynic into a state of permanent delirium.

Take the discovery of the caves of Altamira where our story starts. When the jurist and amateur anthropologist Marcelino Sanz de Sautuola started exploring the caves on the family estate outside Santillana del Mar it took him seven years before he hit paydirt, from the day in 1868 when Modesto Cubillas, a farmhand on Sautuola's estate told him his dog had chased a rabbit into a cave while out hunting to the day in 1875 when his nine-year-old daughter Maria pointed out the famous paintings of bison on the roof of the cave.

"Look, dad, the oxen," she is supposed to have said.

Where Marcelino Sanz's head was all those years till the day his daughter dragged him into the cave, pointed out the discovery of the age, and propelled him to fame, is unknown. Perhaps he was thinking of writing a book. His grandfather Santiago, an early conservationist, published a book entitled *La Conspiracion de Los Jardineros* (The Conspiracy of Gardeners) against the abusive cutting down of trees. As to whether he was referring to the sequoia and the eucalyptus trees the grandfather had on the family estate to create the Historical Gardens of Puente La Reina, or whether he was referring to trees in general or specific trees, we have no way of knowing. The Conspiracy of Gardeners is out of print. For the same reason we have no way of knowing who precisely Santiago Sautuola had in his sights and no way of evaluating the weight of his complaint. Logically he must have been referring to specific instances of yobo tree cutting and to specific yobo gardeners.

Their names are of no real interest. What is of interest however is the fact that Santiago had a bone to pick. Somebody had done Santiago wrong and he had a beef about it, a bone to pick. And it is that beef, that bone to pick that keeps cropping up in the subsequent history of the family.

Modesto Cubillas, the discoverer of the caves of Altamira also pruned the trees on the estate. But he cannot be included in the conspiracy of gardeners as he pruned trees in the grandson's time, in Marcelino's time, not in the grandfather's time, in Santiago's time, the grandfather's time. He too ended up having a bone to pick. Not with outsiders or other gardeners but with his employer, his master Marcelino Sanz, for his lack of generosity. And later the master Marcelino Sanz, would have a beef too. With the entire world when his discovery of the art of the caveman backfired on him.

This "somebody's done me wrong" beef was so strong in the family we need to pin it down, give it a name if we are going to get anywhere with this story. On the one hand we can think of it as a sort of family ghost, howling and wailing in the night, unable to return to the spirit world till accounts are settled in what humans fondly call the real world.

After Santiago died, the ghost or the beef seems to have passed into Modesto Cubillas. Modesto of course knew nothing about this and went about his business on the estate as usual as a day labourer, handyman, weaver, gardener and hunter, a Jack of All Trades, waiting for some kind of recognition or recompense from his master for having discovered the caves while out hunting with his dog.

Marcelino, an amateur archeologist, got the credit and hit the headlines. Modesto got nothing and at the end of the run, when the importance of the discovery was acknowledged internationally, he sent a begging letter to King Alfonso XII in 1881 describing himself as a "poor farm worker," and saying that if the "cave had any merit, he was the first to see it in the present age."

But by that time, the beef had started to live a life of its own. Honour had been impugned, injustice had been done. First to grandfather Santiago, he of the trees, then to Modesto, he of the dog, the rabbit and the cave. Then, when it attached itself to Marcelino, he of the cave and the cave drawings, it became clear that it was not just a simple family ghost wandering lost in the family dungeons but something more ambitious. With tentacles.

A *polypus* in Latin is a sea-animal. In ancient Greek it is *poloupous,* an animal with many feet. In Spanish, it becomes *pulpo:* octopus. The beef was a *pulpo* with its tentacles searching in all sorts of holes. But whereas the common everyday *pulpo's* tentacles are attached to its body, this one had tentacles that lived a life of their own, could inhabit more than one host at a time, take different forms and mutate.

As soon as news of Marcelino's discoveries got round, the wise-noses of the era attacked. Prehistoric man was incapable of any kind of artistic expression, they said, and two of them, led by chief wise-nose Gabriel de Mortillet, founder of a natural history revue concerning *Materials for the Natural and Primitive History of Man* [Materiaux pour L'histoire Naturelle et Primitive de l'Homme] ably assisted by chief editor and assistant wisenose Emile Carailhac, set about destroying Sautuola's reputation. Sautuola's hypothesis was ridiculed by the French experts and by the time it came to the 1880 Prehistorical Congress in Lisbon the Spaniard's name was up to the neck in primordial mud. Sautuola was a forger, they said. Prehistoric man had not done the paintings but Sautuola himself, or some Spanish artist in his pay. Then in 1902, Carailhac, professor by that time at the University of Toulouse, retracted after more cave discoveries were made in France. In a famous *mea culpa d'un sceptique* article published in the journal *l'Anthropologie* he recanted, offering his most profound "excuses."

Marcelino Sautuola was dead by then but the "somebody's done me wrong" beef had long been incubating in little Maria and although strictly speaking she was not entitled to feel wronged since she had not been wronged herself, she had been wronged by association as the daughter of a father who had been wronged.

Now it must be understood that the beef has no scruples, no historical memory and is more than happy to make its home wherever it is invited in. And so it was that fourteen years after the death of her father, Maria invited Carailhac to come down in 1905 to the magnificent new house on the family estate at Puente San Miguel, 16 kilometres south of Santillana del Mar and offer his excuses for having questioned the authenticity of the Altamira cave paintings. Her husband was also there: Mario Botin Lopez. And despite the name –

botin is Spanish for booty – it was Maria who brought the dowry of the family estate of Puente San Miguel which she inherited from her father.

That should have been the end of the tale of a doddery 19th century amateur archeologist and his dear little daughter were it not for the fact that Maria's husband Emilio had a taste for banking. The dynastic union put the beef into booty, transformed it into a high octane *polyp* which it passed down to the offspring during the 20th century from one male to another in a long line of bankers, each naturally with longer tentacles, more inflated than the previous, as the bank, naturally, gained critical mass, expanded beyond the national limits and stretched its tentacles throughout Spain and abroad. The wonder booty gene was passed down the line first to Maria and Mario's son Emilio. Emilio's son passed it to his son, also called Emilio, and his son passed it on to his son, also called Emilio. And so that the family itself would not get confused, the first Emilio became Emilio I, the second became Emilio II and the third became Emilio III. All of them became presidents of the family banking business represented in today's Bank of Santander.

The problem with *polyps*, of course, is that although they have sharp little beaks which in the *pulpo* is fine for crushing the coral and other crustaceous sea creatures that they feed on, they have no brains. Their brains, you might say, are in their tentacles. They expand their reach over rocks and sea creatures. They are compelled to expand by forces beyond them. Sometimes those who are host to the *polyp*, out of a sense of unease, feel called upon to explain the motivation of the *pulpo*. Rarely in life is one granted the privilege of putting one's ear to the beating heart of the octopus and hear it weep.

Emilio I set the precedent when he said "In business you always have to play the game with an advantage, with an ace up your sleeve." This became his motto and it was repeated consistently in the press whenever his name was mentioned, regardless of the subtext which even a halfwit could read as a claim that trickery or card-sharping was something worth pursuing. But that started the tradition of bankable quotes to suggest a philosophy of life. Emilio II, nicknamed, *El Viejo,* the old guy, dropped the cardsharping and came up with a motto with a pseudo-Biblical undertone. The wisdom of Solomon it was not, but at a push you could almost read some sort of altruism in it. "He who gives first gives twice," he was fond of saying. By the time it came to the current president – and just pause to study the historical lineage in the name: Emilio Botin Sanz de Sautuola de los Rios – the family genes had stalled. Emilio Botin Sanz de Sautuola de los Rios, president of Banco Santander since 1986, with the energy of an electric pylon, has been unable to develop beyond a sort of crude Darwinianism.

"Eat before you get eaten," is his motto.

But even sharks have their day. A hundred million years ago they were nearly 20 metres long. They have been shrinking ever since. And since they have started to get smaller, like polar bears they have become cuddly and endearing. Recently on TV I saw a scuba diver trying to kiss a shark. He said it was trying to make contact with him and – I swear to God this is true – said the shark winked at him. They are now so much loved the World Health Organisation is being called in to save them from humans before it is too late. Will the same thing happen to Emilio III? Will he repent, be saved, become loved, come up with a new motto imbued with altruism?

He badly needs to. His current one liner is a pretty depressing admission. Empires have collapsed on less. From aces up their sleeves over a century ago the bank's presidents are now down to dog-eat-dog. No wonder Emilio III only has time to bolt a tin of sardines for lunch before jetting off to another meeting in another country where they do not have days of the week, feast days, bank holidays or Christmas but only virtual or electronic time which is the same all over the planet.

And now that we know that the intelligence quotient of the mighty is no higher than that of the octopus, we can turn to consider how the much maligned caveman was better off upstairs and had a higher IQ than archaeologists and bankers.

43
Archaeology for Idiots

There are two Caves of Altamira. They are close to each other. One is a copy, the other is the real thing. To get there you take the road out of Santillana del Mar going towards Santander. It is about an hour's walk with a pack on your back. If the sun is shining it is a very pleasant walk. Very few cars pass in the early morning and if they do it is probably the staff going to work at the cave-museum. They arrive first. Next come the tourists who get up early to avoid the rush.

The first cave is exactly the same as the second cave. One is a real cave and the other is an artificial cave. The artificial cave is made of polystyrene foam but you will only learn that if you take the time to read the brochure they give you with the ticket at the entrance for which you pay a modest three euros.

You cannot tell it from the real thing. But you cannot see the real thing. The artificial cave is open to the public. The real cave is closed to the public. The real cave is closed to the public because too many people visited it in the past. It opened for the first time to the public in 1917.

In the 1960s and 1970s it was receiving about 4,000 visitors daily in the summer months. A figure of 7,000 was recorded for 1977 but when particles of the paintings of the 200 animals including 38 bison, 10 oxen, 26 horses and a mammoth started to flutter down on the visitors' heads, the cave was closed the next year.

It was opened again to the public in 1982 but only between ten and forty people were allowed in daily. There was a three year waiting list. That was the situation till 2002 when it was closed again to the public because of the alarming signs of human contamination.

When people breathe out, they exhale carbon dioxide. Carbon dioxide is in the blood. It is a heavy colourless, odourless gaseous element found during respiration. It is the waste product of cell respiration. It is found mainly in the air. Carbon dioxide existed as soon as the earth began. Carbon dioxide is responsible for the greenhouse effect. Ergo when you breathe, you breathe in everything that has ever existed, everything that has ever died, including the ashes of your great grandmother, Adolf Hitler's fingernails and the stinking teeth of swamp alligators. And when you breathe out you help poison the planet.

Humans breathing out created fungus on the walls of the Altamira cave. Dust from their clothes covered the rocks and started to decay. The seeds of plants started to grow in the electric light. Grey patches of microorganisms appeared on the roof particularly at the lowest points where humans lingered longest. Had they waited long enough palm trees would have sprouted. So scientists were commissioned to survey the caves and recommended closing them. Vested interests saw it otherwise. Keep the lid off the honey pot, otherwise the tourists will not come, they said. Common sense prevailed and a start was made with the construction of a replica in 1995.

But there was money in the old hole and the Patronage of the Caves, which looks after the caves, were tormented by the sound of cash boxes rattling in unguarded moments. Some more superstitious types said it was the restless ghosts of their ancestors who had been unable to die even when dead because they had failed to get their hands on more money before departing.

After so many sleepless nights, worrying about the money they were losing, the patrons dusted down the "national patrimony" and opened the doors again. That was in 1982. But it wasn't quite the same. What with visitors cut down to between ten and forty a day and a three-year waiting list, they had to close them again ten years later.

Bowed but undaunted the movers and shakers prayed in the dark to Saint Anthony, patron of lost causes, for a revolutionary breakthrough in the molecular sciences or a happy encounter with some wandering savant able to suspend the laws of the universe or come up with a new theory proving carbon dioxide was good for you.

Then Saint Anthony, the patron of lost causes, aroused by the non-stop murmur of wheedling voices from below, woke up and spoke. The vehicle he used was the tongue of President of Cantabria, Miguel Angel Revilla. That was in 2011. The Patronage of the Caves of Altamira met and decided carbon dioxide was just another myth like global warming. The caves should reopen in early 2011, they said.

"We entrust a commission with the task of telling us what sort of conditions we have to comply with," Revilla said, "but we cannot maintain a heritage like that closed … Altamira is an asset that we cannot let go of. It gives us a great card to play."

Ring a bell that last remark? Oh, Oh. Guess who is on the board?

"Every famous person that comes to Cantabria wants to visit," he said.

He had had to say no to Jacques Chirac and no to Calderón, president of Mexico at the time. But now with the good news he had created, he was even thinking of inviting President Obama down to the caves and with his help they just might get them promoted to a number two slot on the World Heritage league and milk that gravy train too.

With the caves in and out of toxic rehab, it was decided in 1995 to start studying the possibility of making a replica. The technique was the same as making a *blanc mange* inside out. Or sticking a big lump of plasticine all over the interior of the cave. And making a mould from it.

Times had moved on. Minolta had come up with a scanner that digitized every detail of the cave. And when it had taken over six million geometrical data points just for the roof section, it moved on to the walls and the floor. And when all that data was on hard disc, the contours of the cave interior appeared on screen showing a complete 3D virtual model of the cave interior.

That was the mould. Next the *blanc mange* in the form of ten tonnes of powdered limestone and two tonnes of synthetic binder to hold the mass together was poured in to fill it. And when it solidified you took out the sections and built an ugly room with them. And now every detail of the interior, floor, and roof, walls, every little bump and protrusion is an exact copy of the original. Computer Numerical Control (CNC Milling) the process is called.

Then there were the paintings. By that time modern artists had twigged how primitive man had done it, the pigments they had used. How they had used templates and sucked up paint through a pipe and blown it over their fingers to get the handprints that were all over the walls like the sticky handprints of candy-gobbling kids and that would have earned them fines for graffiti in another age.

But once you start rooting in the earth or diving into underground streams like a crazy spelunker you're asking for trouble. There's no telling what you will come up with or where you'll resurface. People keep shifting the goal posts, that's the problem. When the visitor numbers to the caves started falling in 2011, St Anthony contacted the Patronage and had them phone the scientists to tell them to get their shit together and get back into the hole, check out the fungus and see if maybe they could look at the figures again, come up with something – you know the one – and phone back with the all-clear sometime in 2014. There's a lot at stake.

Then the news comes out that the palaeontologists, the archaeologists or whoever it is that pegs names on millennia, ten thousand year spans and piles of old bones, have moved the goal posts too. The paintings on the cave roof may not all be human after all. That is the bad news. Some of them might have been done by those pug-ugly Neanderthals. Because down in palaeontology land, the palaeontologists have got together and the top honcho in the palaeontologist pack has checked his figures again and nudged the indicator on the dial back five thousand years. Some of the paintings could have been done 40,000 years ago and not 35,000, they are saying.

So what? So what! You ignoramus! You know what that means? That means the Neanderthals qualified as cave painters. At 35,000 years they had disappeared from the charts but at 40,000 years those low browed, brooding Neanderthals were still walking along with a club over their shoulder, dressed in scruffy, stinking, hairy animal hides as depicted on the wall charts the palaeontologists have hanging in their surgeries. Those big, hairy pug-ugly humanoids, those throwbacks that have nothing in common with us beautiful human beings.

So that means the Neanderthals may have done some of the cave paintings. Not the nicest ones, obviously. The faded ones that were done at the beginning. That you can hardly make out. And what was worse, no one has yet been able to prove they could not speak and if they could speak maybe they'd passed on the secrets of the painting techniques to the humans in their own language. And if they did, their words were passed on to the humans.

The implications for mankind are truly frightening. There is only one thing for it. And so the palaeontologists go back to their bookshelves and dust down the prehistoric bible written by best-selling novelist Jean Auel, the one that fills in the parts Moses glosses over in the Old Testament. Starting with *The Clan of the Cave Bear* they zip through the Stone Age Bible till they get to the last novel in the series: *The Land of Painted Caves*, feverishly thumbing the pages for any reference or bits where Neanderthals socialize with humans.

But it doesn't end there. Oh no! Once the news gets out and reaches the Basque country, it's as if Moses himself has spoken from the mountain. The Basques are delighted. It's only one more proof that, if they are not God's anointed, they were first off the Ark of Noah when it hit *terra firma* after the Flood. They are descended from the Neanderthals and the Basque language was the language of Neolithic man. Or descended from it. Patriotic Basque spelunkers dive back into the primordial depths, deep down into the underground mountain streams up there in the Basque country from which their souls bubble and guess what they come up with? Basque was spoken in the Garden of Eden.

44

The IQ of the Caveman

Socrates: And now, I said, let me show in a figure how far our nature is enlightened or unenlightened: Behold! Human beings living in an underground cave, which has a mouth open towards the light and reaching all along the cave; here they have been from their childhood, and have their legs and necks chained so that they cannot move, and can only see before them, being prevented by the chains from turning round their heads. Above and behind them a fire is blazing at a distance, and between the fire and the prisoners there is a raised way; and you will see, if you look, a low wall built along the way, like the screen which marionette players have in front of them, over which they show the puppets.

Plato, *The Republic*

In the journal of *Trends in Genetics*, Professor Gerald Crabtree a development biologist at Stanford University, positing that mankind reached the peak of intelligence between 6,000 and 2,000 years ago, says:

The need for intelligence was reduced as we began to live in supportive societies that made up for lapses of judgment or failures of comprehension...I would wager if an average citizen from Athens of 1,000 BC were to appear suddenly among us, he or she would be among the brightest and most intellectually alive of our colleagues and companions with a good memory, a broad range of ideas and clear-sighted view of important issues.

Does that sound like anyone you have met recently? And if you are thinking, as well you might – give us a break, what's that got to do with me – just listen to what Kyle R. Skottke of Rochester Institute of Technology has to say in a paper on *The Evolution of Human Intelligence*.

(With) The migration of people to all areas of the earth along with the industrialization of modern society...a greater importance has been placed on cognitive ability and intelligence to allow us how to function in modern society...it follows that someone with a low IQ would have trouble finding a mate and detecting when people are lying...

And that means, if you still do not get it, that watching reality TV, soap operas and reading the yellow press kills millions of brain cells and rots your brain so badly you are a prey to every internet scam going, including those sent by illiterate Nigerians in abominable English telling you you've won the lottery. Or offers of marriage from some nubile young desperado up in Ekaterinaberg, if you will please, please, just sign over your pension because my 45 year-old-mother is dying of stomach cancer in a broken down shack in the tundra of the Urals, signed Veronika, your beautiful golden-haired blue-eyed blonde who just loves you to bits, you pillock. One of the greatest allegories of man's delusion is The Allegory of the Cave which Plato describes in *The Republic.* A work dedicated to discussing the sort of education a philosopher-king should have in the ideal state. And to do that he uses the allegory of a cave in which there is a fire burning at the back. In front of the fire is a passage along which people are carrying objects, rather like people crossing the stage from one end to the other. At the front are people chained so tightly they cannot look round and see what is behind them. The shadows on the cave wall in front of them are reflected by a fire which is burning behind them. When people walk along the passageway behind the prisoners the fire reflects their moving shadows. And it is these shadows that the chained prisoners – mankind in other words – sees.

The moral of the story is simple: this is as close as the prisoners get to seeing reality. A philosopher, Plato says, is like a prisoner, the only difference being he is freed from the cave and when that happens he comes to understand the shadows on the wall do not make up reality at all because he can now see what is happening. He can see the fire and he can see the people pass from one end of the stage to the other in front of the fire.

German film maker Werner Herzog was no doubt aware of Plato's cave allegory when he made his *Cave of Forgotten Dreams* documentary on the caves of Chauvet in the Ardèche province of Southern France, showing some of the beasts depicted in the prehistoric paintings on the walls: cave lions, mammoths, rhinos, bison, cave bears and horses. In the light of the flickering flames of the fires in the cave, the bison and the horses could be seen to run in some instances, rather like that trick you learn in primary school of drawing a little matchstick man at the top of each page of your jotter then zipping the pages like cards under your thumb to animate it and make it run.

Now prehistoric man certainly did not have school jotters, but still at some point, over thousands of fruitful years sitting round the fire watching the shadows like a prehistoric couch potato, he added a profile to the first bison on the wall of the cave or on the roof, a few inches away. Then another and another. So that eventually he had a series of profiles of the bison, one after the other, a dozen or so. And above and below them, more bison, rows of them, a herd of them. And as the flames of the fire flickered in the dark of the cave, the bison appeared to gallop across the endless tundra. And while these prehistoric Flintstones were watching prehistoric movies, some sad sack was playing the blues in the dark, blowing on a flute made from the hollow bone of an eagle's wing like the one found in the cave. With five holes in it, the scale of the flute was pentatonic, the five note scale that many music systems are composed in. From Celtic folk music to blues and gospel. So spare a thought for the cavemen next time you hear poor old Keef Risherts of the Strolling Bones mumble his way through Cocaine Blues because that too uses the pentatonic scale.

But, to take the analogy of primitive man further, relieved of the baggage of internet and TV information, primitive man had the advantage that he could leave the house and come into contact with nature. He could see there was a difference between nature outside and life inside the cave. He could see that when the sun shone it threw shadows, shadows of trees, hills, bison grazing on the plains. When he was inside the cave watching the bison run on the cave wall in the dark, he was indisputably aware of the difference between nature and artefact.

People were possibly schizophrenic up till about 800 BC[5] and the voices in their heads were hallucinated voices. Which is where the 'Voice of God' probably came from too. The caveman may have heard voices in his head and

---

[5]Julian Jaynes, *Origins of Consciousness in the Breakdown of the Bicameral Mind* (Houghton Mifflin, 1976).

imagined they came from the spirits, another word for his experience of the world. He certainly did not watch images on screens, as we do today, designed to blindfold us to the invisible powers that rule our world and assure us all is well in the best of all possible worlds while we acquiesce in our manipulation, degradation and enslavement. Little wonder that man in the scientific age that has been given terms for all things and knows the value of nothing real.

"All is now decadence," artist Pablo Picasso is supposed to have said on seeing the prehistoric cave drawings in Altamira. The remark has led a life of its own since. No evidence can be found that Picasso ever said such a thing. It is about as valid as the dating of the caves made by experts which varies from between 10,000 and 40,000 years, and has about as much accuracy as saying, "Once upon a time" which is how fairy tales usually begin. Another misconception is about who painted them, and how they were painted. To understand that we have to move into another time dimension. Having been trained all our lives to aspire to nine to five jobs, five days a week, that are wiped out from one month or year to the next by technological change and the epileptic fits of capitalism, that should not be too difficult.

There is a nice anecdote in the *Cave of Forgotten Dreams*. In it a young French scientist tells the story of a Western scientist and an aboriginal travelling through the Australian outback. They seek shelter during a thunder storm in an aboriginal cave filled with aboriginal art. The paintings are faded. Looking at them suddenly fills the aboriginal with sadness. The Westerner asks,

"Why do you paint?"

"I do not paint, the spirits paint from me," the aboriginal says.

45

What's Up Doc? Dark Secrets of the Basques

Eeny, Meeny, Jelly Beanie, the Spirits are about to speak.

Bullwinkle Moose

Hello? Hello? Oh, it's you, Horatio. Sorry the line is a bit faint. What's up, Doc? Did I check out that stuff on the Basques for you? About them being descended from the cavemen? Ah, right, Horatio, now I remember: Neanderthals. No, Horatio, not Netherlanders: Neanderthals. Those ugly big hairy cavemen with their fingertips reaching well below their knees. Look like Arnold Schwarzenegger. Right? You remember Arnold? The Austrian guy with the muscles? In *The Terminator*? Yes, that's right Horatio, I've checked it out. Just a sec. I've got it here somewhere. I'll read it out to you.

You listening? It's quite long, so bear with me.

They are named after the Neander Valley in Germany. Tal or thal is German for valley. That's why you get that funny name. No, Horatio, Germany. Arnold was from Austria, he's got nothing to do with it. The bones of one of them were discovered by quarrymen in 1856 digging for limestone. The limestone was for the building trade. It came from a 400 million years old coral reef dating back to Devonian times. They thought maybe it was the bones of cave bear or a soldier who had fought in the Napoleonic Wars which had ended not that long before. They were in a cave with an entrance about 20 metres high. A lovely valley apparently when the caveman had lived there. The glaciers were only 100 kilometres away to the north. At that time, the Thames was a tributary of the Rhine and British Isles were part of the continent. They've discovered about 400 skeletons of Neanderthals since. Spread all over most of Europe, Western Asia and the Middle East. You getting all this?

Palaeontologists say they suddenly disappeared. For obscure reasons: disease, climate change, they couldn't reproduce as many kids as humans. But the woolly mammoth and the sabre-tooth tiger are still going about their business as usual, wandering the steppes for thousands of years after the Neanderthals are gone and nothing happens to them. But its shazam! Boom! And from one day to the next the Neanderthals suddenly vanish from the face of the earth. So what did happen?

Am I asking you for an answer? Of course not. What I'm asking you to do is think. For yourself. The amount of bunk written by mankind is astonishing, you can't believe a word. Historians, scientists, palaeontologist, they're all the same. Simple logic tells you races of people don't disappear abruptly from one day to the next. Your best guess is the Neanderthals were wiped out by humans with superior technology except you have the question of the genetic makeup of the Neanderthal. They interbred with humans, it seems. It is estimated that we all have between one and four percent of Neanderthal in our genes. What's that, Horatio? Yes, I know, it came as a shock to me too when I read it. I'm sorry. You too no doubt. Analysis of DNA taken from Neanderthal bones found in the caves of Europe show that human blood factors A, B and Rh negative are lacking in the Neanderthal who only had blood group O. The Basque people, it is known from various studies, have the highest percentage of blood group O (55%) and the highest percentage of Rh negative blood (33%) in the world.

National Geographic. You know that glossy magazine you like with the glossy pictures and the glossy prose – well, it has been doing a study of the Basques. For years it has been operating a research study called The Genographic Project which aims to map the origins of mankind by following their DNA markers. The Genographic Project, launched in 2005 has nearly 75,000 participants from over 1,000 indigenous populations round the world. Nearly half a million members of the general public have purchased a sampling kit and swabbed their cheeks and sent to it to the National Geographic Laboratory for processing. Eventually we will have a map of where everyone on the globe originated and how they are connected. Of course you can send yours, Horatio, I'm sure they'll be delighted. Can I continue?

In a news release of March 6, 2012 it says that "Comprehensive analysis of Basque genetic patterns has found that Basque *genetic uniqueness predates the arrival of agriculture in the Iberian Peninsula some 7,000 years ago."* Which takes us to the Adam and Eve Project. Researchers are also studying what is known as mitochromial DNA (mtDNA) to reveal Mitochondrial Eve, the female common ancestor of all modern humans who lived in Africa approximately 200,000 years ago.

Who was Eve? Forcryinoutloud, Horatio. Eve. Adam and Eve. In the Bible. Genesis. That's what it says in the Bible. The first man and the first woman. What true? I don't know. It's a myth. What's a myth? Furcrisake, Horatio. A nice kind of story to explain complicated things. Is it true? How do I know? Can I continue? OK, thanks. Mitochondrial Eve? Wheresthenamecomefrom?

The concept of Mitochondrial Eve was introduced in 1987 in a paper entitled "Mitochondrial DNA and Human Evolution," published in *Nature*. The study found that all the lineage of the people alive today falls into one or two branches of the family tree – either out of Africa or not and that people can trace their lineage back to a single common female ancestor who lived around 200,000 years ago.

Eve was a playful misnomer one of the report's authors says and she was not implying Eve was the first or only woman on earth. Mitochondrial Eve does not have to have been human at all, she could have been any of the ancestors of the human race, a primate, a fish or even an earlier, simpler multi-celled organism.

I know, I know. I'm with you all the way there, Horatio. A fish? I know. It sounds pretty awful and I was pretty disgusted too. But that's the good bit. What about some amoeba hanging on the living room wall as a family portrait? You can laugh, all you like. That's what it says. That's what I'm trying to tell you; maybe you're better off with the Adam and Eve story. You want to hear about the mitochondrial bit? Or you had enough? OK, on we go.

What does Mitochondrial mean? Right. Mitochondria are specialized compartments present in every cell in the body except red blood cells and create more than 90% of the energy needed by the body to sustain life. How do I know? I just looked it up on the internet. I'm just telling you what it says. What's it look like? It looks like a sort of cell. Listen, Horatio, if you want to know what it looks like why don't you get your arse into gear and look it up yourself.

OK, so now we've got that one sorted out. The Basques are genetically different. And as far as the Basque language is concerned – the Basques call it Euskera – there have been all sorts of theories about that. That it came from Armenia. Georgia. And I know you'll like this one. You being a Scot, there was even some theories the Basque language was related to the language the Picts of Scotland spoke before the Celts came. The ancestral language of the Basques has been thought to trace back to the languages spoken in Europe prior to the arrival of the Indo-European languages.

Now we've got the scientific bit settled just let me fill you in a bit on the mindset of the Basques.

When *National Geographic* put out the press release on the internet it got some interesting reactions. Just bear with me, Horatio, I'm forwarding you a copy of some emails. As you'll see from the second one they were in the New World before anyone else. They were fishing for cod. They were the greatest cod fishers in history and the most successful because they had salt. But they kept it a secret. No one knew about it for hundreds of years up till the time Columbus discovered America. And they probably landed on the east coast of America before the Vikings. But that's another story. Got to go now. Toodle Pip.

Javier Eguia Beristain
May 10, 1:26 pm

Hello I'm Basque and as far as I know all of my ancestors too. I'm from a little country town where we still maintain some of the culture and language. One of our special things is that our mothers, when we are young, teach us the surnames of our ancestors out of respect for them, so that we know their names is ours.
So my name is Javier
Eguia is my first father's surname
Beristain is my first mother's surname
Urionabarrenetxea is my second father's name 4 Usobiaga is my second mothers name....

All the names have their own meaning. There is another way to distinguish each other. We have the name of the farmhouse we were born in which is 'Baserria' so that my grandpa was Balda. So my father, me and my son. (Well my son is Baldatxiki or little Balda). Both of my sons are blood group Rh-. My brothers and all my family are also Balda. It is like a clan so that so when we go to another village we are Baldina from Markina (town near Guernika). That helps people from other towns to know where we come from. And maybe they don't know me but they know one of the other members of our family so the communication-relation can be better…with internet and the shortening of distances, and the impersonality of relationships, this method loses some of its value. But in rural areas it still lives on. In my town they know me as Balda and not as Eguia…the Basques were very good sailors and there are new studies that conclude that we were in Canada before Columbus. A boat made with the wood of some particular tree was found in Canada and when they studied the wood they noticed that it was from our country. And much older than 1492. I have read about white people in some local tribes in the east side of Canada also.

Now in Basque to say goodbye to you all

Ondo izan ETA beste bat arte. Be well and until next time.

And here's another reply from: San Jose, CA, USA:
February 19, 1:04 am

I have always been fascinated with the Basques. Also, I think you should study the Navajo whose language is said to be very unique. It is a shame the Mandan tribe has died off for they had European blood. Also the Northwestern Tribe the Kwiatal (sorry for spelling) will sometimes have blond/red hair, light eyes and skin when parents are very dark. Interesting where they obtained the DNA for that.

Margaret Easling, California
December 13, 2012, 1:17 pm

I was told by people in Oaxaca, that there were words in Zapotec or Mixtec that were related to basic Basque words. Surely, some peoples sailed from the early Americas to the East.

46
Bilbao in Blade Runner Time

We're trying not to be lost, doing our best, but we're good enough as lost, whipped into the bargain. And the day is moving on fast into afternoon. I don't know how many people we have asked trying to get out of this place called Bilbao. I'm beginning to think I'm in Moloch this high up. Like in *Howl*, that poem of Alan Ginsberg's:

Moloch! Moloch! Robot apartments! Invisible suburbs!
Skeleton treasuries! Blind capitals! Demonic Industries!
Spectral nations! Invincible mad Houses!

I've asked half a dozen people to indicate the road, which is over the hills we can see rising above us, to some place that only exists in Guillaume's guide book. The slope seems a two-to-one gradient. We try this and we try that. We go up, we come back down. I talk with one man; go that way he says for the old Camino road. Five minutes later I check it again with a woman. Go that way she says for the old Camino road, *el viejo camino,* in another direction. There's something seriously wrong. With the language, the directions, the signs, us, them, the weather, the time of day. Any moment I expect an alien spacecraft to flash across the sky and explode on the other side of the hills.

We climb further, meet a dead end. Do a U-turn, come back down, and try another street of tall apartment buildings. All the time checking with anyone we can find. It's taken us over three hours already climbing from the centre of Bilbao, climbing and climbing all the way.

There's a bus stop sign in this dead, soulless street. There's nobody around. We're just about back where we started. Tall dead flats and a high concrete wall holding up the entire mountain and a bus stop that's been put there by mistake.

I go and sit on the pavement by the bus stop. A young guy comes out of a Blade Runner building and I get up and wave to him and cross the road and ask directions. We follow him along the street where there's a big modern glass elevator for bringing people from the street to a lower level.

Going down in the elevator you can see the city of Bilbao sprawled below, the big tower of the Banco Bilbao Vizcaya Argentaria with the letters BBVA where I had an account once, and that I'd noted that morning when we went to the railway station.

Good God, we've been going round in circles, it's right below us in a straight line. What was it? Over three hours ago. When we had the coffee near the main railway station? About ten o'clock and now it's well after one. We'll never get to the next place before nightfall.

So the young guy leads us downhill through the streets ever lower and presently calls in at a corner bar. His mother comes out with him. She's about forty and the young guy is maybe about twenty. And they're so happy to see each other. So happy. And when she comes out of the bar, a few steps lower than the street, she brings a glow to the early afternoon, something nice and warm and caring that is tangible and if you knew how, you'd scoop it up and take it with you all the way back home. Or just stay there for the rest of your life. She smiles and looks up at us and enquires how we are and where we're headed. It's like we've chanced upon two of the last real human beings on earth. The way human beings used to be in some mythical epoch. In the Garden of Eden perhaps, the only ones left with a developed sense of empathy.

I breathe in the precious scent of human kindness like a Blade Runner replicant, meeting a real human being for the first time since we escaped to earth from an off-world colony on Mars. And are trying to keep ahead of the Bounty Hunters who get paid for terminating us because we don't have empathy. Not like all the loving human beings here on earth. Not like the Bounty Hunters.

I've been feeling like I'm from another planet since I arrived in the Basque country. Which is borne out when we wander into the main railway station of Bilbao-Abando half an hour later to enquire about the time of the trains to Guernika. Or Guernica. The conversation is like a Blade Runner applying the Voight-Kampff test to a squirming android to see if its responses are human.

It's Saturday afternoon. Maybe that's an excuse, maybe it's not. Mr. Misery, behind the glass in the ticket office answers in Euskera (Basque language) when I speak to him in Spanish. What? I ask a second time for the name of the station we have to go to. He blesses himself in commiseration. The whole thing: arm sweeping up ostentatiously, fingers touching forehead, a pontifical touch to the left, a pontifical touch to the right shoulder. I'm at least spared the thumb bit. He doesn't kiss his thumb.

I tell him Basque isn't my language, that's why I can't recall the name of the station which he told me just now and which I can't remember because I have no memory for retaining Basque names. I don't even know how to pronounce them. But the miserable Basque fucker says it's the same if he goes to my country. But I'm not even Spanish, I protest, which only makes things worse. He says something again in Euskera.

The problem, apart from the absence of common everyday courtesy, is there are three different train companies and three different stations. We need to go to the Concordia station to get the little FEVE train to Guernika.

It has started to rain. In the train I get out my copy of *Do Androids Dream of Electric Sheep*, the Philip K Dick classic, on which Ridley Scott's classic film *Blade Runner* is based. I picked up the paperback in a hostel somewhere over a week ago and have been reading a few pages whenever I get the chance. You can glean bits and pieces of arcane knowledge from the labels on tin cans if you are so minded.

My fellow replicant is unfazed as always and sits with a satisfied grin as if he's got the Voight-Kampff test off pat in French. As a psychiatric nurse up there in a hospital in that hick village in Normandy, Guillaume has nosed the necessary literature on the subject of human deviance, done the necessary training courses. Handling prisoners from the local state institutions, everything from wackos to suicide cases. Maybe that's what has set him on his six months walk from the North of France to the South of Spain. Or maybe he has escaped from an off-world colony on Mars too. But he's not going to tell me that or anything else and I'm not going to divulge where I've escaped from.

47
Shitting on God in Guernika

It's raining when we stop somewhere and have a coffee and wait in the bus shelter to get the connecting service to Guernika. Pouring down. And the raindrops are running down the bus window when we pass though places the names of which you can't even pronounce. Up here in the hills of the Basque country.

We book into a pension in the centre of town next door to a bar and there's some hassle about the room. The girl wants to put three people in it, the third person out there in the ether of her mind and yet to arrive, but I torpedo that attempt soon enough. Dopey old Guillaume, good as gold, is unfazed as usual. Indifferent to the evil machinations of the world, he does what he's best at, climbs into his sleeping bag and pulls the hood over his eyes.

I've had a thing about Guernika for a long time since I saw Picasso's well-known painting. The one with the screaming horse and the man with his twisted arms raised to heaven. Painted in oil in grey, black and white. It's 3.5 metres high and 7.8 metres long (11.5 x 25.6 feet). You expect it to be bigger but it's not. I saw it in Madrid in the Reina Sophia Museum some years back. A monument to man's inhumanity to man, that's the well-intentioned phrase that comes to mind. That your mind sucked up from a blurb on the back of the book. Or your eyes ingested from a war monument. There's nothing you can ever say that will help except:

> Good morning and welcome to another day of insanity on planet Earth, the demons are loose again as usual, the ground is about to open up and swallow you whole. But be of good cheer nevertheless, things may get better in a thousand years. If we're still here. Mankind is evolving.

But we'll leave discussion of that to another time and place. It's Saturday and tomorrow will be Sunday. The street below is crowded and the bars are full and the food is good. Everyone looks well-heeled, forty and upwards into the pension age. They're tanking up inside and outside the bars in the centre. The rain has stopped and it has become a half decent evening. A few streets up is where the young people hang out. You can smell dope outside the bar where we are. Guillaume has surfaced and is calling his girlfriend. He's just stood up from the table. He's on the phone to his girlfriend up there in some village in Normandy. He's about 35 at a guess. He's a psychiatric nurse. Handles difficult cases. He's done courses. In psychiatry. Studies character. I'm one of them. But his face is always happy and it's nice to watch that bearded ball face talking on the phone. His girlfriend's got a son. Fifteen or sixteen. There's some kind of problem there. And she's older than him. Wants the two of them to set up house together.

Guillaume doesn't exactly pour his heart out. Oh no, that French wise-nose keeps his cards close to his chest. He sits back down again like Buddha himself and we order drinks. I go into the bar to buy him a pack of Marlboro. I normally only smoke other's people's cigarettes and tell everyone I'm a non-smoker. But tonight things have reached breaking point between us on the cig-arette question. His fingers are hovering over the pack. He's not offering. Which he never does. But it's not that he is not offering. There's just a touch of something. Something extra. The way his fingers are clutching the pack, he's trying to tell me something. Even I get the message. The drawbridge has been pulled up. The castle is under siege. I've done courses in psychology too in my time, watch telly occasionally, pick things up, have heard of this thing called body language.

There's an edge to the people here in the Basque country in Euskal Here-dia as the Basques call it. They're carrying baggage. I can guess maybe what it is. But it's heavy baggage just the same. In the bar I put the coins into the ma-chine and get the wrong brand. Not the Marlboro that Guillaume smokes but some Spanish horse shit. So I parley with the barman. He's a bad ass, I get that straight away. But what's new? He protests, so I go nice and courteous on him. The thing is first he has to get the remote control and point it at the cigarette machine. That's to prevent minors from using it. And then he's got to come out from behind the bar and go to the machine and open it and do the money thing. Which is a really big deal when you could be talking to your mates clutching beer bottles at the other end of the bar on high stools. But we get that little contretemps sorted out, overcome some bad will, and I get Guillaume's Marlboro's.

Friendly is not a word you throw about carelessly in this neck of the woods. I've noticed it from three or four little incidents since we arrived. Life here on planet Guernika is probably like most places on planet Earth. People go out in the evening, eat and drink and make a late night of it at the weekend. But if you're not one of them, the barriers go up and they start speaking Basque.

A couple more pilgrims have arrived when we get back to the pension, wandering around the corridors like stun-gunned burglars. Before he gets his head down Guillaume goes through the usual rigmarole, studying the hieroglyphics that will take us along the highways and the byways tomorrow. If it wasn't raining again and it wasn't dark but the moon was full so you could see the stars, he'd be as well going outside and laying on the road and looking up at the Milky Way for guidance.

We're ready to head off in the morning and are having the obligatory *café con leche* and the *croissant* for breakfast in the bar downstairs. There's a pretty girl behind the counter and she's friendly too, which counts for something. And it's also Sunday, the best day of the week as far as I'm concerned. And we'll be leaving soon. But it's been a pretty bum visit. I checked out the museums, the tourist office, and walked round town as far as I could when Guillaume was out for the count but no Picasso. Nothing. I can't get a fix on the place. I'm not disoriented because I've never been here before. I feel cheated, that's it. I've come for nothing. I don't know what I was expecting but I didn't get it.

That's when Ernest Hemingway's ghost wanders in from Sun Valley Idaho and saves the day. From up in Ketchum where he bought a house and went hunting and fishing. Ernest Hemingway, you know? The writer? He was big at one time. If you're under forty and haven't done English lit, you've probably never heard of old Hem. But Hem was good and was very popular at one time. And then he went and shot himself up in Ketchum, Idaho with a shotgun. Blew his head off.

Yep, that was old Hem. Did world wars, did marlin fishing in Cuba. Did bullfights in Spain. And then he did elephants in Africa and blotted his copy book when tree hugging got popular and he fell out of favour and no one reads him anymore. Or so I read somewhere recently in an article by a wise-nose critic in *The Guardian*. Don't believe a word of it.

But look at this! Man alive! It says in the paper, the paper I'm reading at the bar, the Sunday paper, the local paper, the *Deia* (lantern) that two new books are to be presented locally in a few days' time on the bombing of Guernika in 1939. William Smallwood, now 82, is one of the writers. He's an American, lives up in Ketchum and knew Hemingway before he shot himself in 1961. Hemingway, that is. And he's written a book about the atrocity of the bombing of Guernika. It's a collection of interviews he took with survivors in the 1970s. And to do that he learned Basque.

Now if they'd said he'd learned Shoshoni from the Plains Indians up on the high chaparral, I wouldn't have flinched. But Basque? Where dog is txakurra in Euskadi. Where casa in etxea and thanks is eskerrik asko. But that's bye the bye, having heard the story of the Guernika bombing, Smallwood (Egurtxiki), a biologist and writer started to learn Basque from Basque shepherds who had emigrated to the United States and were herding sheep up in Idaho.

What first hits Smallwood, or Egurtxiki (as the Basques call him, a literal translation of the name small wood) when he enters Guernika for the first time in 1970 is that the roofs of the houses in the centre are different from those on the outskirts. They look newer. That might not sound like much till you remember that in Franco's Spain, Guernika hadn't officially been bombed by fascist German, Italian and Spanish planes. The Reds had done the bombing. And the people of Guernika themselves had burned the town down. That was the official line of the Franco regime.

The next year, Smallwood walks into a bar in Guernika. When you walk into a bar, anything can happen. In Smallwood's case, you might say the bar invited him in. Walking through Guernika in 1971, he sees a bar called the Bar Boise and walks in. He walks in because Boise – and you need to know this – is the biggest town in Idaho and sits on the Boise River, so a bar called Boise in Guernika is a bit like 'A Boy named Sue.' It's out of place. It is not supposed to be there. It's supposed to be up in Idaho with shepherds from the Basque country hanging over the bar, shooting the breeze.

Smallwood gets to talking to the barman. This is 1970 in Franco's Spain and it's dangerous talking to strangers. When the barman is sure he can trust Smallwood, he tells him this story.

> After the bombing, the new priest told the congregation in Spanish that they needed to cleanse themselves of sin by doing severe penance for having poured gasoline on their houses and burning them to ashes and reducing the town to rubble. One day, two women, having listened to the service in silence went to the sacristy and tried to explain to the priest in private that they hadn't burned Guernika, that it was Franco's planes that had destroyed their homes. In the morning the Guardia Civil went round to their house, brought them outside and shaved off all their hair in front of the houses, in the middle of the street, out in the open for everyone to see. Then they walked them through the streets of Guernika with their hands tied behind their backs and after a very summary trial they were sentenced to 36 months detention of which they served 27.

Twenty-one percent of the bombers and fighters of Franco's air force took part in the attack on Guernika on Monday, April 26, 1937. They choose market day when the town centre was most crowded. Over 85 percent of the buildings in town were completely destroyed and 1,654 people died. The authorities of the Francoist regime tried to erase all evidence of the bombing and made no effort to recover the bodies of the victims and to register the deaths. United Press covered the story but their reporter said he could find no evidence of any bombing. It took over forty years, seventy-five years after the bombing, before Smallwood could locate the survivors and interview 179 of them in 1972 and 1973, just in time to set the record straight.

And the writer would be here in a few days' time! Here in Guernika!

And I wanted to go and talk to him because it was a chance of a lifetime. But I couldn't. Our paths weren't intended to cross. We had to move on, Guillaume and me. Get out of town. Go follow the Camino up towards San Sebastian and into France.

But I thought about the barman's story afterwards. And how Spaniards say "I shit on god" a lot. *Me cago en dios.* To express surprise. Or anger. Or just for the sake of swearing, like some people I know. As in "I shit on god, this coffee is cold." Or "I shit on god, I didn't know you were coming."

Now before you get all worked up and upset about people saying they're shitting on god, just ask yourself whose god you think they think they are shitting on? It's not their god, it's someone else's idea of god. And to bring it all home, when I run the phrase through the spelling check when writing this, the dictionary refuses to recognize the word shit. It wants to replace shit with sit. Think about that one. Someone out there in charge of the dictionaries has decided shit does not exist.

Everything is connected in life and you can find the connection if you look hard enough. But there's people out there in the world are dead inside and to feel alive need to break the connections. You have to be careful. Evil does exist.

48
Watching Dogs is a Sobering Experience

So the dark shape arises in the semi-dark, outlined against the window at the rear of the stuffy room, and turns the whirling electric fan round so the breeze will blow fully in its direction. And not mine. So from the bottom bunk near the door, I say to The Shape,

"Excuse me, wait a minute..."

But Shape says nothing and heads back to bed somewhere at the other side of the two-bunks-and-a-single-bed room; I pull the ear plug out of my right ear to make sure I actually spoke just now after being abruptly awoken by the saboteur. I get up in the dark and turn the fan stand in such a way it blows roughly into the middle of the room, giving everyone some refreshing air. That seems the fair thing to do. The Shape melts into the dark. I wait for it to make a counter response but it does not. The Shape has its six foot of Australian length stretched out in trunks on the bed at the rear I see later, next to the only window. But since the room is an interior room, it does not count as a window. It opens onto an air shaft. But no air circulates in the shaft, hence the importance of the electric fan.

This is the second time someone has moved the fan. When the Mexican art student was the only one in the room yesterday it was no problem. But today there are new arrivals. Some noisy Australians and an Englishman in the bed above me. The Englishman is a linguist. In the kitchen this morning, leaning over the gas cooker, he points to the burner and says to Fabio,

"Senyor, gasa?"

Fabio, the general dogsbody of the pension, gazes at him in doleful-eyed Italian wonderment. The Englishman repeats the question, raising his eyebrows for emphasis this time,

"Gasa?"

Now Fabio does not look fast on the uptake but when he says pointing at the oven, "Horno... no funciona," I have to thank him silently – God bless you, Fabio – for not saying "Functioning" in English or some other abomination like the Englishman.

Next the Englishman points to the tea mug, which he has set next to the hotplate and says, "Senyor, milka?"

Fabio reaches up, opens the cupboard door and hands him a packet of milk, which all things considered, says much for Fabio's language interpretation skills.

That was in the morning long before the Aussies filled up the kitchen, drinking beer and scheming to hit the bars later and the bearded Mexican student, who swears a lot, threw his bit into the language debate,

"En chew no, hi tink no espanish deefikool..."

To which Bridget the strapping big Sheila who spent the last half hour doing up her face in the mirror, prior to hitting the bars to get wiped out, says,

"No I think Russian and German is better...because that is what I would like to study...and they're more useful anyway."

Useful? Bridget is holed up somewhere in Finland on a student exchange deal. One can only presume Russian will be the *lingua franca* someday down in the Antipodes if the tectonic plates of the earth do a sudden jump.

The pension is crowded since yesterday with Saturday being the start of the big festival week in San Sebastian, or Donostia to give it its Basque name. Donostia is more current and on the signs everywhere. The problem with the name of Donostia is half the time you think you're in the wrong town. Despite that slight drawback, there's a lot of people coming in for the festival.

My bunk bed is no longer sure for the remaining three nights, Fabio says. We are coming up in the lift to the third floor. I look down on Fabio's shaven head. He has a tattoo round his upper arm that looks like some kind of fisherman's net and he's wearing a sleeveless vest: the kind of vest the Latin Kings wear when they go pop each other off down in the *barrio* in Barcelona or Madrid, the colour of coffee when you don't put in enough milk.

"The *patrona* says she wants 25 euros for the room."

"Twenty five? But it was only twenty last night."

So upstairs at his little desk by the door, I pay him the twenty and tell him he will get the rest for the next two nights when I get to a machine. Fabio also works shifts in a bar further up the street and at five when I bump into him later he's with the *patrona* and the runner who are perched against the wall of a bar in the narrow lane across from the pension. "This is the *patrona*," the runner says, nodding to the fat greasy-looking damsel in the black dress next to him. She looks like she has a serious problem of weight distribution. Her bosoms are huge, so big she looks like she's about to topple over from the weight and fall on her face. She's got her feet planted firmly on the pavement, her backside parked on the low window ledge and with her shoulders she's holding up the entire building. If she deflates and relaxes the whole edifice is going to come down on top of all of us. Maybe that's why the runner is not looking too comfortable. The runner is the guy who brings in the clients. He picks them up on the street. Outside the tourist office mostly. He gets commission for each person he fishes out of the tourist pool; anybody with a pack on their back is a potential client. That's how we got here. He netted Guillaume coming out of the tourist office two days ago. And since the pension was central we took it.

Later when I'm back at the pension listening to the talk in the kitchen through the open door, I hear someone say,

"Listen…she's raking it in…"

It could be Fabio, or the runner or the Columbian who helps out in the evening in return for a free bed and spends most of this time after work in the kitchen sweet-talking his sweet Colombian girlfriend.

"And what's she done to the place?"

That sounds like the runner.

"And there's no air conditioning…and she said last year…"

That sounds like Fabio.

Five rooms with four beds apiece for backpackers and sundry tourists. That's twenty beds a night times 30 days a month times 20 euros a night is 12.000 euros a month give or take. Full in July and August. Yes, old greasy bags is doing alright.

The pension is centrally placed, off the Boulevard, next to the lovely big building of La Brexta market where you can sit outside at a big modern glass-

walled cafe and drink a coffee and watch life go by. Downstairs, down the moving stairs, there are market counters with an amazing selection of fish and meat
and vegetables and at the end of the hall there's a big Lidl where you can stock
up on food for next to nothing and tell yourself the only reason you did not
buy from the fishmongers or the butchers is the price. And still regret it. But
not always.

"Lamb's liver?" The butcher repeats. "No don't have any ... got any
lamb's liver?" he shouts across to his mate in the stall opposite. Not much but
enough and he holds up a piece of liver the size of a fist. Attached to it is a white
stringy mass, that if you didn't know better, you'd take for the remains of a
fishing net caught in a propeller.

"You can cut that off," I say. "Two euros...not twelve?" You never know.
You don't want to be making a mistake between *dos* and *doce* just as you don't
want to mistake two for twelve. The budget traveller in foreign climes is fore-
warned.

And so in the late morning I head down to the old part of town where
there's a slipway where you can swim away from the madding crowd on the
beach. Today, Saturday, there are about twenty people there already. Yesterday
there was only a girl with a dog and a guy stretched out on a towel. Today I
count about five dogs. A shaven 'beige poodle or similar,' as it would say in a
lost dog ad, a shaggy-looking mutt that barks all morning jumping up and
down in the water with no clear purpose in mind.

Then there's a big-headed ugly-looking dog, what looks like a pit bull, a
cross between a small black bear and a Christmas pudding, the kind with the
decorations on top. It is not overloaded with IQ content either, because as I
slip into the clear water and swim out between the pier walls, it paddles furiously behind me, thinking I am the guy standing on the slipway with the ball
in his hand: its owner who keeps pretending to throw the ball into the water,
the smart ass, he's got the mutt completely confused.

The rest of the morning is spent to shouts of "Anda." Go get it. "Anda."

And the faithful mutt paddles gallantly in all directions. It needs a lot of
encouragement to get it to distinguish between a human head and a ball, it
seems. So much for His Master's Voice.

On Sunday morning it is quieter out on the quay. Most of the town is probably sleeping off the festivities of the night before. I am the only one there. I swim out in the clear water between the boats and climb up onto a wooden walkway and sun. Later a girl appears with a little dog. It's a ratty looking specimen with a long snout and it seems like is has been cross-bred with a large mouse. It has big ears and they flap about like they are spring-wired as it tears into the yellow tennis ball it has found.

Maybe it is the invisible ball that the Saturday mutt kept paddling after but could never find. Mouse-Dog is a different challenge for its owner. It hates water. There is no way the girl can tempt it into the water. She picks up the ball and makes as if to throw it into the water but Mouse-Dog is too cunning, too lazy or too scared. It refuses to budge. It keeps its eye glued on that ball every second, each time she raises her arm and pretends to throw it in the water. It damn well knows she is hiding the ball behind her back. So she has to face the sad facts of life. That Mouse-Dog is a land-bound dog and not an aquatic dog. And with no one near to witness her shame, she tosses the tennis ball to Mouse-Dog, spreads her towel on the slipway and lays down flat on her back in the sun and dies behind her sunglasses.

And there he is now, proud as punch on the towel, the little rat, tearing with all its might at the tennis ball with his incisors, growling and gulping and getting himself real nice and upset and angry trying to tear off the fabric.

He will too if he keeps it up long enough. Maybe not today but certainly in a day or two. You can see that right off. He is so determined, he will succeed in the end.

Yes, I can see it all before me. He rips off the yellow fabric till he's down to the inner layer, the black rubber underneath. Then, chewing and biting, he's piercing the rubber with his incisors. And when he's done that, a turning point comes. His rage abides and his little eyes drop to the deflated sludge he's created. That isn't moving any more. And he looks up and his eyes say,

"What a clever little dog am I? Doing amazing things no one has ever thought of before. No?"

And when that thought flashes out Sunny Jim's backside, he nudges the dead ball with his snout a couple of times to make sure it isn't a rabbit or a cat or a mouse or a frog playing possum. Then his shoulders droop in disappointment. But only for a second. Undeterred by experience off he goes again and in two shakes of a lamb's tail he's at it again, sniffing at the flotsam and jetsam under the boats on the slipway till his destructive instincts are aroused once more.

But I catch that greedy look in the eye of the little clever billy and having read a thing or two on the transmigration of souls, reckon it just might be another *Ferengi* who has died recently. Maybe one of those Wall Street investment bankers or a hedge fund commodities speculator who croaked it counting his loot, got a Mafia bullet through the head for services unrendered or just threw himself out of a skyscraper window to give us all a break. And having behaved so badly in life, he's sentenced to come back and try all over again to get things right. Condemned to tread the dreadful burning wheel from birth to death one more time. And with Hell barred to him, all his miserable, wretched, unformed soul can do is search for a new home in a pig or a crocodile or some form of life so primitive and base, it doesn't know any better than to let him in.

Some of them end up in monkeys, it is said, others in mules. Even in worms and rats. Dogs too are receptacles. Trapped inside the body of Mouse-Dog, some *Ferengi* or other is now condemned to a lifetime of puncturing tennis balls, sniffing shit and trying to hump bitches in heat. No two ways about it, watching dogs is a sobering experience.

49
Wha's Like Us?

Here's tae us
Wha's like us
Damn few
And they're a' deid
Mairs the pity

Robert Burns

Well, that was that then. We got up fairly early and had breakfast on the pavement at a café this side of the bridge over the river Urumea leading out of town. Three teenage girls passed walking fast and one of them said something about a "lesbo bitch" in French though the accent was American which made me think, the way they were dressed, they were coming from a disco and that it had just closed. Then the Frenchman shouldered his bag, shook my hand and headed off across the bridge in the bluish haze hiding the upcoming sun and the day already starting to get warm.

The way I calculated it, it would take him over two months to walk back to Normandy, and when he got back home he would be gone six months. That's what he said. Six months. Though at this time of year – summer – he wouldn't have the snow to contend with on the high ground like he did on the way down.

First he'd have to go to the post office in Irun to pick up the tent he'd asked his lady love to send down. That was about 25 kilometres from here so he'd get there in maybe five or six hours, maybe less. Then he'd have a stiff climb through the valleys and up over the Pyrenees and into France. I imagined a trail of little red pins on a map, marking out the route. A new pin every night. Like one of those campaign maps generals have. Tracing the march north through France all the way to *La Manche*, the English Channel, where he'd also walked along the coast a few times.

It wouldn't be so easy to get a hostel as there were fewer in France. That was what the tent was for. If need be he could spend a night under the trees or in the fields. And at night he'd take out his guide book and read it in the light of the little LED lamp strapped to his head and study it, though now he was back in France, maybe he wouldn't need to consult it so often. And then when he was settled for the night he'd phone his girlfriend, though he'd only agreed to do that twice a week at the beginning, coming down. Before he left. And his parents, once a week too. Till he got home. Why he had decided to go walkabout for six months he never explained, only that he had always wanted to do it and had done several long walks before along the Channel coast.

I'd head back up somehow. Maybe I'd cross over to Barcelona on the train and go up through France, up through the Rhone valley towards Paris. Or maybe I'd be as well to stay at home in Spain where the Celts came from before they went to Ireland and Britain. All the more so since the Scots lived in Spain when they were Spaniards and prior to that Scythians before they headed for Scotland, though this side of the Resurrection of the Dead nobody was going to prove that one way or another.

But you pick up little gems of wisdom as you go along. Fill in a few gaps. Bryan Sykes, professor of human genetics at Oxford University, recently reported that a majority of Britons are related to the Spanish tribes; that there is no difference between the Picts and the Scots and that even 64% of the English are descended from the Celts. Spaniards in short are more related to the Irish, Scots, Welsh, Britons and Portuguese than any other people.

Another thing is Spanish historians have no problem with the Scythian connection and believe the Scythians crossed the continent of Europe to Spain on their horses centuries before the birth of Christ and bequeathed the Celts of Asturias their love of horses. That was long before the Celts of Spain migrated north by sea from Galicia, Asturias and Cantabria – all on the coast – to Ireland, Britain, Wales and Cornwall from the fifth century BC onwards. Other sources say that after their final defeat by the Romans in the Cantabrian Wars (29-19 BC), the ancestors of the Celts who had fought at the fore for Hannibal in the Punic Wars (264-146 BC), were recruited as auxiliaries in the Roman army and later went to Britain, to work on Hadrian's Wall and the Antonine Wall.

At its widest extent, the Scythian empire covered a vast sweep of territory from the Crimea through Russia and Siberia into Northern India. The Sikhs claim descent from the Scythians and the Hungarians too consider themselves Scythian. Our view of history is being continually reshaped. The claim in the *Declaration of Arbroath* that the Scythians: "...journeyed by way of the Tyrrhenian Sea (Mediterranean) and the Pillars of Hercules and dwelt for a long time in Spain," may yet be validated.

Not too soon, we hope. It's going to take a few centuries for the Scots to get over the shock of being Spanish. But now that one has been sorted out, we can move on to clearing up the Scythian question and whether not they are one of the lost tribes of Israel.

Worst thing is, if you thought raping, pillaging Vikings or cattle-thieving clansmen were bad enough; wait till you hear about the Scythians.

Sometime between December 1993 and April 1994 I visited an exhibition on the Scythians in the Nieuwe Kerk in Amsterdam, organized by the Hermitage in St Petersburg in Russia. The Empire of the Scythians (*Het Rijk der Scythen*) it was called. Two memories I retain from the exhibition of their treasures. The Scythian women were good at sewing. The stitching on the fine textiles they wove was as regular and as perfect as a machine-made garment today. The Scythian men were good at impaling people.

Whenever a king died, his body was borne in a wagon for forty days round the tribes. Great feasts were held in which the participants were required to cut off a piece of their ear, shave their heads, scratch their arms, forehead and nose till they bled and stick an arrow through their left hand. A year later the mourning ceremony was repeated. Only worse. Fifty men of the king's retinue were strangled and fifty of his finest horses were clubbed to death, their intestines ripped out, replaced with straw and raised high like scarecrows on poles and half wagon-wheels. The servants of the king were impaled and raised high in mounted position as though they were sitting on their horses. The horse and men were placed round the burial mound till the wind and the weather reduced them to dust. Such was the terror they inspired that for hundreds of years no one would approach the tombs. It was only when Russian colonists, indifferent to local superstition began to break open the tombs that their treasures were revealed at the end of the 17th century. Czar Peter the Great (1689-1725) was one of the first to show a scientific interest in the "barbarians of the steppes" and managed to amass a collection of over 250 gold artifacts. But much was lost by the tomb raiders. In 1993 a team of Russian and American scientists dug up the body of the 'Ice Maiden' in the Altai Mountains in Siberia near the town of Novosibirsk, close to the Chinese border. It was frozen in permafrost and buried there around 500 BC when Scythians were policing the streets of Athens. In a BBC Learning documentary, Jeanne Smoot of Harvard University, who was with the team, says, "Many people experienced nightmares – pretty violent ones actually. In my nightmare, I was clawing – like hooking the eyes out of people. And the speculation was, perhaps, that the place was testing our will to be there."

The Maiden's eyes had also been ritually removed. But more interestingly, for tattoo lovers especially, she had "some elegant tattoos." Just like the Picts, the 'painted' ones.

Looking on the bright side, we have much to be thankful for to the Scythian-Picts. When the remorseless war machine of the Romans moved into North Britain on three campaigns murdering, plundering and raping to satisfy the insatiable lust for booty of the *Ferengis* of the Roman Empire, the Angel of Death was dispatched regularly to touch the shoulders of the tattooed men to remind them of their killer heritage. But as I say, this side of Paradise, only a tattooist would take a take a bet on proving the connection.

It won't make any difference one way or another to Muldoon. He's a man of the west and the Picts were from the east of Scotland. Only thing he's got in common with the Scythians is they were both fond of cannabis.

And I now know why his name is pronounced "shame-us." I heard on the grapevine that his real name is Harry and not Seamus, that he came from Coatbridge, a chicken-wire hen-run south of Glasgow and plays the accordion in a swanky hotel up in the Highlands during the tourist season. Hence the kilt and the Gaelic name he goes under: Seamus McTavish. Keep a look out for the poster of the imposter if you're up that way in the summer, I hear he moves around.

It was a great blow of course to learn he was just another chancer. Ever since I found out, I keep breaking into song all the time. The same number every time. You know, that catchy, foot-tapping Music Hall number, loved by one and all: *The Ballad of the Highland Tinker*. Goes,

"Oh the lady of the manor while going to the ball, saw the highland tinker pissing on the village wall...."

Maybe it's a way of getting over the disappointment, working out a sense of betrayal. Yes, my dear brothers and sisters, so low has *The Young Lochinvar* sunk in my estimation I have been obliged to reclassify him as a highland tinker. Out of a sense of decorum, I will spare you the lurid details of what the highland tinker does with the lady of the manor.

With respect for Muldoon's extensive family too. Apparently he's impregnated half-a-dozen wenches in his dissolute lifetime up there in the west. Lives in a caravan on the coast in Troon with his greyhound Rocky Raccoon. On his tod in a cloud of weed smoke. That's where the Horatio fellow comes in, though where he fits into the family circle, I haven't a clue.

And having got all that off my chest I can do no more than wish you all sweet dreams, my dear sisters and brothers. Or as Muldoon – God bless him, he had his good points too – was fond of saying, raising a can of beer in toast, "Wha's like us."

Notes

Chapter 2

The English Way (Camino Ingles). In the 14th and 15th centuries, the British mostly came by boat. The first maritime journey, between 1154 and 1159, was made by an Icelandic monk: Nicolas Bergeson. English coins were found in the Cathedral. Offers made to the Apostle include an alabaster tablet by John the Good in 1456. James IV of Scotland donated a cross of pearls in 1488. The English pirate Sir Francis Drake attacked La Coruña in 1589 and stole relics from the cathedral of Santiago.

Pilgrimage in Scotland was largely centred on Fife on the east coast. By the 12th century it was an established tradition and in the Middle Ages it was as big an industry as tourism today.

> The **population of medieval Scotland** was small, rising perhaps from about 200,000 to 400,000 souls between the days of St Margaret and of Mary Stuart ...it is probably safe to say that throughout the Middle Ages, a far greater proportion of Scotland's leading citizens had direct experience of European thought and life than would ever be the case again till we come to modern times. Scotsmen were as much addicted to pilgrimage as any other nation in Christendom
>
> Monsignor David McRoberts, "Scottish Pilgrims to the Holy Lands,"
> *Innes Review*, Spring 1969

King James IV of Scotland was guilt ridden at the death of his father, James III at the Battle of Sauchieburn in 1488. Although only 15 at the time he was used as the figurehead in the revolt by leading nobles to overthrow his father, James III who was thrown from his horse in the battle and killed. As an act of penance, his son shackled an iron chain round his waist which was increased by one link each year. James went at least 18 times on pilgrimage to the shrine of St Duthac in Tain, the last time, two weeks before the battle of Flodden in 1513. The **Codex Calixtinus**, an illustrated manuscript, named after Pope Calixtinus

II is believed to have been written by different authors and compiled by French scholar **Aymeric Picaud** between 1135 and 1139. It consists of five books. Book V is a travel guide for pilgrims travelling to the shrine of Santiago and as such is the first travel guide written.

Hieronymus Bosch (1450-1516) Dutch painter, named after the Dutch city of Den Bosch where he lived all his life, is famous for his fantastical imagery. The painting of the pilgrim on the cover is a side panel of his painting of *The Last Judgement*.

Chapter 3

Alvaro Cunqueiro (1911-1981) Galician novelist, poet, playwright and journalist. The quote is from a story entitled "The Road was Like an Old Beggar" in *Merlin and Company* (Merlin e familia e outras historias).

St Anthony is the patron saint of animals. Special masses are held on his feast day and the priest blesses the animals brought, usually outside the church.

Chapter 4

Puente La Reina is mentioned in the **Codex Calixtinus** as an important town where several routes meet. The Pilgrim's Book (*Libro del Peregrino*), of the Codex says: "Four are the itineraries (passing through France) that lead to Santiago and meet as one in Puente La Reina" *(Chapter 1, Book V of the Codex Calixtinus).*

Chapter 5

The Song of Roland (Chanson de Roland) is an epic poem commemorating the Battle of Roncevaux Pass in the Pyrenees in 778 AD in which Charlemagne's retreating army, laden with booty, was attacked by Basques and slaughtered to a man. Verses of the over 4,000-line poem were declaimed to the Norman Troops of William the Conqueror calling on God's aide before they joined battle with the English at Hastings in 1066.

Coquillards: After the Hundred Year's War, fought between the English and the French for the control of French lands, ended in 1453, France and Spain were plagued by footloose mercenaries who often formed robber bands. Pilgrims on the way to Santiago de Compostela offered rich pickings because of the alms they brought. The band of the Coquillards, whose members came from all over Europe including Scotland, operated the pilgrim routes. Members of the band were arrested and tried in Dijon, France in the autumn of 1455. The band is estimated to have had at least five hundred members and was professionally organised with various levels of membership from a 'king' downwards. Ten of them were hanged, and four boiled alive for counterfeiting.

Bordoneros: Robbers of pilgrims in Spain were known as **bordoneros** a name also used for thieves, vagabonds and street urchins. A *bordón* was a staff with a steel tip used by pilgrims to ward off dogs and wolves. Fake pilgrims were already a problem in the 11th century. By the 16th century things became so bad that Philip II banned the pilgrim's dress in 1590.

Chapter 6

Pata negra (black hoof) ham is the finest Iberian ham and is the official designation the food board gives to cured ham from the black-hooved Iberian pigs that feed on acorns and grain in the south and southwest of Spain. Cafes and restaurants in Spain are quite cavalier with the name, so like much else the *pata negra* is often fake.

Chapter 7

Poitou and Cajuns: Many of the Acadians (Cajuns) that settled in Nova Scotia and later New Brunswick from 1604 onwards came from the Poitou region which is on the west coast of France above the port of La Rochelle.

The Book of Miracles: Book II of the **Codex Calixtinus** describes 22 miracles. These include:

> The Pilgrim that fell into the sea and was seized by the Apostle by the scruff of the neck and brought to port after three days; Guillermo (William) the captive knight that a count struck on the bare neck with his sword and was unable to harm him; the pilgrim who out of love for the Apostle killed himself at the devil's instigation and was brought back from death to life by Santiago with the aid of Mary, the holy mother of

God; the hanged pilgrim that the holy Apostle saved from death even though he had been hanging from the gallows for three days.

Chapter 8

Qwhen Alexander our kynge was dede: The poem *Scotland After Alexander* (Anonymous) was sung after the death of King Alexander III who was thrown from his horse and killed at Kinghorn in Fife in 1286. Edward 1 of England then insisted he be made feudal overlord of the Scots till a new king was chosen. His brutality earned him the nickname of *Hammer of the Scots* and invoked rebellion leading to the Wars of Independence.

Excommunication and death for robbers: As early as 1095, Pope Nicolas II instructed bishops in Galicia, the Basque country and Aquitaine in France to excommunicate robbers of pilgrims. The Lateran council of 1123 condemned them to excommunication. The royal charters (fueros) of Castile the oldest legal records of Castile report that in the 13th century report that:

> Andres, son of Arnalte, stole bags and money from a traveller and was arrested. He confessed that had done it at the instigation of his brother the abbot Don Esteban de San Pedro who was charged with looking after the money; the Abbot took refuge in the holy church of San Pedro and had to repay the money to the traveller. Andres who was of very ill repute, was hanged, and the clergyman was deprived by Bishop Don Mauritius (1213-1238) of his office and benefices and even had to journey to Rome twice, until, after four years, he was pardoned by the bishop to pray for good men (*Fueros de Castiella*, no. 27).

Cornish men with tails: The text here in Spanish is *cornubianos caudados* and refers to the *caudata* (salamander) a reptilian creature with a tail, a mythical monsters in antiquity and a basic symbol in alchemy since salamanders can live on both land and in water. It was an association with the devil in the early Middle Ages and probably comes from antiquity. The Cornish are also referred to in British sources as having tails. How the Cornish in particular got the name is not known.

Getae were Dacians, a branch of the Thracians who fought with Hector in the defence of Troy. Herodotus mentions them in his *Histories*. Their territory roughly corresponds to modern day Romania, Moldavia and Northern Bulgaria.

Chapter 9

Alexander *Sawney* Bean is legendary as the only cannibal cum fornicator in Scottish history. The story goes that he was born in East Lothian in the 1500s, took up with a wife as vicious and depraved as himself and sired a string of offspring including grandchildren, the gross of them through incest. He lived with his self-created 'clan' in a coastal cave in Bennane Head, between Girvan and Ballantrae on the south west coast of Scotland. It can be visited today if you care to scramble down the cliffs but apart from the associations it is not much to look at. King James VI of Scotland and I of England, when he heard of Bean's evil ways, is supposed to have led a manhunt with bloodhounds to track them down to their cave which was found scattered with human remains. After being taken to the Tolbooth Jail in Edinburgh on the other side of the country, they were executed. The men had their genitals cut off and their hands and feet severed. After watching the men bleed to death, the women and children were burned alive.

Robert Burns, the national poet of Scotland, was born near here in a little cottage in Alloway in 1759, two miles south of Ayr. In his poem *Tam o' Shanter*, Burns describes how Tam is chased one sullen dark night brewing up a storm with witches and warlocks dancing round the local church and the devil playing the bagpipes.

Robert Louis Stevenson, another Scottish writer, wrote a novel called the *Master of Ballantrae* about the place, supposedly inspired by the fact that he was stoned by local throwbacks when visiting the town. This area of Scotland has a dark folk history of witchcraft and some dark inhabitants even to this day. Drop into a local pub and with a bit of 'luck' get into conversation with a local throwback for an insight into the dark side of the Celtic mind. Having done that you will conclude that Sawney Bean was probably real enough.

Chapter 10

Pilgrim traffic. Nearly 216,000 people from 156 different countries travelled the various pilgrim routes to Santiago de Compostela in 2013, most of them (70%) taking the French Way, the *Camino Frances*. With about half only doing the last 100 kilometres, starting from Sarria. Spaniards were the biggest group, accounting for about half, followed by Germans. About 3% were American. The oldest 'pilgrim' was an 85 year old Belgian man. This according to the Pilgrim Office, *Oficina de Peregrinos* which only records the number of people who pick up the *Compostela* certificate at its office in Santiago so the total is certainly higher.

Commercial exploitation: As early as 1993, the Council of Europe warned against the 'commercial exploitation' of the Way of St James by local and government authorities (*El Pais*, 5 February 1993).

Chapter 13

Cajun The term Cajun derives from Acadian. The Cajuns of Louisiana speak a variety of French that is mostly derived from the Acadian French spoken in the French colony of Acadia or what are now the maritime provinces of Canada, and the U.S. state of Maine which borders on the province of New Brunswick, Canada. Jack Kerouac, author of *On the Road*, was born in Lowell, Massachusetts, south of Maine of French-Canadian parents. Hence the connection.

Chapter 15

Vannoccio Biringuccio (1480-1539) was an Italian metallurgist, best known for *De La Pirotechnia* (Pyrotechnics) a manual on metal working. He is considered the father of the foundry industry and is credited with starting the tradition of technical writing. In 1538 he became head of the papal foundry and director of munitions.

Chapter 16

John Brierley is the author of a series of guides on the pilgrim roads to Santiago de Compostela. A former chartered surveyor, based in Dublin, a mid-life crisis forced him to seek a new spiritual path, meaning and direction for his life which brought him with his family to the community of Findhorn in Scotland in 1987. He has since made the Camino and its spiritual dimensions his life's work and expresses this in his popular guidebooks.

Chapter 18

Erasmus (1466-1536) the great Dutch scholar of the early Renaissance was born in Rotterdam and brought up twelve miles away in Gouda, both small country towns at the time. An illegitimate child, his father Gerard was probably a priest, a fact that he took pains to hide. His Christian name is taken from St Erasmus of Formiae, one of the fourteen Holy Martyrs venerated in the Middle Ages. He is also known as Desiderius Erasmus Roterodamus or Erasmus of Rotterdam. The most plausible explanation of his name and origins is given by Dutch historian Johan Huzinga in *Erasmus and the Age of Reformation*.

Poilus (hairy ones) was the name given to French infantrymen in the First World War because of their beards and moustaches. *Boche* is a disparaging term for German soldiers. The word comes from *caboche* – cabbage.

Chapter 19

Delmore Schwartz (1913-1966) was an American poet and short story writer, star of the New York literary scene in the 1930s and 40s, and remembered more for his wretched life than his great talent. Novelist and friend Saul Bellow portrayed him in *Humboldt's Gift*. He taught musician Lou Reed at Syracuse University, New York, where he was professor of English literature. "You were the greatest man I ever met," said Reed, who like Schwartz came from a Jewish background. *In Dreams Begin Responsibilities* was one of Russian writer Vladimir Nabokov's favourite short stories.

Chapter 21

The **credencial** is a card issued by the cathedral authorities in Santiago, by hostels and other institutions along the way to people making the journey 'for spiritual purposes' and is a record of the trip. It is required for staying at pilgrim hostels where it is stamped. Many 'pilgrims' only do the last 100 kilometres. To ensure they do it on foot, the Pilgrim Office requires two stamps a day on the *credencial* as proof on the last stage. When the trip has been completed the *credencial* is presented at the Pilgrim Office close to the Cathedral and you get a Compostela certificate, a document in Latin with your name on it, confirming you have done the trip. Or at least 100 kilometres.

Chapter 22

The **Internationale** has been the most popular song of the socialist movement since the late 19th century and was intended to be sung to the tune of the Marseillaise. It was written by Eugene Pottier, a member of the Paris Commune which ruled Paris briefly for ten days in 1871. The Paris Commune considerably influenced Marx and Lenin.

Chapter 26

The Aberdeen Bestiary is an illuminated manuscript bestiary dating back to the 12th century. It once belonged to King Henry VIII. Bestiaries were popular in the Middle Ages and gave a description of animals, birds and even rocks accompanied by an illustration and a moral tale. The earliest bestiary is an anonymous 2nd century AD Greek manuscript called the Physiologus summarizing the treatment of animals in the writings of classical Greek and Roman writers such as Aristotle, Pliny, Solinus and other naturalists.

Chapter 27

The **Botafumeiro** is the biggest censer in the world. It weighs 80 kilos and is 1.60 metres high. It is normally on view in the Cathedral library. Brought out on special occasions it is filled with 40 kilos of charcoal and incense. Eight robed *tiraboleiros* pull on the ropes, pumping the censer with precision so it reaches a maximum speed within a minute and a half. Most dangerous point is when it reaches its highest point, almost touching the roof of the transept, reaching speeds of up to 80 km an hour. The first recorded accident was on 25 July 1499 when flying at an arc of 82%, 8 degrees less than that needed to make it vertical. At a speed of 68 kilometres an hour, one of the chains broke and the rest could not hold the weight. The problem seems to have been that whenever it swings to the left or the right, the weight falls on three chains, and if any one chain breaks the rest get a 50% increase in weight.

Princess Catherine of Aragon (born December 1485) was married by proxy on 19 May 1499 at the age of nearly 16 to Arthur Prince of Wales, eldest son of Henry VII (born September 1486). They could not communicate, it is said, as each pronounced their Latin differently. Officially married on November 14th,1501, Arthur died less than five months later on April 2nd 1502, at the age of 15 in the sweating sickness epidemic. In April 1509 Catherine became the wife of the future Henry VIII.

In the **Discourse of the Dogs** (*El Coloquio de los Perros)* of Miguel Cervantes, published in 1613, Cipion and Berganza, two dogs that guard the Hospice of the Resurrection in Valladolid, have a chat about their adventures with their human masters.

Erasmus was **tutor** to two of the illegitimate **sons of James IV** of Scotland: Alexander Stewart and James Stewart whom he instructed in logic and rhetoric in Padua, Italy in 1508. Alexander who was archbishop of St Andrews was killed at the Battle of Flodden in 1513 in which the elite of Scotland: 15 earls and 20 barons and between 10,000-20,000 men, were wiped out at Flodden Field by a smaller English Army sent by Catherine, then regent. Erasmus wrote an obituary for Alexander Stewart who was his patron.

Alms and donations: The poor got a share of these after a percentage was creamed off by the clerics from the top down. In the high Middle Ages, half a million and more pilgrims trudged the pilgrim roads every year, taking money or other valuables to the holy shrine of Santiago on their own behalf or on behalf of others.

Chapter 29

William Dunbar (1460-1520) was a Scottish Court Poet to James IV. **Fear of death** (*timor mortis*) is a common theme in late Medieval Scottish and English poetry. The phrase here is from a prayer for the dead in Latin:

> Peccantem me quotidie, et non poenitentem, timor mortis conturbat me. Quia in inferno nulla est redemptio, miserere mei, Deus, et salva me.
> Sinning daily and not repenting, the fear of death disturbs me. Because there is no redemption in Hell, have mercy on me, O Lord and save me.

The Big Sleep is the title of a hard boiled crime novel by Raymond Chandler set in Los Angeles, featuring private detective Philip Marlowe. The title is a euphemism for death, or 'sleeping the big sleep.'
Hollywood has filmed it several times, the first by director Howard Hawkes in 1946 featuring Lauren Bacall and Humphrey Bogart.

Chapter 31

The Forgotten Armada was a fleet of 15 galleons from Castile and 9 from Portugal, 53 German and Flemish boats, 5 pinnacles, 1 caravel and nearly 11,000 men. Under the command of Admiral Padilla it set out from Lisbon in October 1596 heading for La Coruña to meet up with other ships for the invasion of Ireland. It ran into a heavy storm off Cape Finisterre. Among the ships that went down were the La Capitana de Levante and the Santiago el Mayor each carrying 30,000 ducats probably to support the Irish in their war against Isabel. (Hiram Morgan, *The Battle of Kinsale*). Earlier the same year: in June 1596, Sir Walter Raleigh sailed from Plymouth with over a hundred vessels to attack and sack Cadiz.

Chapter 34

Taino Indians:

Arawak Indians from the Orinoco Delta who spread from Venezuela through the Antilles and are estimated to have been a population of 3 million on the island of Hispaniola, now the Dominican Republic and Haiti. The Taino so impressed Columbus, with their generosity he said: "They will give all that they do possess for anything that is given to them, exchanging things even for bits of broken pottery." Like the Picts of Scotland, the Taino Indians of Cuba were supposedly wiped out by the invader, in their case the Spaniards. Dictator Fulgenicio Batista nicknamed El Indio (the Indian) and overthrown by Fidel Castro in 1959 is said to have been descended from Taino Indians. For obscure reasons, Cuban sources have long claimed that the Taino Indians were wiped out and left no traces. Recently and somewhat miraculously their descendents, ignorant of the writings of historians have surfaced and spoken.

"Todavia Tenemos Aborigines en Cuba?" Osviel Castro Medel,

Juventud Rebelde, January 2011

Chapter 35

German tribes and Scythians:

Vandals and other East Germanic Tribes were differentiated from the Germans and were referred to at times as Scythians, Goths or some other special name. Prior to that Greek ethnography, the teacher of the Roman writers, had differentiated among the northern Barbarians only the Scythians from the Celts, or at most had mentioned the Celto-Scyths in between the two

Herwig Wolfram, *The Roman Empire and its Germanic Peoples*

Chapter 40

The Population of Europe during the Roman Empire in 4th century AD was about 50-60 million. In Europe in 1340 it was about 70 million. The Black Death Pandemic decimated the population by about 60% between 1346 and 1353.

The Plague of Justinian (541-542 AD) was named after the Eastern Roman Emperor Justinian I, who contracted the disease in Constantinople where he was based, but survived. The plague, which seems to have been a form of bubonic plague, spread from the east to Europe and Arabia. It was the first pandemic and flared up intermittently until the 8th century. The minds of people living in this period were conditioned by impending death. The number who died of the Justinian plague is estimated as high as 20 million. A contributory factor to death was the scarcity of food occasioned by starvation. Farmers were wiped out.

Chapter 42

The Historical Gardens of Puente San Miguel are open to the public from May to September.

Picasso is supposed to have said to his secretary Jaime Sabat:

> Primitive sculpture has never been surpassed, have you noticed the precision of the lines engraved on the caverns?

Chapter 44.

The mind of the caveman The voice of God came from the non-dominant side of the brain, and the men who obeyed these voices, to put it in Freudian terms, would have a superego and an id but no ego at all. Therefore no responsibility says William Burroughs referring to his reading of *The Origins of Consciousness in the Breakdown of the Bicameral Mind*, by Julian Jaynes who proposes that the first voices people heard in their heads were hallucinated voices, that everyone was schizophrenic up till about 800 BC. Victor Bockris, *A Report from the Bunker with William Burroughs*, 1982.

The False Discovery Rate (FDR) of a set of predictions is the expected percentage of false predictions in a set of predictions.

Chapter 45

Neanderthal genes: "About 2% of genes found in people of European, Asian and Far-Eastern origin come from Neandertalers," says Svante Paabo of Leipzig's Max Planck Institute of Evolutionary Anthropology following his study of ancient DNA (*The Observer*, 15 February 2014).

Basques and the secrets of cod:

> But medieval Basques were the top cod traders. They were whalers, able to travel vast distances whaling because they had learned to salt-cure cod, a better technique than the Vikings' air-drying. They also had a secret source: by the year 1000, the Basques were supplying a vast international market in cod, based on their fishing fleet's surreptitious voyages across the Atlantic to North America's fishing banks, a cod cornucopia about which they kept mum... During the Middle Ages, when Europeans ate great quantities of whale meat, the Basques traveled to distant unknown waters and brought back whale. They were able to travel

such distances because they had found huge schools of cod and salted their catch, giving them a nutritious food supply that would not spoil on long voyages...The Basques, unlike the Vikings, had salt, and because fish that was salted before drying lasted longer, the Basques could travel even farther than the Vikings...By the year 1000, the Basques had greatly expanded the cod markets to a truly international trade...for the Middle Ages it was remarkably long-lasting... Not only did cod last longer than other salted fish, but it tasted better too... For the poor who could rarely afford fresh fish, it was cheap, high-quality nutrition. Catholicism gave the Basques their great opportunity. The medieval church imposed fast days on which sexual intercourse and the eating of flesh were forbidden, but eating "cold" foods was permitted... But where was all this cod coming from? The Basques, who had never even said where they came from, kept their secret. By the fifteenth century, this was no longer easy to do, because cod had become widely recognized as a highly profitable commodity and commercial interests around Europe were looking for new cod grounds. There were cod off of Iceland and in the North Sea, but the Scandinavians, who had been fishing cod in those waters for thousands of years, had not seen the Basques. The British, who had been fishing for cod well offshore since Roman times, did not run across Basque fishermen even in the fourteenth century, when British fishermen began venturing up to Icelandic waters. The Bretons, who tried to follow the Basques, began talking of a land across the sea...Jacques Cartier arrived (In Newfoundland, Canada), was credited with "discovering" the mouth of the St. Lawrence, planted a cross on the Gaspe Peninsula, and claimed it all for France. He also noted the presence of 1,000 Basque fishing vessels. But the Basques, wanting to keep a good secret, had never claimed it for anyone.

Mark Kurlansky, *Cod: A Biography of the Fish that Changed the World*

Chapter 49

Scythians is the general name given to a wide variety of people and races that lived between the Carpathian Mountains and Mongolia during the first millennium BC. In the popular conception they were nomadic Indo European tribes that at their widest extent ranged across an area covering the Crimea,

Kazakhstan, Russia, Poland, the Ukraine, Belarus, Romania and Northern India. They became a general term for horse nomads and even barbarians by the supposedly superior Greek and Roman civilizations. Just as this sweeping term of Scythian, which was given to a tract of land, was also given sweepingly to the peoples it encompassed: from light-haired Europeans to Mongolians. Another tradition has that they are one of the Lost Tribes of Israel that had come from the east, moving into Iran and later Turkey. Herodotus, the Greek historian, the main source of information on the Scythians, says they lived in Anatolia before the 7th century BC and then moved to the Kuban region early in the 6th century BC and the Pontic Steppes (Black Sea). Later they sailed from the Black Sea into the Mediterranean. Scythian was the term loosely applied by the Romans also to some of the Germanic tribes they sought to conquer, the same 'barbarian' cultures that would eventually overrun a decadent, imperialistic Rome. The Venerable Bede, the historian, says that the Scythians arrived on the north coast of Ireland in long ships having sailed from Scythia. Since there was no land for them to settle there they settled in the north of Scotland (Caithness).

Scythian monk Dionysus Exiguus (470-544) aka Dennis the Dwarf, the Small or the Humble, because of his size, was a 6th century monk born in **Scythia minor** in modern Dobriya, now shared by Romania and Bulgaria. He was a member of the **Scythian monks' community** in Tomis, the major city of Scythia Minor, between the lower Danube and the Black Sea, and is best remembered for the Gregorian Calendar. From about 500 AD he lived in Rome, was a learned member of the Roman curia and translated over 400 ecclesiastical canons from Greek into Latin. He was admired by Bede.

Scythians and Celts

> At the time of the Roman contact with Spain, the peninsula was shared by a large number of fairly barbarous peoples, probably belonging ... to two main primitive races....Three civilized peoples, the Phoenicians, the Greeks and the Carthaginians had been in contact with some of them.... About twenty of the Hispanic nations of this period are worthy of particular mention: the Cantabrians, Asturians, Galicians, Lusitans, Bastetans...The first five of these are without a doubt Scythians and

Celts.... It is impossible to state with any certainty that the Asturians were one of the peoples of Gallic blood; like the Cantabrians, they seem to belong to a race of more northerly origins. One is inclined, on the basis of their passion for horses, and the devoted way they took care of them, to believe they were of Scythian origin.

Antonio Pardo, *The World of Ancient Spain*

Bibliography

Almagro-Gorbea, Martin, *El Origen de Los Celtas en La Peninsula Iberica: Protoceltas y Celtas.* Universidad Complutense, Madrid 1992.

Araguz, Antonio Martin, and Bustamante Martinez, Cristina, "Visiones Apocalipticas de Beato de Liebana," *Ars Medica. Revista de Humanidades*, 2003.

Arribas Briones, Pablo, *Picaros y Picaresca en el Camino de Santiago*, Burgos 1993.

Brierley, John, *A Pilgrim's Guide; From St Jean Pied de Port to Santiago de Compostela; A Practical and Mystical Manual for the Modern Day Pilgrim*, Findhorn Press 2010.

Cummins, W.A., *The Age of the Picts*, Stroud, Glocestershire 1995.

Cunqueiro, Alvaro, *Merlin and Company*; from *Merlin e familia i outras historias*, 1955, translated by Colin Smith, London 1996.

Henderson, Phinella, *Pre-Reformation Pilgrims from Scotland to Santiago de Compostela*, The Confraternity of St James, London 1997.

Herwaarden, van, Dr J. (red). *Pelgrims door de Eeuwen Heen, Santiago de Compostela in Woord en Beeld*, Turnhout 1985.

Jacobs, Michael, *The Road to Santiago de Compostela, Architectural Guides for Travellers*, London 1992.

Keay, S.J., *Roman Spain*, Berkeley, California 1988.

Kurlansky, Mark, *Cod: A Biography of the Fish that Changed the World*, New York 1999.

MacDougall, Carl, *Scots the Language of the People*, Edinburgh 2006.

Malone, Kemp and Baugh, *The Middle Ages, A Literary History of England*, volume 1, London 1972.

Montes, Ana Ainsa, *The Way of St James in Aragon, The Pilgrims Guide*, Zaragoza 2009.

Murado, Miguel-Anxo, *Otro Idea de Galicia*, Barcelona 2008.

Pardo, Antonio, *The World of Ancient Spain*, Geneva 1976.

Pombo, Anton, *El Camino Norte de Santiago en Tu Mochila*, Madrid 2010.

Rembert, Virginia Pitts, *Hieronymus Bosch*, New York 2012.

Schwartz, Delmore, *In Dreams Begin Responsibilities and Other Stories*, London 1978.

Tate, Robert Brian, *Pilgrimages to St James of Compostela from the British Isles*, Liverpool, Liverpool University Press, 1990.

The Aberdeen Bestiary, Aberdeen Bestiary Project, Aberdeen University; www.abdn.ac.uk/bestiary.

Toureille, Valerie, "Les Coquillards, archives d'une société criminelle," *L'Histoire*, Sept. 2004, no 290.

Wolfram, Herwig, *The Roman Empire and Its Germanic Peoples*, Berkeley, California 1997.

Woodworth, Paddy, *The Basque Country*, Oxford, 2010.

Lightning Source UK Ltd.
Milton Keynes UK
UKOW04f0903300315

248742UK00001B/42/P

9 789076 660400